UNRAVELLING THE SILK ROAD

UNRAVELLING THE SILK ROAD

Travels and Textiles in
Central Asia

CHRIS ASLAN

ICON

To my parents, who raised me adventurously.

This edition published in the UK in 2024 by
Icon Books Ltd, Omnibus Business Centre,
39–41 North Road, London N7 9DP
email: info@iconbooks.com
www.iconbooks.com

ISBN: 978-183773-120-6
eBook: 978-178578-987-8

Typeset by SJmagic DESIGN SERVICES, India

Printed and bound in the UK

CONTENTS

LIST OF ILLUSTRATIONS

Map of the whole of the Eastern Med, through to China
Map showing the modern-day borders of Central Asia

COLOUR PLATE SECTION

1. Cherchen man
2. A burnt-out courtyard in Osh
3. Down from a yak
4. The *jailo*
5. A yak herder with a newborn yaklet
6. Interior of a yurt
7. Weaving palas
8. Trialling American and Mongolian combs
9. Making felt
10. Embroidering *suzani*
11. Folio from a manuscript of Layla va Majnun by Jami, Harvard Art Museums/Arthur M. Sackler Museum, Gift of John Goelet, formerly in the collection of Louis J. Cartier. Photo © President and Fellows of Harvard College, 1958.75
12. Soviet poster
13. Silkworms
14. Teal atlas silk warp threads
15. Atlas silk warp threads drying
16. The last Emir of Bukhara, photographed by Prokudin Gorsky around 1908. Prokudin-Gorskiĭ photograph collection, Library of Congress, Prints and Photographs Division. LC-P87- 8086A-1
17. Samarkand locals photographed by Prokudin Gorsky around 1908. Prokudin-Gorskiĭ photograph collection, Library of Congress, Prints and Photographs Division. LC-P87- 8002
18. Dhakka Muslin
19. Detail from a *suzani*
20. A bride wearing seven veils
21. The author with local boys on the prow of The Karakalpakia
22. A cotton boll

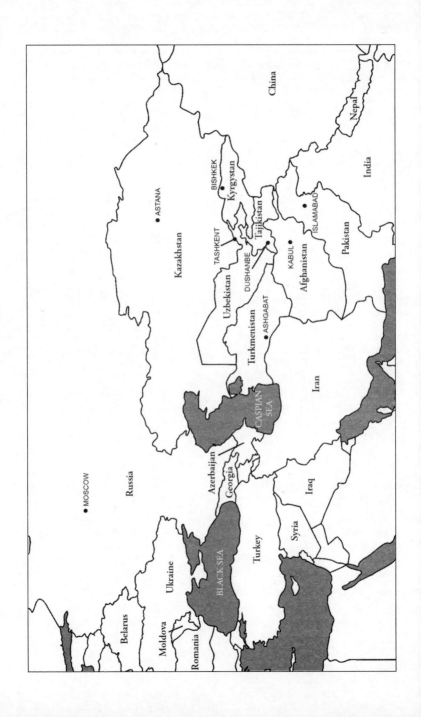

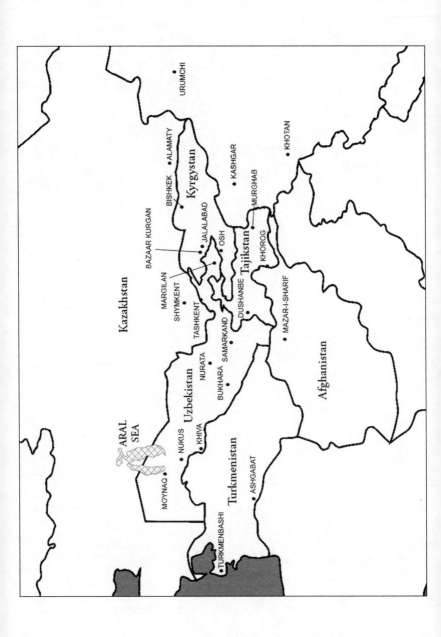

AUTHOR'S NOTE

There is a glossary of terms at the end of the book. All temperatures are in degrees Celsius.

As for pronunciation, Russian loanwords with 'zh' are pronounced with a soft 'j', like the 's' in measure or pleasure. 'Kh' sounds, such as Khiva or Khorog, are pronounced the way Scots say the 'ch' in 'loch'. I've generally aimed for consistency in the spelling of place names, so that Bokhara and Bokhoro have given way to the standardised Bukhara.

The area of Central Asia has been called different things over the years. In ancient times it was Transoxiana, or the land beyond the Oxus River. Medieval Europe knew it as Tartary, then later it became known as Turkestan, or Russian/Chinese Turkestan once under colonial rule. I've used different terms depending on which period I'm writing about. Today, Central Asia is generally understood to refer to the former Soviet -stans, possibly with the inclusion of Afghanistan and Xinjiang province.

At the end you will find a bibliography with books that I found particularly helpful highlighted in bold.

PROLOGUE
Crossroads

It's a bold claim but I'm going to make it anyway: everything is about textiles.

As the only mammals without brown fat layers to metabolise for warmth or adequate hair or fur to insulate us, we've had to compensate by using our cunning and creativity. Our need for covering may have sped up our evolution, as early humans required tools to transform animal skins into clothing, and more sophisticated methods to create woven cloth.

Our preoccupation with textiles kick-started the Industrial Revolution, and even before that, the primary preoccupation of humans – using more man-hours (or more commonly, women-hours) than any other activity (including farming) – was textile production. The ghosts of textile words are present even as you read this book. The very term 'text', for example, comes from the word 'textile', thanks to the ancient orator Quintilian who described the Greco-Roman art of rhetoric as the weaving together of words, much as fabric gradually takes shape on a loom.

The most iconic textile to transform the world, ushering in the first era of globalisation, was silk. The network of trading routes it spawned, connecting East and West, is known as the Silk Road. At its heart lies Central Asia, a region that for fifteen years I called home. An estimated 10 per cent of the Roman Empire's wealth was frittered away on silk and other eastern luxuries, causing consternation in the treasury. Eventually, silk became so associated with decadence and debauchery that Roman men were banned outright from wearing it, lest it corrupt or effeminise them. Also passing along these new trading routes were unfamiliar fruits, vegetables, animals, fashions, artistic styles, inventions, ideas and religions. Globalisation is not a new phenomenon.

However, this is not the only textile road to tangle its way across Central Asia. There is an older road which allowed the vast and often inhospitable landscape to be populated in the first place. It is the Wool Road. It followed the Great Eurasian Steppe which stretched from Hungary all the way to Mongolia and Eastern Siberia. This wild, treeless sea of grass, far from caves or other shelter, could not be traversed in one summer. Winter temperatures of -60 degrees, with howling winds and no natural shelter, meant that the only way to survive along this road was to live in houses light enough to carry but insulated enough to provide warmth. These houses were made of wool.

This Wool Road spawned highly mobile people who were almost impossible to vanquish. Nomads could attack a town or village and then melt away, able to traverse vast distances with rapidity, sleeping in their saddles. Some nomadic people, such as the Xiongnu, the mountain barbarians, or the Yuezhi, the hairy barbarians, harried China so much that the Great Wall of China was built in response. A few nomadic leaders had greater ambitions than merely raiding. They formed vast empires, becoming the scourge of those they conquered. Most infamous were Attila the Hun, Genghis Khan and Amir Timur. Nomads have always been treated with suspicion and misunderstanding by sedentary people and the consequences for nomads during the Soviet era were devastating.

A third textile road winds across Central Asia, passing diagonally through the other two roads, from India to Russia. It is a road which decided the fate of Central Asia in the 19th and 20th centuries; one that made fortunes, exploited people and natural resources, brought down governments and killed a sea. It is the

Cotton Road. While Russia exploited Central Asia for its cotton, a longer, parallel exploitation took place in India, until one man turned cotton against British colonial rule and brought down an empire. Cotton has inspired countless examples of Soviet and post-Soviet art and propaganda. Its effects on the Aral Sea and the health of both the surrounding people and landscape have been even more catastrophic than that other Soviet-made ecological disaster, Chernobyl.

So, this is a book about three textile roads, focussing on their crossing points rather than any terminus. I've also embroidered each of these roads with my own experiences of living in the region. I spent seven years living in the desert oasis of Khiva in Uzbekistan, where I founded a silk carpet workshop to create livelihoods at a time of chronic unemployment. My remit was to revive silk carpet-weaving, natural-dye-making and 15th-century Timurid carpet designs rediscovered in the illuminated pages of contemporary manuscripts. We ran out of space in the 19th-century madrassah that had been repurposed as our workshop, so I started a second workshop producing the same designs in silk embroidered onto cotton and became the largest non-government employer in town. Then, in 2005, popular protests in the city of Andijan were brutally supressed, leading to the deaths of hundreds, if not thousands of ordinary people. The Karimov regime needed a scapegoat and decided that International Development Organisations were somehow to blame, and I was expelled and blacklisted from Uzbekistan. I discovered five or six years later that others who had been expelled were no longer blacklisted and were able to return. So I do, whenever I can, leading tour groups and reconnecting with my Uzbek family and friends in Khiva. I wrote about the workshops in my first book, *A Carpet Ride to Khiva: Seven Years on the Silk Road.*

I then moved to Tajikistan and spent several years in Khorog, a border town nestled in the mountains of Badakhshan. Every morning I'd open my curtains and gaze across the valley at Afghan villages on the other side of the Panj River. I worked with a local professor to write a textbook for foreigners wanting to learn the local language, which had no official alphabet. I also made regular trips up to the high-altitude plateau known locally as the High Pamirs – meaning 'Roof of the World' – with similar topography to Tibet. Here, I taught herders how to get down from their yaks. Of course, they were more than capable of dismounting from their beasts themselves, with many boys learning to ride a yak before they could even walk. The 'down' I speak of is the soft cashmere-like undercoat that can be combed from a yak in late spring when they moult. When I arrived, herders were generally throwing it away. I wanted to start a knitting cooperative, turning this luxury waste product into adventure knitwear.

Next came a spell in Kyrgyzstan. I moved to a small mountainous village famed for its waterfalls, for its Islamic conservatism, and for being surrounded by the world's largest walnut forest. Determined to rescue beautiful logs of walnut wood from the firewood piles of the village, I started a school for woodcarving.

Although I'm reluctantly based in Britain, I spend as much time as I can in Central Asia, leading tours there and reconnecting with friends. It is, after all, a place where I've left a large chunk of my heart.

INTRODUCTION
Spinning a Yarn

If I unpick my own road to Central Asia, it begins in the school library as I studied Soviet politics. In 1990, every world map was dominated by a huge red smear that crossed all the way from Europe to the Pacific. This was the Soviet Union. Lazily, I had assumed that it was just the communist name for Russia, and often people used the terms Soviet or Russian interchangeably. However, halfway through my course, the Soviet Union collapsed, and I decided to write my dissertation on the role of nationalism in its break-up. Reading more, I began to discover just how varied the peoples of the Soviet Union were, in terms of religion, language and ethnicity, and that a more accurate description of it was the Soviet Empire.

The Kazakh Socialist Republic alone was roughly the size of Western Europe. These were significantly large areas of non-Russian Soviet presence. I discovered Abkhazians, Georgians, Turkmen, Chechens, Tartars and Kalmyks, and found illustrations of these people in their national dress.

I was gripped. Although my parents are English, I was born in Turkey and spent my childhood there as my father was a professor at a university in Ankara. I knew that the Turks had originally come east from Central Asia, but hadn't realised that there were so many other Turkic peoples out there, all sharing linguistic similarities.

Ruling over the largest contiguous empire the world has ever known was a centralised government that made economic decisions which I couldn't understand. I read how in the twilight years of the Soviet Union, Gorbachev's policy of *perestroika* allowed greater economic freedom, combined with subsidised public transport and a burgeoning unofficial market. This meant that a Georgian villager could pick two buckets of apricots from the trees in her orchard, get on a bus to the airport, fly over three hours to Moscow, sell the apricots on the street and then fly back to Georgia again that evening. And still make a tidy profit.

Now, though, these new countries, still vastly overshadowed by Russia, were having to make their own way in the world.

My interest in the region continued. I was determined to travel along the Silk Road and see some of these exotic former Soviet countries for myself. I managed to get a travel bursary from Leicester University, on the proviso that it funded something related to my course. I was studying media and journalism, so I contacted some of the development organisations that had proliferated in these new republics and offered to write news articles for them in return for bed and board. A few took me up on the offer.

With youthful certainty, rather than any actual financial accounting or a proper understanding of visa systems, I exchanged my earnings and bursary money into new US dollars – for some reason old notes were unacceptable – and stuffed them into my money belt, hoping it would be enough for the trip. I look back now in amazement at my readiness to head off with only the vaguest of plans for where I would end up, and with no contingency plan in case I was robbed. There were no ATMs where I was going, so the cash would simply need to last. I hoped to get as far as China but was relatively hazy about where I'd go after that, thinking I might try to get to Russia and return home on the Trans-Siberian train.

Or not. I wasn't entirely sure.

In the end, I was persuaded by a New Zealander in Tashkent to avoid Russia completely. He assured me that the Trans-Siberian was just a really long and fairly tedious journey through featureless landscape dotted with the occasional onion-domed church. Much better, he said, would be to head for China and then traverse the Karakoram Highway from Kashgar down to Gilgit in Pakistan and fly out of Islamabad. I took his advice but was to have a near-death experience as a result.

My main concern before I left was that I might run out of books. So, I packed *War and Peace* in my hand-luggage – an epic novel for an epic journey – and a few other books I was happy to discard along the way. I'd borrowed an old rucksack from my dad, which he said had served him well as a student. It was a mistake. The rucksack was both heavy and uncomfortable and – as I discovered while in a bazaar in Turkmenistan – fairly easy to pickpocket. I also had a Russian phrase book, which might have been useful for ordering opera tickets, but other than that was fairly limited. It was my rusty childhood Turkish that was to prove more helpful.

It was 1996 and a privilege to lift the Iron Curtain and peek behind it, visiting countries just five years old that were coming to terms with their own national autonomy. As these new identities were being forged, there was still a reeling from the sudden collapse of a centralised system which had in no way prepared these former Soviet countries for independence. Even oil-rich Baku was struggling economically, despite the influx of oil companies keen to get drilling.

There were many highlights along the way, and moments I still remember clearly. The first was the thrill of reaching the border between Turkey and Georgia. Turkey felt very familiar, but just a few hundred metres away was a country that had recently emerged from behind the Iron Curtain. I joined the queue and passed through checkpoints fairly quickly on both sides, my passport scrutinised and stamped. There was a bench on the Georgian side where I waited for the bus, feeling nervous excitement at signs everywhere in bold Cyrillic or exotic Georgian script. But my excitement dampened as the hours went by. It was just before dawn when the bus finally arrived. Most of the other passengers were women, and were either traders or prostitutes. They all looked exhausted, and I wondered what money or other services had been extorted from them in order to let them pass. I soon learnt that the Soviet Union, and the new republics it had spawned, survived on the tenacity and determination of Soviet women, who did whatever was necessary to feed their families.

I saw little of Georgia on that first trip; it was only on subsequent visits that I discovered the amazing food and wine, the love of complicated toasts, and the stunning mountain scenery of the country. From Georgia I took another bus, this time to Baku, the capital of Azerbaijan. There, on the shores of the Caspian Sea, was the classiest of the capitals that I would pass through. The city was divided into three sections. The outer section was Soviet-era and largely grey blocks of flats. The inner section was a walled city, which was as large as Baku would get until the mid-19th century when the city overflowed with foreigners flocking to the world's first major oil boom. The middle section, or 'Boom town', was a cacophony of different European architectural styles built around the same period, as former peasants – now millionaires – returned from tours of Europe with postcards of their favourite buildings, which they handed over to architects to reproduce, along with wads of cash.

Baku was about to experience another oil boom, but it hadn't quite started. Taxi drivers were still university professors or opera singers, trying to make ends meet now that state salaries were virtually worthless. Those who could got jobs as cleaners or receptionists in the offices of the new international oil companies.

I spent a week in Baku waiting for the 'daily' ferry to actually leave for Turkmenistan. Arriving in the dusty port town of Krasnovodsk, I bit into my first slice of Turkmen melon, which was incredibly crisp and sweet, thanks to the searing desert temperatures. Later I learnt that skilled melon growers could even grow their crops in the desert itself, digging down to the root base of a camel-thorn shrub and making an incision into the main stem and inserting a melon seed. Not all would take, but those that did were able to draw on the camel-thorn's extensive and deep-running root system, producing melons with a unique flavour.

Ashgabat, the Turkmen capital, was a fascinating study in presidential megalomania. Saparmurat Niyazov, the first secretary of the Turkmen Communist Party, had reinvented himself after independence as Turkmenbashi, or 'leader of the Turkmen'. Everywhere there were slogans stating, 'People, Nation, Turkmenbashi!' His portrait was ubiquitous, and his golden revolving statue dominated the skyline. Shops may have had a limited amount of consumer goods, but there was plenty of Turkmenbashi aftershave or vodka (later I regretted not buying a bottle as a souvenir). This presidential cult had barely got into its stride – Turkmenbashi went on to write a holy book entitled *The Rukhnama*, promoted as equal to the Bible and Quran. Great swathes of this drivel had to be memorised and regurgitated in lieu of job interviews or university exams, or to pass a driver's test.

After Niyazov died, the presidential cult continued with his successor, who managed to bankrupt the country through further mismanagement before handing over the reins to his son, a prince in all but name. Serdar Berdimuhamedow now rules a country with the world's sixth largest gas reserves at a time when global gas prices are surging. Despite this, the people of Turkmenistan live in abject poverty. Water and power cuts in the searing summer temperatures are the norm, and most have to queue for hours outside state shops in the hope of buying cooking oil, flour or water. Meat is a mere memory. Unsurprisingly, these repressive and isolationist policies, along with a presidential cult, have led people to draw many parallels with North Korea.

I took a further train through Bukhara and Samarkand to Tashkent, the capital of Uzbekistan. I was learning how to navigate police corruption. 'Problema,' said a policeman as I got off the train in Tashkent, just before dawn. He ominously tapped my passport before walking off with it, beckoning me to join him in his office. A few weeks before, I might have panicked. Instead I simply told him, 'Problema niet,' got out my tatty copy of *War and Peace* and read for an hour or so in the police office, as it was still too early to call my hosts. Eventually, the irritated policemen chucked my passport at me with what I presumed was a muttered curse and shooed me on my way.

Jon, my host in Tashkent, arranged for me to work on a commemorative newspaper celebrating Uzbekistan's fifth anniversary of independence. I had to turn the nominally translated English into something that was actually comprehensible, and enjoyed wading through the pages of nationalist propaganda. An article comparing the historical figure of Amir Timur with present-day President Karimov contained sentences such as 'Historians note that the "General of Genius" did a good works amongst the European peoples.' I wasn't always sure what it was actually trying to say.

While the Soviet architecture of Tashkent was more concrete brutalism than anything oriental, the Silk Road came alive when Jon took me to Chorsu bazaar. Under retro-futuristic domes was a riot of colour and smells. I tried to keep my wits about me, mindful of pickpockets or garrotting myself on the strings that held awnings over the stalls, designed for people shorter than myself. I was intoxicated. The smoke and sizzle of *shashlik* wafted over us as a portly man skilfully rotated the skewers of six cubes of mutton. There are always six pieces, sometimes alternating between meat and mutton butt-fat; the word for six in Persian is *shash,* giving *shashlik* its name. We wandered through curtains of fabric, much of it silk, but with an increasing amount of glittery or sequinned polyester from China, while women bought metres to take to their local tailors for dresses.

It was late August and the fruit and veg section of the bazaar held an embarrassment of riches. Colourful mounds of bright red and green peppers, carrots strung together by their bushy green tops, and a whole section devoted to piles of enormous melons in all shapes and colours. There was a bed beside each stall as the heavy fruit could not be easily moved and would have to be guarded at night. A woman squirted bundles of fresh herbs with a plastic water bottle to keep them from wilting in the heat. Tomatoes were so large that three was already a kilo. We filled the string bags Jon had bought for the purpose. Plastic bags cost extra, and I was amused to find Morrisons bags for sale, wondering how these Northern British supermarket bags had ended up there.

'Why's it so busy?' I asked Jon.

'It isn't,' he explained. 'You should see it on Sunday, which is called Bazaar-day. Then it's really heaving.'

'But why are there so many people? You said that there are plenty of other bazaars in Tashkent.'

Jon shrugged. 'It's where people go for something to do, or to meet a friend. Plus, most people like to buy their produce fresh, so they'll come several times a week.'

Annette Meakin, a British travel author who stayed in Tashkent for a while at the turn of the 20th century, put it thus: 'When a Sart*wants amusement he turns his steps instinctively towards the bazaar; when he wants news of what is going on in the world, he is off to the bazaar, and when in fact there is no urgent reason why he should be there, you will find him in the bazaar.'[†]

I got up early one morning and caught a bus to Samarkand for a day trip. After all, this was the heart of the Silk Road. I marvelled at the stunning Timurid architecture – a relief after the brutalist concrete architecture of Tashkent. At the Registan – a square with three sides dominated by the most incredible tiled madrassahs – renovation was taking place. Beneath a scaffold I noticed a broken piece of glazed green brick tile in the dust. Furtively, I pocketed it, breathless with transgression and the knowledge that I now possessed a 15th-century treasure in my bag. I didn't. I discovered later that the Soviets regularly renovated these monuments, particularly as some of the Registan was destroyed in a large earthquake in 1886. The tile was probably younger than I was.

In the afternoon heat I passed by wheeled stalls offering carbonated water mixed with violently coloured cordial from medicinal-looking glass bottles, served from a communal cup. I stopped for refreshment in one of the teahouses and tried not to stare too obviously at those around me. There was still evidence of the great melting pot of varied people, brought together under Amir Timur's ruthless reign. Women wore gypsy-style headscarves, some looking Mediterranean, others Mongol. They seemed a lot busier than the men, or perhaps just harder-working. Other than a group of stout older women,

---

* Russian term for sedentary Central Asians.

[†] Meakin, A., *In Russian Turkestan* (1903), p. 204

marked as pilgrims by their long white headscarves, seated in the teahouse that looked out at the Timurid-era Friday Mosque, most of the idlers were male. Older men sat cross-legged on raised seating platforms, resplendent with long white beards, striped robes and turbans wrapped around grubby skullcaps, playing backgammon or simply nursing a bowl of green tea, gossiping and watching life go by. At another seating platform were middle-aged men in greasy, well-worn suits, wearing black skullcaps adorned with four white embroidered chillies. The young men in the teahouse wore polyester tracksuits made in China with misspelt brand names and were undoubtedly uncomfortable in the heat.

I then travelled from Tashkent through the fertile Fergana valley, across an open border with no passport checks and into the city of Osh in Southern Kyrgyzstan. The famous market was filled with Uzbek men in their familiar black skullcaps and Kyrgyz men with more Mongol features, sporting tall bonnets made of white felt with black velvet trim. I experienced my first trip by UAZ. These high-clearance, khaki four-wheel-drive Soviet vans were both incredibly sturdy and extremely uncomfortable. Ours had a habit of breaking down, but when it did, there was usually someone selling melons nearby, or possibly *kumiz*. The passengers seemed happy to sit around and chat by the side of the road while the driver tinkered with the engine. I was offered a swig of *kumiz* and the other passengers laughed as I tried not to wrinkle my nose at the sharp, fizzy taste. It's fermented mare's milk and mildly alcoholic. After several bottles had been consumed and the engine fixed, the rest of the van sang Kyrgyz songs lustily and revelled in my applause, insisting that I sing a song from 'Angliya'.

We climbed steadily in altitude heading for a mountain pass, and I could feel the heat radiating from the labouring motor under my front seat. At some point during the night, the driver stopped to get a few hours of sleep. I woke, sore and cold – my one warm top packed in the rucksack strapped to the van's roof-rack – and stepped out of the van for a pee, greeted by steaming breath and a spectacular sunrise. Before a backdrop of soaring mountains, the hills were dotted with yurts and splashes of colour from clothes on washing lines. Smoke curled up from their chimneys and doors opened as girls went to milking and boys took their herds to graze.

We eventually arrived in Bishkek later that day, but I saw very little as I didn't know anyone there and needed to get to Almaty, still the capital of Kazakhstan at that point, before nightfall. In Almaty, my favourite experience was a trip to the Arasan Baths. These were no run-of-the-mill Russian *banyas* but an opulent and yet distinctively Soviet complex of saunas and bathing pools. I had to wait a few days for my remaining visas, before taking a 36-hour train journey on the Genghis Khan Express from Almaty in Kazakhstan to Urumchi in China.

There were growing numbers of ethnic Han Chinese arriving in the city from Eastern and Central provinces of China every day; the park was filled with pagodas and red lanterns glowed outside Han Chinese restaurants, and yet Urumchi still felt surprisingly Central Asian. Uzbek phrases that I'd picked up along my travels seemed to work just as well with Uighurs, the largest indigenous people-group. Chinese influence, like the legacy of Russia in Central Asia, was more noticeable in municipal spheres such as hospitals, schools and universities rather than in the bazaars, teahouses or domestic settings. Certain parts of the city were where the Han lived, and other parts still retained their Turkic identity.

Even with my limited understanding as a tourist, I was aware of the ethnic tension, and it turned out that even the time you set your watch to was political. I walked naked out of my hotel bathroom as a Han cleaner opened my bedroom door without knocking, looking unapologetic given that she considered it ten in the morning and that I should already be out and about. My watch, as with most local people, was set two hours behind, which made far more circadian sense but was considered 'separatist' for being on local, not Beijing time. There was a constant cultural tug-of-war between Mohammed and Mao.

As more Han arrived daily, Urumchi, the regional capital, was filling up fast. Cranes bristled on the skyline, and Uighurs and other Turkic peoples were now a minority in the city. I still found streets where the smoke from sizzling sticks of mutton *shashlik* wafted in the air along with steam from fresh rounds of bread cooling from the oven, and the slap of *laghman* noodles being expertly hand-stretched and then whacked against a metal tabletop.

The one place where Han and Uighur seemed to mingle, or at least tolerate one another, was the People's Park. I'd expected perhaps some older Han moving sedately together in communal tai chi around the beautiful ponds and pagodas. Instead, I was passed immediately on my arrival by a diminutive Han woman walking backwards and clapping loudly. Another woman strode by, waving her hands in the air, shouting. These were both time-honoured methods of improving circulation.

Then there were eager groups of Han retirees learning Uighur dancing, the men happily mimicking the coquettish flourishes of the women's parts. There were also traditional Chinese dance classes, some involving swords, as well as line dancing, communal body-slapping and tai chi. I passed a ballroom dancing group where partners were optional. An old man swirled by holding an empty waist of air.

Young Uighurs and Han skateboarded together or did tricks using two sticks connected with string and something akin to a disembodied yoyo. In a shaded section of the park, older Han used giant broom-handled paintbrushes with water bottles attached above the brush to write out poetry in large watery Chinese characters onto the pavements. By the time they were finishing their last characters, the first ones were drying and disappearing.

Later I endured a 30-hour bus ride through the Taklamakan Desert to Khotan. The Jade City – as Khotan was known – was famous for its Sunday Bazaar, which had not been commercialised and commodified by the local authorities, as had happened in Kashgar. I joined herds of fat-tailed sheep trotting at pace with their large backsides wobbling as shepherds slapped them with sticks. There were carts drawn by horses resplendent with bright tassels, pompoms and sleighbells, blending with the clank of the cowbells as cattle and camels ambled slowly to market. The other bazaars I'd visited in Central Asia still had a distinctively Soviet feel to them, but here I felt swept up in the real Silk Road. Clanging resounded from the copper section of the bazaar as craftsmen hammered at their water ewers, basins, cauldrons and plates. Many were covered in beautifully intricate patterns. The carpenter section was full of lathes and more hammering, decorative gourds, painted wooden cradles, carved spoons, wooden stamps bristling with nails and used for decorating bread, and much more.

The livestock bazaar was just as noisy. Sheep were carefully lined up with odd numbers pointing in one direction and even numbers in the other, as if they'd just been expertly shuffled. There were spice spellers, and makers of fur hats and square embroidered skullcaps plying their trade. There were also reams and reams of gaudy atlas silk, made with a distinctive warp-resist method.

It was wonderful.

Perhaps the most memorable part of the whole trip was the bus journey from Kashgar, the historic Uighur capital, to Pakistan. Most of the passengers were pot-bellied, bearded Pakistani traders in *shalwar kameez*, who spent the journey gossiping, belching and spitting. The rest were backpackers from an assortment of countries. At first, the bus was stiflingly hot as we passed cotton fields being harvested by Uighurs. Gradually, we left the plains behind and climbed into the foothills of the mountains. We passed a caravan of shaggy Bactrian camels, heavily loaded with bales of merchandise, and I took blurry photos through the bus window. This was the Silk Road of my imagination.

We climbed further and the road opened onto high summer pasture studded with yurts, yaks, camels and sheep. My neck got sore from craning out of the window at this beautiful, raw landscape. By the time we'd reached Tashkurgan that night, we were already at 3,000 metres. The air had a nip to it and our rooms were equipped with bright pink thermos flasks and thick blankets.

We continued to climb the next day until we reached the Khunjerab Pass, the highest paved international crossing in the world, at almost 4,700 metres. We all disembarked and the Pakistani traders wrapped woven woollen *pattus* around themselves and stamped their sandalled feet to keep warm, while the tourists took photos. I wasn't wearing enough.

The descent was quick and steep, with the road zigzagging sharply down hairpin bends. Then there was a sudden clatter behind me. One of the large panes of glass had fallen out of the bus and now cascaded in ever-smaller pieces down the side of the mountain. But the driver seemed unperturbed, and we continued, mountain air sweeping through the bus, down to the first habitation, a small village called Sost. This was where the bus terminated and where our passports were officially stamped.

The village consisted of flat-roofed mudbrick houses and lush green terraces full of orchards and poplars that already blushed yellow, as autumn started early up here. Flanking us were jagged, snow-capped peaks. I headed for a cluster of minivans, finding one going further down the valley to a village with a recommended guesthouse. A Japanese backpacker sat at the back and several local people had also taken their seats. I picked a spot and hoisted my hand luggage onto my lap, pulling out my tattered copy of *War and Peace*, and wondering if I'd finish it before the trip ended.

A few minutes later, my chest was stabbed with pain. It didn't feel deep enough for a heart attack, but the pain was worse than any bee- or wasp-sting I'd experienced before. I shook the neck of the baggy T-shirt I was wearing in the hope that the hornet, or whatever it was, could fly out. There were two more stabs in quick succession. Peering down I saw, matted in my chest hair, a pale-cream scorpion, pincers moving and tail poised to strike for a fourth time.

I shrieked loudly and ripped off the T-shirt, flinging it and the scorpion out of the open sliding door. Staggering outside, I peered at three marks on my chest where blood had begun to trickle. 'There's a scorpion in my T-shirt,' I announced to no one in particular, feeling a little faint. 'I think I'm going to die.'

A crowd formed, alerted by my scream and curious about my state of undress. I tried to ignore the pain and think quickly, given this was a life-or-death moment. 'Look,' I told the crowd, pointing at my chest. 'I've been stung three times by a scorpion. On my heart! I need a doctor. I'm going to die. Please, take me to a doctor.'

This elicited a wave of sympathetic head wobbling, and someone picked up my T-shirt, shook out the scorpion and squished underfoot it before handing the T-shirt back to me. 'Very sorry sir,' said one of the younger men who spoke a little English. 'Clinic closed.'

'Clinic?' I asked, seizing on this vital information. 'Yes! I need to go to the clinic. Now! I don't have much time. Please, I need a doctor.'

'Very sorry sir, clinic closed,' said the man again with an emphatic wobble of the head. One of his friends offered me a pill of some sort, which I swallowed unquestioningly. Another offered me tiger balm which I dutifully rubbed onto my chest. I felt my left arm grow numb and become difficult to move. *It's starting,* I thought to myself, forlornly. All I knew about scorpion stings was that in a film I'd seen as a child, a woman stepped on a scorpion and then just minutes later went into a fevered shock before dying. I had just minutes. *Why was no one helping?*

'Please, take me to the doctor,' I pleaded again, trying to keep my bottom lip from trembling.

The young spokesman for the crowd declared, 'Not possible sir. You are okay. Many pain, no problem.' Then, with an apologetic smile, he and everyone else began to disperse. I was left with the Japanese backpacker who spoke no English, but was furiously flicking through his guidebook in a bid to find information. I did likewise. Both our searches proved fruitless. I gingerly flopped my limp arm through the armhole of my T-shirt and pulled it back on.

The lack of concern was a good thing, I reasoned. No one wanted a dead tourist in their van, and they knew scorpions better than I did and didn't seem to think I was in particular danger. There was nothing for it but to sit back down again. As the shock wore off, the pain kicked in, and it felt as if my chest had been stabbed with a white-hot poker. We set off, passing spectacular scenery, and I glanced out of the window, half-heartedly, my chest throbbing. I really wanted my mum.

An hour or so later, the van deposited me, still alive, outside the guesthouse. I was wobbly on my feet and couldn't use my left arm properly, but I was alive. There were Americans, and now I had someone who would listen to my story and give me sympathy and, more usefully, a tube of antihistamine. My chest felt tender that night, but the following day I was fine and went trekking, crossing the river over a bridge made of steel wire and sticks.

Later, when I actually lived in Central Asia, I learnt that a sting from these small scorpions might kill a baby, but for an adult, it was merely a case of severe discomfort. In many ways, I was lucky to be stung on my chest and not somewhere more sensitive.

These scorpions were particularly common in mountainous regions. When I helped my local friends in Khorog to build a house, we often found scorpions resting beneath the boulders we were using instead of bricks. 'Look, it's a scorpion!' I said, the first time I spotted one. My friends looked at me quizzically, wondering if I would also comment on the ants, or occasional centipede, given how commonplace scorpions were.

There was an older American couple who lived in Khorog, and on a visit to their traditional Pamiri house, our hostess, Melinda, suddenly yelped and ran out of the room, unbuttoning her blouse as she did so. This was unexpected, but then something caught our eye and we saw, twitching on the carpet in its death-throes, a small pale scorpion. It had fallen from the roof-beams into her cleavage, where it had stung her and then been crushed by her bosoms. I now know, should I ever get stung again, that whacking the offending scorpion until it's turned to mash and then smearing this on the sting will help reduce the effects, as scorpions carry antibodies to their own poison in their bodies, in case they accidentally sting themselves.

I stayed for a week in the Hunza Valley, trekking and enjoying fresh chapattis and dahl drizzled with apricot-kernel oil. I would have stayed longer, but term was starting and I still didn't know if I had enough money for a flight home. I think the Hunza Valley might just be the most beautiful place I've ever been. The mountainsides were covered in boulders that spelt out greetings to the Aga Khan, as most of the inhabitants were Ismaili and revered him.

After a terrifying overnight bus journey from Gilgit to Islamabad, the driver careening at speed around blind corners as we wove our way down from the mountains, I arrived in Islamabad. I was dishevelled and dirty but managed to purchase a last-minute flight that evening back to the UK, with just enough money left to get all my rolls of film developed.

I had 'done' the Silk Road.

Although, of course, all I'd done was skate across the surface. I blush at photos of my youthful self in inappropriately short shorts blithely standing beside the holy tombs in the sublime necropolis of the Shah-i-Zinda in Samarkand with no sense of my own cultural insensitivity. I have a photo of a man taken in Osh; on the back, I've written that he is Kyrgyz, when I can now see from both his features and dress that he is clearly Uzbek and that a border does not signify an ethnicity. The cotton fields had been obvious as I travelled through during harvest time, but I'd missed the significance of the many pollarded white mulberry trees I'd passed, not realising that they were grown for a thriving silk farming industry, also known as sericulture.

In Soviet museums I enjoyed cutaway yurts showing their fabulous textile trappings, but never questioned why there were so few nomads left now. As for the cotton-pickers, they simply added drama to my photos. I hadn't stopped to think about their working conditions or whether they were actually getting paid, or why the children amongst them weren't in school.

Instead, having ticked 'The Silk Road' off my bucket list, I got on with writing up news stories for the various development organisations who had hosted me, and a report for the university travel bursary board. I was in Leicester for two more years and had largely forgotten about Central Asia, until one of the development organisations I'd written for contacted me. It was a small Christian Swedish organisation called Operation Mercy and they had just opened a new branch office in the desert oasis of Khiva, which also happened to contain a walled old city considered by UNESCO to be the most homogenous example of Islamic architecture in the world.

The Mayor of Khiva had heard about this thing on computers called the interweb or something, and that it might be a good way of promoting his city to the outside world to garner more tourists. He approached Lukas, a Swedish graphic designer, asking him to create something. Lukas assured the mayor that he could make it look nice, but that he wasn't a writer and would see if he could find one who would volunteer on the project. Lukas asked me if I was interested.

And I was.

So, this was what brought me out to live in Central Asia in the first place. It really was a journey into the unknown, and I had absolutely no plan to stay longer than my initial two-year commitment – and definitely not for fifteen years. If I'd known during my student trip along the Silk Road that I would return to live in these countries and get gored by a yak, swim illegally to Afghanistan and back, unsuccessfully smuggle gems, share a cage with a snow leopard, weep with survivors of ethnic cleansing, and get expelled from two countries, I'd have been as surprised at that as the fact that I'd develop a passion for 19th-century Central Asian embroidery.

PART ONE

The Wool Road

roving
/ˈrəʊvɪŋ/

adj: **roving**
        constantly moving from one area or place to another.
noun: **roving**
        a sliver of cotton, wool, or other fibre, drawn out and
        slightly twisted, especially preparatory to spinning.

1. TARTAN IN TARTARY

I step into a large, windowless room in the Urumchi museum in Xinjiang on that first trip along the Silk Road to see the museum's star attraction. Gentle spotlights focus attention on the family that lie before me. There's a hushed, reverential air, as if no one wants to disturb the rest of those we've come to see. Remarkably preserved, they look as if they died mere weeks ago.

They didn't. This particular family were around at the time of King David.

They are part of a collection of corpses known as the Tarim Basin mummies, although they're not wrapped in strips of linen or mummified at all. Their incredible preservation is due partly to the desiccating air of the Taklamakan Desert, and partly thanks to the expert way in which the bodies were originally laid to rest over salt flats, allowing air to circulate under them and salt to dry and preserve them. Many of the bodies are so well preserved that the unclothed ones are now displayed with strategically draped modesty cloths.

I wait until a tourist group moves away before I draw closer. Lying on a bed of white felt is a tiny baby, lovingly wrapped in a loosely woven blanket and wearing a snug indigo felt bonnet trimmed with madder red wool, with unspun madder wool stuffed into its tiny nostrils to protect it from cold air. Flat blue pebbles are placed over its eyes and next to it, a milk bottle – the oldest known in the world – made from a sheep's teat and udder. At roughly three months old – or three thousand years old, depending on your perspective – I find it incredibly moving to witness a life curtailed and yet prolonged for millennia.

The twill blanket has additional overspun threads woven in that writhe and kink to create an unusual decorative detail. It was made from brown sheep wool dyed in madder, giving it a dark plum colour. This same cloth, minus the additional overspun threads, was used to make the robe worn by a tall middle-aged man, possibly the baby's father. They were found together with several females in Cherchen, an oasis settlement on the south side of the Taklamakan Desert. The man lies with his knees and back bent, but if he stood upright – and it almost appears as if he might wake up and do just that – he'd be two metres tall. His brown hair is flecked with silver. Ochre burial whorls, matching the reddish tinge to his beard, still spiral at his temples.

He wears supple deerskin boots that have worn away in places, revealing puttees beneath made from brightly dyed strips of combed wool. Knitting has yet to be invented, but the puttees wrapped around his feet have naturally felted due to sweat and friction, and now provide a warm insulative layer.

Of the three women, two have badly decayed but the third is better preserved. She is also remarkably tall, and wears a striking scarlet robe with a cashmere sheen to it. Her brown and silver hair has scarlet wool woven into it. The burial chin-strap designed to keep her jaw closed after death had failed, and her mouth now gapes open. Facial reconstructions have been kinder, revealing an oval-shaped face with high forehead, prominent nose, chiselled cheeks and full lips. She's unmistakeably European. This is a problem. Although we're in Xinjiang, which means New Province, the communist government is creating a revisionist Han-centric version of history which claims that the first people to settle the Tarim Basin came from the East, not the West.

When these tall, red-haired mummies with prominent noses were first discovered, they soon became emblems of Uighur nationalism. Popular songs were written about them and their reconstructed faces were printed on posters like Bollywood movie stars. In reality, the DNA of Uighurs doesn't share much with these older inhabitants of the region, but it was enough for Chinese academics who wrote about the mummies to include obligatory warning against the dangers of ethnic separatism and attempts to divide the motherland.

The concept of China's current borders having always correlated with Han settlement is also somewhat undermined by the very existence of its Great Wall. It was, after all, built specifically to keep out the inhabitants of this region, known as the hairy barbarians, with their blonde beards, blue eyes and tall stature.

Visit Urumchi now – if China will let you – and, along with all the trappings of a dystopian surveillance state, and a systemic oppression of Uighurs akin to Jewish persecution in 1930s Nazi Germany, you'll find that the old museum has been replaced with a shiny new one. Its star attractions, however, have been relegated to one of the upper floors.

'We go straight up to the mummies,' our Uighur guide announced to my tour group on my most recent visit, which was before the persecution had really started to heighten. He headed purposefully for the stairs, waving dismissively at the queue of Han Chinese waiting to enter the ground-floor exhibits. 'Everything there is just Chinese propaganda.'

We passed a prominent sign in English and Chinese that declared: 'Xinjiang has been an inalienable part of the territory of China.' The first floor was dedicated to traditional costumes of the different minorities of Xinjiang, with pictures of happy Uighurs, Kyrgyz, Kazakh and Pamiri living in inter-ethnic harmony. Up another flight of stairs, we found a jumble of glass display cabinets with corpses in them, including more recent Han Chinese in beautiful silk brocades, as well as the Cherchen family, in what seemed like a deliberate attempt at confusing any sort of timeline. The simplicity and beauty of the original exhibit was gone. The bodies had been buried again, but this time among disinformation.

How did these Caucasian people end up living along the rim of the Tarim Basin? The answer may lie in the textiles they wear, which are surprisingly sophisticated for their time. Rather than plain weave, many of the robes and blankets are woven in twill. While plain weave is a case of weft threads going over-under-over-under the warp threads to create a checker-board effect, twill is different. The weaver must go over one warp, then under two, and repeat. This allows the weft threads to nestle closer together, creating a denser, warmer and more durable fabric. It creates the distinctive diagonal ridges you see in fabrics such as denim. In the case of Cherchen Man, his robe is an extended form of twill, with the weft thread going over two warps and then under three, to form a flatter diagonal pattern.

In some of the fabrics, brocaded mountain sheep with impressive horns form the borders of the textile. These additional threads have been added purely for decoration. There are vibrant dyes that remain colourfast to this day. There are painted textiles. And then there are woollen plaid twills, also known as tartan.

While the concept of each clan in Scotland having their own tartan is a Victorian fancy, used now to sell overpriced kilts to American tourists exploring their ancestry, the Celts in general knew the value of thick woollen twills to protect themselves against the elements. They were particularly fond of plaid, making use of stripes in a variety of widths and colours to create enormous variation. Bronze-Age proto-Celts lived in Central Europe before expanding westwards to Gaul, Brittany, Scotland, Wales and Galicia, as well as eastwards, through Thrace and Greece, and possibly a lot further.

Although ancient textiles rarely suvive, there are some exceptions. When items of clothing were accidentally dropped in the dimly lit salt mines used by proto-Celts in Hallstatt, near Salzburg, Austria, scraps of cloth sometimes snagging on protruding rocks, they were preserved by the salt. This gives us a rare glimpse into clothing from that time. From the various scraps found, it appears that a cream background with blue and white plaid stripes was a particularly popular tartan design.

In burial chambers contemporary with the Cherchen family in nearby Hami, tartan twill has also been discovered. The similarities are striking. Both have the same kind of weight and feel, and both employ the cream background with blue and white stripes. Given the enormous variety of patterns possible with twill, this similarity suggests a common weaving tradition. As the proto-Celts of Central Europe began to expand rapidly outwards, some may have travelled a lot further East than we previously thought.

How to survive traversing the grass steppes stretching over 5,000 kilometres from the mouth of the Danube in Eastern Europe, all the way to Mongolia and Eastern Siberia? It was too great a journey to complete over one summer, and in winter there were few trees for fuel or natural caves to shelter in. Nomads would have collected dung from their herds and flocks to use as fuel and could milk their animals or slaughter one occasionally to keep themselves fed. Hunting, possibly with hawks or eagles, would have provided further sustenance. Their main issue, though, was surviving the cold.

Woven tents, made with a sturdy blend of goats' hair and wool, are the most popular nomadic dwelling in the world, found everywhere from Northern Africa to Western Asia. However, the buffeting winter winds of the steppe would blow right through them. These nomads needed to make houses out of wool that were water-repellent, windproof and incredibly insulating, and yet light enough to transport. The only building material that could achieve this was felt.

While Cherchen Man's puttees had naturally felted, the beautiful felt indigo-dyed bonnet worn by Cherchen Baby was no happy accident. Felting is the most insulating way of using wool. If sheep lanolin is retained during the felt-making process, then felt can be not only water- and wind-resistant but also breathable. Felt has provided shelter to nomads in some of the toughest landscapes of the world.

To understand felting, we first need to explore the structure and origins of wool. Wool – as it turns out – is more of a man-made fibre than I'd realised.

There are at least 260 pure breeds of sheep today, but their DNA can be traced back to just two common ancestors. One of them is the Asiatic mouflon, which can still be found in Eastern Turkey and Western Iran. The other is unknown and became extinct at some point in the past. I've seen a mouflon or two in my time and they're impressive, with males sporting a decent goatee and curly horns. However, their coats are more goat-hide than anything I'd consider woolly. We know that around 10,000 years ago, early humans began to domesticate the animals they'd hunted; it proved far more efficient to take your larder with you, rather than expend energy hunting it. The domestication of the horse allowed humans to keep pace with their livestock, as did domesticated wolves, the precursors to sheepdogs.

Sheep were particularly good candidates for domestication. They aren't picky eaters, they mature quickly (which suits a nomadic lifestyle), they're adaptable to different environments and can be found in deserts, valleys or mountains. Crucially, sheep have a social hierarchy, led by the alpha sheep. A shepherd can usurp this role and the sheep will then happily follow a human instead.

According to bone fragments, up until around 5,500 years ago most sheep were slaughtered young, while their meat was still tender. However, shepherds began to learn that there were benefits to keeping their sheep alive for longer. Their dung could be used for fuel and their milk could be shared with humans. Shepherds also noticed how the fur on some proto-sheep hides was thicker than on others. With selective breeding over the next two millennia, these traits were magnified. Sheep became woolly – so much so that most breeds today no longer moult, as yaks, camels or cashmere goats do, but need to be annually sheared each spring.*

Today, nearly all sheep in Europe are white, rather than their original tan or brown, as white fleeces produce the most vibrant

---

* In 2004 at Bendigo Station in New Zealand, a Merino ram named Shrek was discovered, having evaded capture for six years. His face was virtually invisible under his shaggy fleece, which weighed a whopping 27 kilograms. In Australia, another Merino was found living in the wild with a fleece weighing 40 kilograms. Had they not been discovered, both sheep would likely have died from overheating or from the sheer weight of their fleeces. So, the domestic sheep is locked in a symbiotic relationship with humans.

colours when dyed. Different breeds produce different kinds of wool. The Karakul sheep, native to Central Asia and found particularly in Southern Uzbekistan and Tajikistan, has been bred to produce wool with just one crimp per inch, giving it a soft curl that has made its pelts extremely popular. At the other end of the spectrum is Merino, with one hundred crimps per inch. These extra crimps make the wool easier to spin and allow for thinner, finer yarn. Crimps also create pockets of trapped air, making the yarn an excellent insulator.

The importance of wool's ability to insulate us and keep us warm cannot be overestimated. As naked apes, we're particularly poorly designed for the cold. Our core body temperature is 37 degrees, but just a 2-degree decrease will lead to hypothermia. If our body temperature reaches 29 degrees, we quite simply die. Not only do we lack fur, we also lack brown fat that other animals – particularly sea mammals – metabolise to create warmth.

So, for humans to survive beyond the tropics, clothing, bedding and shelter is essential. All of these can be made from wool, particularly when it maximises its insulative properties as felt. Wool also has some other near-miraculous qualities:

- Wool has incredible elasticity and can stretch over a third its own length but still return to its original shape. This was one of the qualities that made wool the textile of choice for sails, as they could stretch in the wind and therefore tore less easily.
- Wool has a much higher UV protection rate than cotton and most synthetics.
- Wool has a high nitrogen content, making it virtually fire-retardant. It ignites at a much higher temperature than most other textiles and even then, the flame spreads slowly. It chars rather than melts, making it much safer underclothing for astronauts, firefighters or soldiers. It's also why carpets on planes or trains are typically made from wool, as they're far less likely to combust.

- Wool is more hydrophilic than any other natural fibre, which means it can absorb up to 40 per cent of its weight in water without feeling damp to the touch. Not only does this make it an effective insulator even when damp, but when it gets sopping wet, wool releases chemicals that make the wearer feel warmer. This is done through a process of sorption, where wool takes in vapour and generates heat. If you sweat a lot, wool will absorb this and wick it away from the skin. That, and its breathability, make merino running gear the choice of many top athletes.
- Wool is extremely resilient. Fibres can be bent back on themselves over 20,000 times and still not break.
- The outer layer of wool is covered in scaly cuticula that can open or shut to help regulate the sheep's temperature. This is key for felt-making, because the scales also open when warm soapy water or whey is applied. If the wool is then agitated, the fibres tangle so much that by the time the scales have closed and interlocked, you have a strong, insulating material that can be cut or stitched. Shepherds in Turkey have long known the benefits of felt for both warmth and protection from rain, and traditionally wear large felt caps over their heads with wide brims.

My first experience of felt-making took place in the village of Porchinev, just outside Khorog, six months after I'd arrived in Tajikistan. I was there with the Swedish development organisation, Operation Mercy, conducting village surveys all over the region. I had spent the first four months in Dushanbe, the capital, learning Tajik, despite my concerns that this wouldn't be very useful in the Pamir Mountains. Sure enough, when I arrived in Khorog, the regional capital of Eastern Tajikistan, I discovered that not only did the locals speak Shugni, their own language, but that unsuccessful attempts to break away from the republic during the recent civil war had left most Pamiris feeling actively hostile towards Tajik speakers. So, I set about trying to learn another new language; in this case, an oral one spoken in only three valleys. Living at 2,200 metres above sea level, I learnt that Pamiris have three words for 'to' and three for 'from', depending on whether you're going upwards, downwards or along; altitude is woven into the very fabric of their language.

Our new Operation Mercy office was small, so we wanted to make sure we invested in the right projects. The surveys allowed us to hear from the community themselves about their greatest needs, rather than making assumptions for them. It was, after all, an unusual region. Stalin had decreed that the Pamirs would be a beacon of communism to the world due to the area's strategic proximity to Pakistan, Afghanistan and China. As such, the region was lavished with a disproportionate amount of Soviet development, with a proliferation of small factories and workshops that made little economic sense. These largely collapsed when the Soviet Union did.

'All these mulberries you see now,' explained one of the older men in the Rushan Valley, 'they may have been a bad business idea, but they saved our lives during the civil war in the nineties. Originally these mulberry trees were planted to feed silkworms, but when the Tajiks blocked the main road and we didn't have enough food, we let the trees bear fruit and learnt to dry the mulberries and grind them into powder which we used instead of flour or sugar. It was a stupid idea to make us rear silkworms up here in the mountains. Even indoors, our houses are still not warm enough to rear the worms. So, in the Soviet times, each spring, diesel trucks would arrive and fill our heating tanks to overflowing. When they gave us too much, we simply poured the excess diesel into the river. Can you imagine?'

Similar waste had occurred in Porchinev village, where a clothing factory was set up that transported cotton chintz which had been manufactured in the north of Tajikistan and then transported across appalling roads to be cut and sewn into clothes in Porchinev before being transported back again. Of course, the factory was empty now – the machinery cannibalised and sold as scrap metal to China.

In the Soviet times, there had been six or seven flights from Dushanbe to Khorog each day in tiny unpressurised planes that flew through rather than over the majestic Pamir mountain range. By the time I lived in Khorog, there was the possibility of one flight a day, although this was often cancelled due to poor weather conditions and you generally needed to have connections to get hold of a ticket. The few times I did manage to fly, the propellers would skim so close to the mountainside that they would sometimes create flurries of snow, and the plane would often swoop up and over the mountain at what seemed like the last minute. The journey was still preferable to travelling by road, which took fourteen hours on a good day along pitted gravelly paths. My record was a three-day journey in winter, where all passengers had to get out and help dig our way through the road during a blizzard, before getting stuck for a day in Rushan – where I was welcomed into the home of a kindly village English teacher – due to a major avalanche.

During Soviet times, Khorog was full of top Russian military stationed there to maintain border integrity with Afghanistan. Unusually for a Central Asian regional capital, there was no bazaar back then, but the shops were full of luxury products flown in from Moscow and unobtainable even in Dushanbe. So, an overpopulated, remote mountainous region propped up by a command economy suddenly found itself in serious trouble when the Soviet Union collapsed. Initially, farmers on the Tajikistan side would call across to their neighbours in Afghanistan, asking 'What should we grow?' For so long, Moscow or Dushanbe had made such decisions, and they weren't used to thinking for themselves.

Then the situation got much worse as the newly independent state of Tajikistan descended into civil war in 1992. Pamiris, keen for independence and with no shared ethnicity, language or religion with the majority Sunni Tajiks, allied themselves against the lowlanders with catastrophic results. Pamiris in Dushanbe had to flee and were picked off at checkpoints, given away by their accents.

'They would ask you which number comes after six. If you said 'haft', then they let you go. But if you failed to pronounce the 'h' sound, then they knew you were Pamiri and put a bullet in your head,' explained one local friend who had escaped from the capital. These terrified families fled south into Afghanistan and then swam over to Khorog across the Panj River, because the main road connecting the region with the rest of the country had been blockaded by the opposition.

Khorog now had twice as many inhabitants. They were stuck there, as the border to Kyrgyzstan was closed due to the war. Only 10 per cent of food consumed in Khorog was grown locally. The shops were quickly picked clean.

My friend, Rashid, told me how he would join the queue outside the bread factory each night, waiting for the ration of one roundel of bread in the morning which was shared amongst his extended family. Another friend, Bunyod, told me his own experience of this turbulent time. 'We were lucky because we lived up in the Tang Valley and had our own land, so we could grow carrots, which we had to guard. Each day, my mother would carefully wash and then divide a single carrot into quarters, for me, my brother and my parents. It was all we would eat that day. I was just a kid and when I handed my portion of carrot to my dad and told him to eat it as he was regional school director and needed it more than me, I couldn't understand why he started crying.'

Although access to the rest of the country was blocked, the river border with Afghanistan was no longer rigorously patrolled. Afghan heroin and hashish flooded Khorog. 'I don't think there's a man over thirty in Khorog now who wasn't taking heroin during those times,' stated one of the professors I worked with. 'It stopped you feeling hungry. Of course, later, there were problems with addicts, but it helped us through those difficult times.'

Any tree that didn't bear fruit was chopped down for firewood. The days of excess diesel poured into the river were now nothing more than a bitter memory. Things were looking grim. Mass starvation seemed inevitable, until a man whom many Pamiris now worship as a god stepped in.

Spiritual leader of the world's 15 million Ismailis, the Aga Khan – a Persian princely title inherited from his great grandfather – is known as the *Hazir Imam*, which means literally 'the Imam now'. While Ismailis refer to themselves as Muslims, the majority of Sunni and Shia are not so generous, considering their veneration of the Aga Khan as idolatrous. The Aga Khan persuaded a warlord farmer from the south of Tajikistan – who became the unlikely new president of Tajikistan – to end the blockade and allow aid deliveries through. This aid came from a number of sources, and most villagers still plant their geraniums in tins that once held USAID vegetable oil. However, only one person is remembered for feeding the hungry, and that is His Highness, Prince Karim al-Husayni, Aga Khan IV.

If you're wondering what he looks like, imagine a bald old man with the clipped intonation of Captain Jean Luc Picard from *Star Trek*, but with considerably more bulk. His mother was of British nobility and his father half-Italian, half-Persian and a playboy who was briefly married to Rita Hayworth, among others. He grew up in Kenya and was then sent to Switzerland's most expensive boarding school. A close friend of King Charles, he has one of the best racing stables in the world; he is also a keen philanthropist and one of the top fifteen wealthiest royals, owning a decent chunk of Sardinia. He's been married and divorced twice, to an English model and then, much later in life, to a German model. According to Ismailis, he is the 49th Imam in an unbroken line of succession that can be traced back to the Prophet Mohammed.

As part of his philanthropy, the Aga Khan set up a network of development organisations focussing on poorer areas of the world where Ismailis live. As such, the Pamirs have received a generous amount of help with their healthcare system, education and more. I wondered whether our new branch office was needed at all, and if we had anything special to offer. I hoped we might find our niche through the village survey.

Having previously started two textile workshops in Khiva, I was keen to discover what textile resources were available in this region and how they were being used. Together with Vasila, our office administrator and translator, we approached village houses, clipboards in hand, and were usually ushered inside. There we were seated on one of the platforms and given bowls of *shir choi* – strong, black, salty milk tea with a dollop of ghee plopped in. I wasn't a fan, but to refuse would cause offense. We gifted each participant with a packet of tea to thank them for their time.

The survey began with questions about how many people lived in the household and then explored their needs and those of the village as a whole. What could they do about those needs themselves? What did they think we could do? Expectations were often unrealistic. A popular request was for us to open a mining company nearby, as the mountains were reputedly full of gems. There was one village near the southernmost tip of Ishkashim where old ladies would head up to the nearby mountain with their pickaxes and find *laal* – a rare red gem, highly prized in India – as well as the usual rubies.

I discovered that to take an uncut precious or semi-precious stone out of the country was considered gem-smuggling. This made me understandably hesitant when my language helper handed me a handkerchief full of large uncut rubies.

'Just see if you can sell them for me when you visit your sister in Mumbai,' he asked.

'But I'm not allowed. What if I get caught?'

'No one's going to check you. Just stick them in your washbag in your hold luggage.'

Stupidly, I agreed. The following week I took my illicit bundle and went through two security doors into Mumbai's main diamond trading centre.

'Every good family needs three things,' the jeweller told me smoothly. 'A good doctor, a good lawyer and a good jeweller.'

He examined each purple-coloured rock in turn, showing momentary interest in one. 'They're quite big, aren't they,' I offered, hoping that would aid a good sale.

It didn't. They were all poor quality and couldn't be used in jewellery. So, I smuggled them back again to their disappointed owner in Khorog.

Further down on our village questionnaire were the questions about textiles. 'What do you do with the wool from your six sheep?' I'd ask. Men would look blank and summon their wives. Women would disappear and return with drop-spindles – usually simple constructions made from a stick and a potato – and balls of their hand-spun yarn. Some had heirloom spindles with carved wood or stone flywheels instead of a potato. These flywheels add weight and momentum to the spindle, so that when you give it a turn, it spins for longer in the air. The combed strands of wool that are fed out evenly to the spindle are twisted by this momentum into yarn. Most women could get at least half a metre from one spin and would then wind the new yarn around a growing ball that covered the flywheel. For a durable two-ply yarn, two balls of yarn would first be spun separately, clockwise, and then spun together but counter-clockwise, which evened out the tension.

It's a laborious process, but spindles are highly mobile; spinning can be done while watching children play, or walking to the fields or orchards. The spun wool is then dyed and crocheted using short copper hooks with beautiful curving hand grips, polished with use. The main items of crochet are Pamiri socks. These are sold in bazaars and along roadsides and are a popular gift to anyone visiting from the lowlands. They're sturdy, warm and intricately patterned. But they don't actually require a massive amount of wool.

'And what about the rest of the wool?' I'd persist. 'If you have six sheep but crochet only three pairs of socks each winter, what do you do with the rest of the wool?'

As Vasila translated, the interviewee would assume an air of vagueness. Sometimes, we were told, they would stuff mattresses with it, but for the most part, they just put it on the roof.

'And then what happens to the wool, once you've put it up on the roof?' I wasn't giving up.

There was usually a shrug at this point. 'The wind takes it.'

'But the quality of wool from mountain sheep is really good. Can't you do something with it?' I asked.

That was how I heard about the felt-making workshop in Porchinev.

The workshop was situated at the top of the village, which sloped up from the Panj River towards the mountains. Channels of water irrigated apple and apricot orchards, as well as vegetable plots. On the other side of the valley was the largest Afghan village in the area, with a sparser population and better terracing of fields. Chickens pecked and scratched, and cows or sheep grazed in some of the fields of meadow flowers.

I knew I was close when I heard the whir of machinery. Ahead of me was a large, dilapidated warehouse and next to it several smaller buildings. Carpeting the ground between them were hanks of dyed wool in vivid greens, purples and oranges.

I introduced myself to the director of the workshop, Rashida, who offered to give me a tour. We started in a smaller side room where large clumps of sheared wool were fed into a noisy Soviet-era carding machine. A series of spiked wheels fluffed and combed the wool, so that all the fibres faced in the same direction, making it easier to work with.

We went into the main warehouse where an older head-scarfed woman wearing colourful baggy pants and a long kurta was laying down a large sheet of cotton cloth on the scuffed wooden floorboards that had once been painted municipal brown.

'Can I help?' I asked. Rashida nodded indulgently.

'You'll be making a large wedding felt. These are very popular at the end of summer when the boys come back from working in Russia and the marriage season starts.'

Rashida handed me over to the older woman and I watched as she took clumps of freshly combed magenta wool and began to tease them together to form a long, somewhat lumpy tube, known as roving. She gestured for me to do likewise, although my attempts at roving were fairly amateurish. This colourful roving was then placed onto the sheet in the outline of a large rectangle. Rashida made a second smaller rectangle, completing the frame for our felt.

More magenta roving created three diamond shapes within the inner frame. By now, a middle-aged woman had joined us and was busy forming long rovings in orange. The older woman took these and created cruciform patterns within each diamond that branched at their ends into ram's horns – a powerful magical design to keep away the evil eye. Gradually, different colours were added with garish but impressive results.

Finally, the older woman stood back and looked at her handwork critically, before nodding with the flicker of a satisfied smile. We collected handfuls of carded undyed wool with which we created a second and then third layer, the fibres of each laid perpendicular to the layer before. We now had what looked like a black, lumpy mattress, given a decorative touch with the last of the coloured rovings which were pinched and then sprinkled like confectionery over what would be the underside of the felt.

'Aslan,' Rashida said, and handed me an old empty paint tin full of holes which she filled with a bucket of hot, soapy water. The water began to stream out of the holes and I swung the tin like a censer in an Orthodox Church, until the whole felt was well sprinkled. Then reinforcements were brought in. There were five of us now. We were directed to one end of the cloth and began to roll it up tightly, as you would a sleeping bag, water seeping from the cloth and wetting our knees.

'Aslan, keep it tight,' Rashida grunted, and I tried to comply. Once we'd reached the other end, one of the women wrapped string tightly around the oozing sausage of wool, and we dragged it outside, leaving a soapy trail in our wake. Now came the hard part.

A flattened, well-worn cotton seating mattress was laid in front of the rolled-up felt, and the women began to pull rubber tubes up their arms and over their elbows. I think they were made from a car tyre inner tube. I was handed a pair and tugged them on, still unclear why I needed them. Then we knelt in a row on the seating mattress, leaning forward with our elbows on the rolled-up felt.

'Ready?' said Rashida. I wasn't, but the other women nodded and off we went. We rocked forward, rolling the felt under our elbows, and then rocked back again, repeating the motion as we found a steady rhythm. It reminded me of the ab wheel I used for core strengthening exercises and, indeed, my abs were really sore for the next few days, although they fared much better than my elbows. Despite the so-called protection, I would have large scabs on my elbows for weeks.

After 45 minutes, the women paused briefly, wiping sweat from their brows, and then undid the winding rope around our felt and unrolled it. There were still places where the wool hadn't fully felted, and these were rubbed with a nub of soap. The whole thing looked a little spongey, but our design was worked into the felt's very fabric.

'Are we finished?' I asked hopefully. The old lady shook her head. We rolled up the felt again, this time landscape instead of portrait, and began to rock again. I was very aware of a throbbing pain in my elbows and abs, but didn't want to be shown up by a far hardier 70-year-old woman. None of them were out of breath or seemed in the least bit exerted. We stopped, finally, and the wedding felt was unfurled and laid in the sun to dry. We stepped back briefly to admire our handwork.

'It should have dried by tomorrow, and then it will be ready to sell,' Rashida stated matter-of-factly.

I wondered if the gaudy patterns would be appreciated by the couple who purchased it, or whether it would simply provide insulation underneath a synthetic factory-made carpet from China, which had become the new fashion.

This way of creating felt is known as the 'fulling in' method, as the design is worked right into the felt itself. The Kyrgyz of the High Pamirs sometimes employ this style as well, although they use a reed mat as their underlay. Once rolled up, they employ a system of pulleys to roll the mat back and forth, which is far kinder to your elbows. If they're feeling lazy, they simply tie the reed mat to the tail of a yak and send it off to graze, letting it do the work instead.

However, most Kyrgyz felt is made using a patchwork appliqué method to create the wonderfully colourful *shyrdak*. I was very familiar with these from my travels in Kyrgyzstan and Kazakhstan, but had never seen them actually being made. That only happened on my first trip up to the High Pamirs, the roof of the world.

2. THE ROOF OF THE WORLD

Itook a break from the village survey to head to the High Pamirs with some foreign friends. It was near the end of July and they were happy to escape the heat of the lowlands. We borrowed our organisation's vehicle, loaded up, and left for a road trip.

Over a couple of hours, the road works its way steadily up the Ghunt Valley, studded by villages and cramped parcels of agricultural land in places where the valley is a little wider. We passed the hydroelectric station that had frozen solid the previous winter, leaving Khorog dependent on a small station in the town itself. This had led to rolling blackouts, with most households getting just two hours of electricity a day. Those who lived in blocks of flats and relied on electric heaters fared worse, and many moved in with relatives in stone houses who had wood-burning stoves. Nine months later, there was a record number of births after those long, cold, dark nights with no TV.

Eventually the trees peter out and only wheat and potatoes grow. We followed the Ghunt River upwards. The wider valley here was covered in clumps of sea buckthorn bushes. Their orange berries look like Tic Tacs and have a sharp, bitter medicinal taste, and make for a good local source of vitamin C. Upwards still, we passed the treeline altogether, seeing nothing but scrub until we reached the greenhouses of Jelondi.

Here, at over 3,000 metres, is the only place for hundreds of kilometres where you can buy fresh tomatoes in winter. A small settlement has sprung up alongside the hot, sulphurous water that gushes and bubbles out of the ground. Greenhouses heated by piped hot water from the springs are full of tomatoes and cucumbers. We stayed the night in a sanatorium, with two large indoor pools separated by gender, as swimwear is forbidden and considered unhygienic.

The following morning, we enjoyed an early morning soak before heading onwards and upwards, getting a puncture just as we reached the high pass. At this point, the road was just a mud track flanked by purple puddles of alpine flowers nestling close to the ground. Over the pass, we reached the wide glacial valleys of the roof of the world. Most of this plateau is around 4,000 metres high, and the air is so thin and clear that the distant hills and mountains seem close enough to touch. The stark landscape is studded with yaks, goats and tiny splashes of colour where a cluster of yurts have drying clothes laid out on the clipped meadow around them. Rivers move slowly and are often flanked by lush bogs that make for excellent yak-grazing. Eagle vultures, known locally as bone-crushers, wheel in the sky, occasionally dropping carrion bones onto rocks below to break them open. The air is filled with the shrill birdlike warning calls of plump honey-coloured marmots sitting near their burrows. The region is breath-taking, and not just because of the altitude.

We spent a night in the village of Alichur, where the ethnic divide within the region was clearly marked. The eastern side of the town and all settlements beyond it were mainly populated by Kyrgyz, while the western section housed Pamiris. It was a desolate village with no vegetation other than some stunted willows huddled in the shelter of a school-house, and boxy flat-roofed houses surrounded by gravel and dust.

You expected tumbleweed. Most villagers were semi-nomadic yak herders and had already left with their yaks and yurts, chests and churns, decamping to their summer pasturage until September.

One area of summer pasture could be accessed by a track off the main road from Alichur to Murghab, the regional capital. Here, there was a cluster of several yurts and we stopped for a visit. The Khorezm dialect of Uzbek that I'd learnt in Khiva has been influenced by the proximity of the oasis to the nomads who lived around it, which meant that I could more or less make myself understood. I spoke to the head of their *aul*, or settlement, and we negotiated a price to stay in one of their yurts for the night.

The outside of our yurt, as is usually the case, had little decoration other than some patchwork squares that rimmed the dome. The only other outer decoration was a patchwork appliqué felt that was draped over the doorway at night, when temperatures could still dip below freezing. We slipped off our shoes outside and ducked through the small wooden door – careful not to step on the threshold as this is considered unlucky – and then marvelled at the textile beauty all around us.

Underfoot were warm appliqué felts, rich in design and vibrantly coloured. There were also woollen flatweave strips sewn together to make decorative wall rugs that ran behind the wooden latticework of the curving wall. These flatweaves were traditionally woven with a portable loom made of three sticks that fit together to form a pyramid, with the warp threads pegged out behind. Today, women recycle the headframes from Soviet-era hospital beds instead, repurposing them as looms. The resulting warp-facing patterns utilise two or three colours to great effect, with a predominance of deep blues and rich reds. The narrowest flatweave bands are used to tie together the sections of wooden latticework, painted red, and to fasten the dome beams that slope out of the walls. These converge as spokes around the central wheel, or skylight, known as a *tunduk*.

The willow or poplar boughs used to make the wooden frame of a yurt are steamed to bend them into the correct shape, in a highly skilled process practised by sedentary people who expect payment in livestock. The central *tunduk* has at least four crossbars that form an X across the skylight wheel, although some yurts sport more decorative *tunduks* with up to ten crossbars. The *tunduk* is considered the soul of a yurt; if it breaks, the whole yurt frame is replaced to avoid bad luck. It's up in this skylight that the ancestral spirits reside, and some yurt-dwelling Kyrgyz and Kazakhs still fry diamond-shaped pieces of *borsok* dough each week to feed and honour them with its aroma.

Sunlight pooled through our open *tunduk,* creating criss-crossed shadows on the felt rug beneath. A flap of felt can be tugged across the skylight at night to keep it warm inside. Our yurt also had a decorative reed screen near the entrance. These are beautifully adorned by wrapping each individual reed in different-coloured bands of wool, building up complex carpet-like patterns. Each yurt has them on the left side, which is the women's section, and they are used for changing behind or storing things out of the way.

Along the far curve of the yurt wall were three large wooden chests. Piled atop these were wool-stuffed seating mattresses, sleeping mattresses, quilts, cushions, pillows and bolsters. Some of these were embroidered and others were richly patchworked. Not only is patchwork a way of repurposing scraps of material in beautiful and intricate ways, but the abrupt shifts and tessellation in the design are thought to confuse the evil eye, providing additional magical protection.

At night, these piles would decrease as mattresses and heavy quilts were laid out. Traditionally men sleep on the right side and women on the left. Similarly, saddles and weapons are kept on the men's side and kitchen implements on the women's side. Newly married couples would usually be given their own yurt as part of the betrothal. Hanging on the latticework of the walls and from the lower dome rafters were felt and synthetic velvet bags of various sizes, some used for storing food and condiments, others for clothing. In past times, the chests would be made of cured leather, which is both light and durable. Today, as summer migration usually involves a vehicle or two, larger wooden chests or cabinets are brought. Fancier yurts boast solar panels and small TVs, LED lightbulbs and phone-charging stations inside.

Nomadic Kyrgyz had lived in yurts like these for centuries, until Stalin began to forcibly settle Central Asia's nomads in the 1930s. The Austrian adventurer Gustav Krist was one of the last people to record their ancient way of life on the eve of its demise. He first arrived in Central Asia during the First World War as a prisoner of war, interned in a camp between Samarkand and Bukhara. He managed to escape and eventually made his way to Persia where he became a carpet seller. A chance encounter with a Turkmen fishing vessel on the Caspian coast, and a debt that needed repaying after Krist helped one of the fishermen to rid himself of guinea worm, led Krist to sneak back into Soviet Central Asia at the end of the 1920s and witness the dramatic changes being forced by the Soviet Slavic rule.

In Kyrgyzstan he encountered a great horde of Kyrgyz who had just returned from their summer pastures in the High Pamirs, only to discover that a Soviet army contingent was looking for them, planning to tax and then settle them. They simply turned back around, inviting Krist to join them. Once in the Pamirs, Krist marvelled as the women began unloading folded felt and all the yurt-poles while the men simply lounged around. The women would usually position chests and larger items inside the stone circles that marked out each yurt before erecting the frame around them, as the doors were often too narrow to fit the chests through.

> 'The Kyrgyz made merry over me when I tried to help the women erect the felt tents. Mahmud Sharaieff explained to me that setting up the yurts was women's work and unbecoming for a man ... The yurt is unquestionably one of the greatest inventions Asia has brought forth. Its circular structure and dome-like roof combine maximum comfort with extraordinary stability. During my stay in the Pamirs the heaviest storms raged over the *aul* without a moment's cessation all through January, yet never once was even one yurt blown down.' *

* Krist, G., *Alone Through the Forbidden Land* (1992), p. 143

To keep the cold from rising up, Krist noted how the women laid thick felt on the floor of the yurt, covering this with layers of dung and grass and then more decorative felts on the top. Doorways faced south, to make the most of the sun, and he found that even when the outside temperature was -50 degrees, the yurt was tolerably cosy. The hefty felt, up to ten centimetres thick, would be hauled over the dome when the hearth fire was not burning, and tied firmly in place with yak-hair rope.

The common word that most nomads used to describe their felt homes is *ui*, which simply means house. The term 'yurt' does not actually refer to the structure at all. Instead, it simply means home. For traditional nomads in Central Asia, their home would be in four different locations as they rotated their pasture with each season in a practice known as transhumance. So, for example, when arriving back at their winter pasture, an extended family would see the stone circles that marked out where to set up each felt house, as well as the nearby stream and the graves of ancestors who had finally ceased roaming and now lived in elaborate tombs, and possibly a yak pen. This is *yurta,* or home. When Russians first interacted with nomads and pointed in the direction of these *auls,* or settlements, asking what they were, the reply was 'home' – so the Russians began to refer to the domed houses of wool as yurts.

Before the invention of metal yak-dung stoves, with chimneys that poke jauntily out from the dome, the centre of each yurt was the open hearth, ringed with rocks. Smoke escaped through the skylight above and meals were eaten around the hearth, although it was bad manners to pass anything directly over the fire. Guests and elders would sit in the place of honour with their backs furthest from the door, away from danger (and drafts – which for elders was almost the same thing).

Yurts were not only the main dwelling places of the Kyrgyz mountain people, but also the Kazakhs of the steppes, the Karakalpaks of the marshy reed kingdom of the Aral delta, the desert-dwelling Turkmen and the Lakai tribe of Uzbek speakers who roamed the hills of Southern Uzbekistan and Northern Afghanistan. Most yurts look largely the same from the outside, although Turkmen yurts have pile carpets that drape over their front doors, and Karakalpak yurts usually deploy an intricate web of decorative outer bands to keep the felt in place. The Karakalpaks, who live in a mosquito-infested region of marshland, traditionally utilise the profusion of local reeds to create reed mats for the outer walls of their yurts. On hot days, the felt is rolled up around the bottom of the yurt, to allow air to circulate but keep the sun out. Back-yard yurts are still popular in Karakalpakstan today, and I enjoyed lunches in several while living in nearby Khiva. They're a great place to sleep in summer, providing the yurt has been kept closed during the day, as felt insulates against the heat as much as the cold.

And so it was that houses of felt enabled nomads to traverse the steppes of Central Asia, even in winter. They were light enough to transport and protected from extremes of both heat and cold. By the 19th century, these felt houses could be found from Eastern Anatolia through to Mongolia and the Gobi Desert, stretching a quarter of the way around the world.

Some of the ancient civilisations spawned by the Wool Road are finally getting better treatment in the history books, which have traditionally been written by the sedentary, whose accounts of nomads tended to be condescending, depicting them as little better than the horses they rode. The words 'Scythian' and 'barbarian', for example, have often been interchangeable, but now we're discovering just how sophisticated Scythian burial customs were, even though we know little about their culture as they never developed writing. Assumptions about them only began to change in the 1940s when some intact Scythian burial mounds, or *kurgans,* were discovered in the Pazyryk valley in south-western Siberia, dating back to the 4th–3rd centuries BC. One of the most impressive finds, which caused the rewriting of all books on carpet history, was the Pazyryk Carpet. It is thought to be one of the oldest surviving carpets in the world, and contains a far higher knot count than most high-end silk carpets made today. Its central field bears a striking resemblance to stone relief patterns found in ancient Persepolis in Iran, but along the border are large elk and Scythian hunters on horseback. It's likely that the carpet was woven in Persia, either commissioned by a Scythian or marketed to one wealthy enough to afford such a masterpiece. It completely contradicted the accepted narrative that carpets of this complexity were only created after the rise of royal workshops in Persia, less than a thousand years ago.

The burial mounds also revealed that Scythian chiefs, wealthy from their vast herds and flocks, had developed expensive and far-ranging tastes; artifacts were found in the *kurgans* that ranged from as far afield as Turkey, Armenia and Iran. Bowls of coriander seed – which only grows in warmer climates – also indicated widespread trade. And there was so much gold; from tiny golden beads sewn onto leather slippers or fine tunics, to gold harnesses for horses, and from gold dagger handles to lavish jewellery that depicted animals of the steppe such as enormous stags with flowing antlers.

Another find was an intricate felt wall-hanging that appears remarkably contemporary, with a repeated border depicting a mounted warrior standing before a king. The Scythian hunter sports a moustache and the kind of skin-fade haircut popular with today's footballers. He wears a close-fitting indigo jacket, tan riding trousers and a short red cape, unexpectedly covered in large blue polka dots.

It seems appropriate to capture the likeness of a nomad in felt, given that felt-making was what made this Eurasian way of life possible. The discovery of new *kurgans* continues and has revealed a myriad uses for felt: burial shrouds, socks, coats, boots, cushions, elaborate and incredibly warm horse-blankets, decorations for harnesses, and patterned floor coverings. Some of the felt is thick and utilitarian, while other items are lighter and embroidered. We tend to think of the Silk Road as the first age of globalisation, but the Scythian *kurgans* reveal dyes from the

Mediterranean, woollen textiles from Armenia and wild silk from India that were traded long before the Silk Road, proving that nomadism is anything but backward.

In our yurt, we watched the slanting rays of the late-afternoon sun pour through the open door, as we unpacked and made ourselves at home. Then the yak calves, still just a month or two old, began a frantic commotion. The herd was returning from grazing and the calves cried out to their mothers, who answered not with lowing or mooing, but with pig-like grunts. We went out to watch. Most of the yaks were chocolate brown, but some were piebald, caramel or a striking slate grey. One of the women pulled up a simple stool and began to milk a yak. They only produce around six or seven litres a day, but the milk is much sweeter and fattier than cow's milk and tastes vastly superior.

The fresh yak milk was poured into churns and some went into a cream separator. I've never fully understood how this Soviet-era contraption worked, but the turning of a crank whisks the milk so that buttermilk goes in one direction and thick globules of cream and butter in the other.

Some of the buttermilk was kept for drinking or making yogurt, but most was poured into a large metal vat over a smouldering fire of dry yak-dung bricks. Once warmed, a little vinegar would be added to curdle the mixture, and then the whey would be drained off. The curds were poured into woven plastic rice sacks hung up on a wooden platform, which acted as sieves, allowing more whey to drain away. After a day or so, the remaining sludge would be mixed with salt and rolled into large balls about the size of a mozzarella cheese. These curd balls were then placed on a high platform, out of reach of huskies and rats, where they would dry in the sun and wind. They would then be stored for winter consumption, crumbled into black tea with a dollop of yak butter, into which bread would be dipped. This would do for two or even three meals a day during the long winter months.

As our host was busy milking, I noticed the wool or fur – I wasn't sure what it was – flaking off the flanks of the some of the yaks. Others had moulted entirely. I knew that it must be incredibly warm if the yaks survived such cold winter temperatures, so I asked her what it was called and what she did with it. '*Tiwit*,' she said. A word I'd come to use a lot. As for its purpose, they sometimes used it for felt-making, but the felt of a yurt lasted for such a long time that usually, the wind just took it. Not the wind again.

'Could I have some?' I asked. 'I'm happy to pay for it.'

Soon the Kyrgyz family was chasing down their herd, lassoing the yaks with yak-hair rope. Once captured, we helped tug these flaky layers from their flanks. I collected several bags of caramel, grey and dark-brown fibre and wondered what I might do with it. I didn't realise it at the time, but this was to be the genesis of a new project.

That evening, as we sat around a plastic food-cloth spread over a beautiful felt, enjoying the rich, fatty sweetness of fresh yak milk and cream, I asked our host and two other men who had joined us how much a new yurt would cost. This provoked a heated debate, discussing the variations of yurt size and whether the price included the flatweave textiles around the lattice-walls, or a reed screen, and what furnishings would come with it. Then they had to decide upon a currency. Most Kyrgyz could think in Tajik somoni, but were also familiar with Kyrgyz som and Russian roubles. Larger purchases were usually made in US dollars – my host thought that $3,000 would be about right.

'What's that in sheep?' asked one of the other men, using a currency I was less familiar with.

During the night I went outside to pee and got distracted by the stars. The high-altitude air was so thin that the Milky Way – or Star Path, as it's sometimes referred to locally – was lit up above me, and I ended up staying outside for far too long. One of the huskies came and curled up at my feet as I stared upwards. They're never allowed inside a yurt. Finally, I was driven in by the cold, my teeth chattering. The stove still crackled a little as the dried yak-dung bricks shifted and smouldered inside. The crown above us was covered in a thick layer of felt, and the front door had a felt and reed mat that draped over it, keeping out the cold. It felt very different from the flimsiness of a tent. This was truly a house, just one made from wool.

We stayed an extra day in the *jailo,* or summer pasture, enjoying a taste of nomadic life and trying our hands, or thighs, at yak-riding. Our clumsy efforts drew much merriment from the children who had all been riding before they could even walk. The day after, we visited the village of Bash Gumbaz. Our arrival was greeted with village-wide interest, particularly when they heard that I was interested in their handicrafts. Family heirlooms were unearthed from the bottoms of chests and proudly displayed to be photographed, and I was ushered over to one house where the women were busy making felt in the dirt yard outside.

I never saw how they cleaned wool in the Porchinev workshop, but it's a tricky process. Wash wool too vigorously and it'll start felting. Herders would sometimes wash the fleece while still on the sheep, by moving their flock across streams or rivers just before shearing. A more common way to clean wool is to avoid water altogether and dry scour the wool. The way these Kyrgyz women were scouring their yak wool also made use of another part of a Soviet hospital bed, this time the interlocking wire mesh that made for a sagging support to the mattress. Clumps of raw wool were placed on top of the mesh and then whipped with metal rods. This fluffed up and separated the fibres, causing dried sweat, burrs, dried dung and other impurities to drop through the mesh, leaving the scoured wool ready for felting.

We left them to it and visited another woman who was in the midst of making a patchwork appliqué felt, known as a *shyrdak.* Initially, it was much more straightforward than the 'fulling in' method that I witnessed in the Porchinev workshop, with just two large rectangles of felt made to identical size but one in red and the other in black. The same design was cut out of both rectangles and then switched over to fit inside the rectangle, creating red ram's horn motifs with a black background on one, and black ram's horn motifs against a red background on the other. The felts were then stitched together with bright orange wool, and the same process used to create longer pieces to frame this main design. Once assembled, the whole patchwork would be placed on a larger rectangle of undyed felt and then elaborate quilting stitches would fasten it all together.

The motifs themselves included deer horns, broken horns or the leather flasks for storing fermented mares' milk. They were always cursive, because straight lines, particularly when stitched, weaken the felt and act like perforated tear-off slips. Felt-makers claim that standing on felt reduces aggression; traditionally, *shyrdaks* would be placed beneath the feet of warriors returning home, hoping for a more peaceable domestic life. Every bride will need huge amounts of felt both for her new yurt and for the *shyrdaks* that will carpet it. A traditional Kyrgyz admonishment states: 'If you want to join in with the celebrations, then you have to help out with the felt-making.'

All this stitching gives the *shyrdak* its name, which means 'stitched'. The result is a large felt appliqué that is strikingly beautiful and extremely warm. In fact, as I type this at my dining-room table, my feet are warmed by a *shyrdak* that I haggled hard for from an old woman that day in Bash Gumbaz.

We left the High Pamirs and travelled back to Khorog along the Wakhan Valley. The Pamirs had been starkly beautiful, but had also given me a fresh longing and appreciation for trees and gardens, fresh fruit and vegetables.

The next time I visited Dushanbe, I took my bags of yak down to show an American woman who was a textile artist and spinner. The yarn she produced had a sheen to it and felt very soft, but also very scratchy. This was because yaks and cashmere goats have two coats; an outer hairy coat which is rugged and can handle the elements, and a much finer undercoat of soft down. Any method of down collection will inevitably have guard hairs and outer hairs mixed in with it, which is what caused the scratchiness.

'Still, this is an amazing fibre, and you should definitely do something with it,' the textile artist said. 'They're crazy to be throwing it away.'

I agreed. After all those village questionnaires, it was a chance encounter with a moulting yak while on holiday that was the beginning of my new project. Surely there was a way to collect this fibre each year and either export it or, better still, find a way of dehairing it, spinning it and knitting or crocheting it into something warm and wonderful?

It wouldn't be easy. Cashmere had first become a luxury fibre because to hand-separate the hair from the down was such a labour-intensive job that Babur, founder of the Moghul Dynasty, had workshops full of Mongol slaves who could manage a pound a day. We had no Mongol slaves, or modern machinery to dehair the yak down, but these were bridges to cross later.

Perhaps, I thought to myself, a project like this could go some way to preserving the remnants of nomadism that had been all but wiped out in the 20th century.

3. HOW TO GET DOWN FROM A YAK

Several challenges were clear right from the start of this new project. I would need to travel widely across the High Pamirs before the annual migration to the summer pastures to gauge yak herders' interest in this project and research the best method for collecting the yak down. Then, most importantly, I would need to find an effective method of dehairing the fibre that wouldn't entail buying and importing expensive and cumbersome factory equipment.

I'd had the ball of yak wool knitted into socks by the mum of one of my friends in Khorog, but they were scratchy next to the skin, as expected. Yak hair is tough and excellent for making ropes, but not so great for, say, knitted underwear. The most popular local uses for the straight yak-hair tails were either to hang as a marker over the graves of holy men or to use as a fly whisk, which had historically made them much sought-after in ancient Rome. But dehairing was a problem for tomorrow. For now, I was focussed on collecting more than a plastic bag or two of yak down.

So, the following May, I went with my language helper and two colleagues back up to the High Pamirs to conduct a proper survey of yaks and yak down. Although it was sweltering in Dushanbe, winter had barely finished in the Pamirs and there were still patches of snow on the ground. The yaks looked gaunt.

The Kyrgyz didn't look much better. They complained about losing teeth due to the cold, but I suspected that the lack of vitamin C in their diets might be more the cause. We'd brought vitamin tablets to distribute, and I shared my stash of radishes with an elderly Kyrgyz man who'd never seen one before. In villages we asked who spun wool and discovered that many women had Soviet-era spinning wheels as well as homemade drop spindles. They favoured sheep wool over cashmere or yak down as the fibres were longer and easier to work with.

Yak herders varied in their reactions to our proposed project; some were initially sceptical about whether we would be able to deliver, others were incredulous, stating: 'We've been herding yaks for centuries. Why has no one told us until now that we're throwing away something so valuable?'

I found one enterprising Pamiri in Khorog who had previously collected a harvest of yak down but could find no buyers for it. After four years in a warehouse, it became infested with moths and had to be burned. Everyone agreed that they would happily try harvesting their yaks if we would buy the down.

Since the previous summer I'd tried to learn more about yak down. Yaks, I discovered, generally live at altitudes of between 2,000 and 5,000 metres, with 90 per cent of the world population in China and Tibet. Their down is considered one of the lightest, warmest fibres in the world, being three times warmer than sheep wool, and yet it was only harvested commercially from the 1970s. It's still often passed off as cashmere. In fact, if you own a cashmere jumper that was made in China, chances are that it's been blended with yak down, which still doesn't seem to sell so well in its own right. What do you even call it? Yakshmere?

Our trip the previous summer had been at the end of the moulting season and the yak down had simply flaked off in clumps. Now, yak herders were busily tugging the down off the flanks of the yaks, often leaving patches that looked raw and painful. Sarah, an engineering student from Cambridge, joined us – she made our technical challenges of down collection and processing the subject of her dissertation. She agreed that harvesting by grabbing handfuls of down and hair was cruel, as well as ineffectual, as it meant a much larger ratio of hair to down.

Sarah ended up returning to work with us, and the following June we made a much longer trip up to the High Pamirs to trial three different styles of cashmere combs to figure out which one worked best on yaks. The first comb was from Kashmir and was pretty and ornate. It proved utterly useless, so we stopped trying to use it after the first day. The second type were from America and looked a bit like miniature rakes with nice wooden handles. They were okay, but not great. By far the best combs were the ugly, hand-soldered, metal-hooked wire ones from Mongolia.

Our main aim for the five-week trip was to visit as many settlements as possible throughout the High Pamir plateau and show herders how to use the combs, spreading the word. Then, the following spring, we would return with more combs and distribute them so that herders could harvest their own down, which we would buy off them.

We discovered that there were an estimated 15,000 yaks in the High Pamirs and that they played an important role in the ecology of the region because of the way they grazed. The high plateau was at risk of turning into a high-altitude desert. One of the few shrubs that grew prolifically, but slowly, was teresken. At this altitude, a bush might take 50 years to grow to a height of 40 or so centimetres, with an extensive root network that anchored the topsoil in place. However, what took 50 years to grow took around 50 seconds to burn: dried teresken bushes were widely collected and sold in Murghab for fuel. As well as man-made damage, goats also destroyed teresken, clipping it to the nub rather than picking off branches as yaks do, which allows for better regrowth. In fact, the use of yak dung as biofuel was the main reason more teresken hadn't been used for domestic fires. So, a project that encouraged the herding of yaks rather than goats would be better for the environment.

Yearling yaks produce the highest yield of down, with a 70 per cent ratio of down to hair, while a six-year-old mature yak only produces 20 per cent down to hair. With adult yaks, the best down comes from the neck area, and just under the long hairy mane that follows a yak's spine. Yaks don't like being combed, so we became adept at hobbling them. This required grabbing a yak by the horns and giving its neck a sharp twist of 45 degrees, then tying the downward-facing horn to a front leg, which disorientated and immobilised the animal. With herds of 50 or more yaks in pens, it soon became impossible to determine which ones had been combed and which hadn't. So, we took to spray-painting the tip of one horn red if a yak had been combed.

On the whole, yaks are good-tempered, if shy of humans. There are exceptions. The first time I saw a newborn yaklet, still glistening and wet, its legs all wobbly, I knelt on one knee, a little too close, to take a photo. The mother, hovering nearby, became agitated, but I was oblivious to this. Then she charged me. Her horn took me in the groin, just missing my balls and leaving me with a large, vividly blue bruise along my inner thigh. I tumbled face first into dried yak dung and broke my glasses.

Once I'd stopped rolling around in agony, I dusted myself off and then rummaged around in my bag for my prescription sunglasses. I had to wear these as we drove back to Alichur, the nearest village, to scour the little stalls set up as makeshift shops inside people's houses, searching among the misspelt bottles of 'Haed and Shoulders' and the unfortunately named Fux shampoo, boxes of Barf detergent (*barf* meaning 'snow' in Tajik), Mars Bars, sunflower seeds, oil, macaroni, tins of sweetened condensed milk, candles, plastic dolls, cigarettes, radios, batteries, playing cards and other life essentials for some superglue. Eventually we found some, and Victor – my American colleague – used it to repair my glasses as best he could.

Another challenge was washing. Aluminium ewers and decorative basins were usually available, although designed for hand washing rather than something more all-over. It was usually possible to squat behind the reed screen in each yurt to wet and wash the essentials, but the only public bathhouses were in Murghab, so we were generally reliant on hot springs. Sometimes these were open-air and scarcely more than warm puddles, but no less a welcome sight.

My favourite hot spring was just north of the tip of the Wakhan Corridor on the Tajikistan side. Due to its proximity to the border with Afghanistan (if you can call a long fence of barbed wire which the local villagers have snipped and would roll back each morning to let their yaks graze a border) the spring was next to an army barracks, and the soldiers inside considered it theirs and we were told to ask permission before using it.

We dutifully did so, and soon Victor and I were wallowing in bubbling hot water like a natural jacuzzi. We were surrounded by snow-capped peaks and found it hard to drag ourselves away. We crossed the river and spent a day or so teaching a border village about getting down from their yaks before returning the way we'd come.

We had assumed that having asked for permission to use the spring two days ago, we were still covered, and Sarah went to use the spring first. Then it was our turn, and I was desperate to wash my hair. I had barely lathered up when two soldiers stalked over to us, guns slung over their shoulders, demanding to know why we were trespassing and ordering us out. I told the soldier that we'd already requested permission.

'That was for before, not now,' one of them barked at me.

'Okay,' I said, 'Once we're finished, I'll go and speak to your commander and apologise for the miscommunication.'

'No, you must get out now,' demanded the more annoying of the two, and then pointed his gun at us.

'Okay, okay,' said Vic, holding up his hands and trying to calm soldier boy down.

I was getting riled. 'No,' I said. 'I'm going to wash my hair. It'll only take five minutes, and then I'll go and see your commander.'

Gun-boy (as we later christened him) cocked his gun and pointed it at me, glowering. 'Go for it,' I told him. 'Then explain to your commander why you shot a foreign guest and got his hot-spring all bloody.'

I ducked under the water and gave my hair a quick scrub, but when I came back up, Victor was looking at me, concerned and naked, so I accepted defeat and dragged myself out.

'Is this how Tajiks treat guests in their country?' I hissed at gun-boy as I towelled off. He looked a little chastened. Hospitality in Central Asia is practically sacred.

We were marched to our vehicle, the roof rack towering with bags full of yak down and some ibex horns that Vic had found and wanted to keep. It was a fairly new four-wheel drive, but with low clearance that was woefully inadequate for our off-road driving needs.

'Okay, we're leaving,' I announced gruffly, and said no more to the soldiers. We drove off down the main track, but thought it might be worth taking a shorter route off-road. This proved to be a mistake, and we soon found ourselves stuck in mud. We placed boards under the tyres, as this was not the first time this had happened, and dug around them, but to no avail. Eventually, I realised that we'd need help and went back to the army barracks, feeling petty and sheepish at having left in a strop, and now asking for their help. The soldiers were quick to pick up spades and come to our aid, even gun-boy. It was hard work, but we eventually managed to get the vehicle shifted and onto firmer ground and by the end of it, gun-boy and I had become friends, the hot-spring incident well behind us as we took a photo together.

Another hot spring was near Bulunkul, a village with a majority Pamiri population. A young Pamiri man offered to show us the way as he fancied a soak and the spring was a short drive away. We left the road and bounced over hummocks and tufts until we reached a spot that looked down at the valley below. He pointed to what looked like a small pond and Sarah went first while Victor and I chatted with our new local friend. When it was our turn, we took soap, towels and shaving gear with us. Dipping our toes into the shallow water, it was the perfect temperature. We started to strip, and I did my usual sucking-in of the belly. I was fairly trim by Western standards, but Pamiris are impressively lean. I glanced over at his enviable six-pack and he caught my eye.

'I'm sorry I'm so thin,' he said. 'It's just, we don't have that much food up here.'

I wasn't sure what to say to that. After all, life at this altitude was tough.

In one village, we stayed with a yak herder called Horsand and his family. His name means 'joyful'. Like most herders he was semi-nomadic, wintering in Kyzyl Rabat, a cluster of three simple houses, and spending the summer months in a yurt up in the hills. He was particularly welcoming towards us as their settlement was one of the most remote that we visited and guests were rare. We entered through a sort of storage shed into his one-room house, which stood on a packed-dirt floor covered in homemade flatweave *kilims* and *shyrdaks*.

Horsand apologised for the poor condition of his home while we marvelled at how neat it was, with pyramids of upturned tea-bowls displayed prettily in a glass-fronted cabinet, neatly folded wool-stuffed velvet bedding piled on top of a chest, and a small solar-powered TV – their one luxury – taking pride of place on a table. He explained how winters were bitterly cold and his flock of sheep and herd of yaks were at constant risk from wolves. Of course, only ten of the 100 yaks in his herd actually belonged to him. The rest belonged to a wealthy businessman in Khorog. He was merely their custodian, and if any were lost to wolves or disease, then the loss was docked from his meagre wages. While the meat and skins belonged to the owners, the dung, dairy and down belonged to him, so he was particularly interested to discover that down had such a commercial value.

As Horsand sat us down on wool-stuffed mattresses around a food-cloth, his wife poured out bowls of yak cream for her unexpected guests and added another dung brick to the stove, stoking it, and then kneading a batch of dough. She put a large aluminium cooking pot upturned on top of the stove, which seemed odd. Once it had heated up, she lifted it quickly and deftly slapped a roundel of dough onto its sides where it began to puff and brown. The upturned pot had become an ingenious bread oven. We were soon enjoying hot fresh bread, delicious golden yak-butter sliding over it, as Horsand told us more about his life.

'It's not easy for us to herd yaks for other people,' he explained. 'We work so hard to take care of the yaks through the long winter, but we don't get to eat their meat, and the pay isn't enough for us to live on. The merchants who come here can charge us whatever they like for food basics. When we complain at the prices they just say that it's expensive to drive all this way. So, one sack of flour costs three-quarters of my wages. It's hard for us to afford tea or sugar.'

I noticed that there was no mention of purchasing onions, potatoes or even some dried fruit.

'I want to stop yak-herding, but what else could I do here?'

I asked if he'd ever consider living elsewhere.

'How could I leave the land of my ancestors?' he replied. 'This is our land; this is where we've always been and this is all I have to give to my children.'

We told him about our project and explained how much we paid for one kilo of combed yak down. His wife glanced up from her baking and caught his eye. This was something they normally just threw away. The timing of the payment also turned out to be ideal. Yaks moult just before the migration to the summer pastures, which is when herders need extra cash to stock up on flour, sugar and tea, as no merchants will drive up to their summer pastures. Selling yak down to us would make that transition much easier.

After lunch, Horsand and his brother who lived next door were keen to get combing. We spent two days with them – by the time we left, he'd earned the equivalent of a whole month's wages from yak down. He and his wife discussed how to spend the money. There were so many immediate needs, but his dream was to invest in a wooden floor to keep their home warmer in winter.

'You will return next year, won't you?' Horsand asked as we left. 'This time you came as guests. Next time you return as friends.'

In another remote settlement near Jarty Kumbaz, we arrived at a series of farmhouses and pens which had once been a Soviet collective farm. Eyes lit up as we explained our purpose and soon five or six women joined us in a spacious yak-pen, combs in hand and cotton bags over their shoulders.

Towards the end of the afternoon, as our bags were bulging with high-quality down, a Soviet-era jeep – the travelling bazaar – arrived, and there were squeals of delight and hopeful pleas that we might weigh and pay right then. While we handed out wages, the back door of the jeep was opened and goods displayed as temptingly as possible. Most of the money was taken by one of the older men, but each woman was allowed enough to buy Snickers bars, hair scrunchies, bottles of nail varnish, batteries or a bottle of cheap perfume.

Jarty Kumbaz is a region where many argali still roam. These enormous wild sheep, also known as Marco Polo sheep after they were described in the explorer's 13th-century travelogue, can rival a llama in size. Their huge, curled horns make them one of the most sought-after trophies in the hunting world. Until recently there was a ban on hunting them, but, as numbers increase, a few high-end hunters are granted permits for a price, with the money being used to subsidise conservation efforts.

I was served argali stew, which I declined, several times. I only ever saw one alive in the distance; it was magnificent. Ibex also roam the craggy mountains. The main predators for yaks, argali and ibex are wolves and snow leopards. The wolves usually only attack yak herds at the end of winter and are generally unsuccessful, chased off by the yak bulls. There are richer pickings for wolves in Khorog. Dogs aren't castrated and each year unwanted puppies and other strays proliferate and form feral packs, which can sometimes become quite aggressive. However, once the first snow falls, wolves from Afghanistan swim across the Panj River and eat the local strays. Team-mates reported horrible sounds in the night, the only trace in the morning being a red patch of snow with some tufts of fur around it.

As for snow leopards, it is hard to monitor their numbers as they generally stay away from humans. However, a backpacking couple visiting a Kyrgyz village in the High Pamirs were told that if they paid ten dollars, they could view a snow leopard cub. They paid up and the poacher, who had obviously killed the cub's mother, took them into his backyard. Inside a large wooden box with chicken wire mesh over the top, with virtually no space to move and no peripheral vision, was a pitifully thin snow leopard cub. Sensibly, the couple said nothing, but took photos, made a note of the address, and as soon as they had access to the internet contacted an international snow leopard charity.

They, in turn, contacted Stefan, a diminutive and bespectacled Swiss man who lived in Khorog and worked in conservation. He then arranged a confiscation order from the local government and drove up to the village. He hadn't entirely thought the confiscation through. The wooden box was far too big to fit inside a car, so Stefan ended up bundling the cub up in his leather jacket and then transferring him to a cage. The 'owner' protested, demanding compensation for the thousands of dollars he swore he spent feeding the cub, and only shut up when Stefan mentioned prison sentences.

Stefan named the cub Pamir. Back in Khorog, with nowhere to house Pamir, Stefan put him in the unused chicken coop in his back yard. Pamir, unused to any visual stimulation, began pacing and exploring. Initial estimates of his age were miscalculated. Although he looked six months old, he was over a year in age but severely malnourished. As Stefan began feeding him up, he tried to figure out what to do with this beautiful creature. Snow leopard mothers spend four years training their cubs how to hunt. Pamir had no hunting skills; when Stefan stuck a live chicken in the cage, Pamir got excited but only managed to kill it eventually by sitting on it.

Stefan set about building a proper enclosure in the botanical gardens in Khorog – the second highest in the world. The new enclosure was spacious and included a cave. It also happened to stand next to a building used by my colleagues for a mushroom-growing project, so they saw Pamir daily. I visited him several times, with just wire mesh between us, marvelling at his beauty and his enormous tail that was as long as his body. The zoo in Dushanbe wanted to take him, which was an appalling thought, only marginally better than his wooden box. Stefan was exploring options to send Pamir to a zoo in England which specialised in snow leopard breeding.

However, all reputable zoos have signed up to international conventions that refuse to pay for endangered species, as this simply creates a market for them. Dushanbe were unwilling to part with a snow leopard without someone's pocket being lined, so as legal wranglings continued, so did my visits to Pamir. I offered to write a story about him for a British newspaper and Stefan arranged for Nowruz – a chemistry student who lived in the flats nearby and had been hired as a part-time keeper and feeder – to let me inside the cage to take photos. Nowruz wore a padded jacket which Pamir loved to bite, and while his jaws were fastened around Nowruz's forearm, I took photos and stroked his incredibly soft fur.

It was the last time I'd see Pamir. As I prepared to write the story, Stefan was alerted by two of our staff working on the mushroom-growing project that someone had apparently given Pamir vodka, as he couldn't stand up properly. It turned out that Pamir had been given meat laced with rat poison. He died soon afterwards. I was full of rage and bewilderment at how someone could commit such an act, particularly when snow leopards are on the verge of extinction. The culprit was never caught, and the empty enclosure was all that was left.

Our yak-down-collecting trip continued. The late-spring weather was unpredictable. It never rains in the High Pamirs, even in summer. It only snows. On most days we were slathering on factor 50 sunblock and still burning as the air was so thin. Local men often wore balaclavas and sunglasses, and local women wore head scarves that left just a slit for their eyes, more out of necessity than piety. Some days we woke up to snowy landscapes, although the snow had usually melted by lunchtime.

In a few of the most remote areas, we came across people who were still truly nomadic, living in their yurts all the year round and moving to different seasonal grazing grounds. Despite the forced settlement of nomads under Russian and then Soviet rule, some had managed to keep the old ways alive. I knew of true nomads in some of the desert regions of Uzbekistan and Turkmenistan, but they probably numbered in the hundreds at most. I wondered how long semi-nomads, who lived in houses during the winter months, would continue their annual summer migration.

We tried to offer lifts whenever someone flagged us down, which sometimes involved taking their livestock as well. At one point we had two kids with two kids on the backseat, chatting or bleating. Occasionally we received lifts as well. In order to get to one herd, we were required to cross a river. It was a cold, overcast day, and I found myself clinging to a Kyrgyz herder as the yak beneath us waded through the icy waters, while I tried to keep my legs raised and dry.

Much as I love the superior taste of yak milk, it isn't something I'd want to subsist on. We brought jars and jars of apricot jam and tomato relish that we'd made the previous summer, along with Thai curry paste and coconut blocks. Not to brag or anything, but I can make a mean Thai curry on a yak dung stove.

I was aware that our brief foray into this world was very different from actually living in it. I only visited the High Pamirs once in winter. It was late October, but already the landscape was white with snow. Our vehicle's fan packed up during the trip, so we had to drive with the windows open. It was awful. I had no intention of ever going back in January or February, by which point the roads were often impassable.

So, I was surprised by what I heard while chatting with some of the Kyrgyz men in Alichur after I asked them what they thought about living there. The Pamiris, who all lived at the other end of the village, had complained bitterly about their hardship and how they'd much rather live in Khorog. The Kyrgyz, though, were enthusiastically positive.

'It's the best place to live in the world,' said one of them.

'When I go down to Osh, or to Khorog, the air is like a wet towel around my face and I can't breathe. Up here, the air is clear, the land is open and it's much better,' said another.

Although they were officially Muslim, the reality was that Islam rested very lightly on what was a more traditionally Shamanistic culture. Despite new mosques funded by Saudi Arabia, few prayed namaz regularly and it was the Kyrgyz historical epic of Manas that was memorised over the Quran. By the end of our five-week trip, we'd spent long enough at high altitude that our blood would have tested positive for doping. I noticed the effects of these additional red blood cells as Victor and I climbed up the mountainside in the Wakhan Valley, a good 1,500 metres lower, to get to the Bibi Fatima springs, which gush, hot and fizzy, from the recesses of a cliff. We weren't even out of breath as we strode upwards, chatting.

That Christmas I returned to the UK with several bags of yak down and took them to a mini-mill in Lincolnshire for dehairing. I caressed the dehaired down that collected at the end of the mill, marvelling at how incredibly soft it was. It seemed that importing the machinery for a mini-mill like this might be our only option, despite the fact that a it still took up a large warehouse and would undoubtedly cost a lot of money.

Back in Khorog, several village women hand-spun the dehaired down for us. We'd purchased several second-hand knitting frames from Scotland and started frame-knitting our first yakshmere beanies. The engineering student Sarah – whose father is Chinese – was able to locate a factory in China that sold mill equipment and we sent them a large sack of our down for dehairing. If the results were good, then we would start fundraising for the equipment and begin researching defunct Soviet factories that might be suitable venues for our mini-mill.

Meanwhile, I found a metal workshop in Porchinev that could copy the metal yak-comb from Mongolia. However, unable to provide the quantities of combs we wanted, I resorted to a larger factory down in Dushanbe and ended up with several hundred. By the following April, we'd laminated photos demonstrating which parts of a yak to comb in order to get the highest percentage of down, we'd stitched hundreds of cotton satchels and we'd transported all the combs back to Khorog.

We were ready to make a trip up to the snowy High Pamirs to start distributing the combs and provide training before late spring, when the yaks would fatten up on fresh fodder and begin to moult. We even had a new vehicle which had decent ground clearance and seemed fairly indestructible. We'd brought plenty of jars of jams and relishes to share and had a much better sense of what we were doing now. Our project was on course for success.

Families crowded round, listening eagerly as we knelt in their one-room houses, demonstrating which parts of a yak they should comb on a new British team-mate crouching on all fours. We discussed the fixed price per kilo of yak down, the necessity of a high down-to-hair ratio and the separating of colours.

It was all going well until we returned from one of the valleys to Murghab. Before we'd head to some of the more remote valleys, we were treating ourselves to egg and chips in one of the ramshackle restaurants. We'd just finished lunch when I received a phone call from Dushanbe. Murghab, the regional capital, was the only place in the High Pamirs with a mobile phone signal. It was Andrea, the Operation Mercy country director for Tajikistan. Her voice was shaking and she was close to tears.

'I've had the authorities in my office, and the KGB are making all sorts of crazy accusations,' she explained. Although the secret police had changed their name, everyone still referred to them by their Soviet initials. 'They say that you've got a month to leave the country permanently or they take us to court. And you know what that means.'

'But what am I supposed to have done?' I asked.

'They say that you caused the suicides of two teenage girls in Khorog, that you've translated the Bible into Pamiri and that you're a Swiss spy.'

'Swiss?' I asked, 'Why Swiss?' This seemed just as baffling as the accusations of espionage, the suicide of girls I'd never even met, and the very generous assessment of my Pamiri translation skills.

'I think they got Switzerland and Sweden mixed up,' Andrea stated. We were, after all, a Swedish development organisation. 'Anyway, you need to come back to Khorog straight away and we'll see if we can find out what's really behind this, and how we can fight it.'

There was stunned silence in the car as I explained the accusations being brought against me, followed by a clamouring of questions and then subdued confusion as we began the two-day trip back to Khorog. We speculated on the way back what might have motivated these accusations. Was it the language textbook I was co-writing with a Pamiri professor, to help preserve the language, standardise spelling and enable foreigners to learn Pamiri? Perhaps this book was seen as fanning the flames of separatism? Of course, we would never be told the truth.

We gathered character references from my host family, from the Pamiri professor and from local friends who were shocked at the allegations, particularly about the teenage suicides. Everyone had been shaken a few months before when the two girls hanged themselves from the same rope, both leaving only simple text messages reading, 'Forgive me, mother.'

It became clear from regular calls with Andrea that the KGB weren't going to budge, even with embassy pressure. Rather than grief, I felt an unexpected sense of relief. I had found life in Khorog tough. It wasn't just the seemingly endless snowbound winters and the threats of avalanches, or mudslides in spring and rockfalls in summer; I'd also struggled to connect with Pamiri people and culture. After seven years living in Khiva and coming to love the culture and community there, Khorog never quite matched up. I used to watch the river flow past as I tramped along the pedestrian bridge to our office each morning, knowing that these waters would join the Panj that would in turn become the Amu River and eventually flow past the Khorezm Oasis, and some would end up in the canal branch that flowed to Khiva. I still missed Khiva like a physical ache, but was banned from returning to Uzbekistan in the aftermath of the Andijan protests. The only thing that was keeping me going in Khorog was an unwillingness to quit, and a

strong sense of obligation towards the yak herders we had part-
nered with.

But now I had no choice.

So, I gave away much of my stuff, kept essentials and left the
rest in storage in Dushanbe, unsure if I'd see it again. I also spent
those last weeks attempting to prop up our yak project as best I
could. We were trying to stay positive, but I was the only one who'd
been able to communicate in both Kyrgyz and Pamiri and had been
the founder and driver of the project, so it wasn't going to be an
easy transition. My colleagues tried to keep things going over the
subsequent six months, but the project floundered and was then
officially closed down. I tried not to think about the hopes we'd
raised or the promises made to Horsand and the other yak herders. I wished that I could have returned in person to apologise and
explain, but I couldn't.

Instead, I returned to the UK, unsure what my next step would
be, or whether I might return to Central Asia. Mere weeks later, I
saw Kyrgyzstan feature on the ten o'clock news, which didn't happen often. Orchestrated violence had broken out: rural Kyrgyz from
the mountains around Southern Kyrgyzstan were attacking urban
Uzbeks in the towns and cities of Osh, Jalal-Abad and Bazar Kurgan.
Thousands of Uzbeks, carrying their wounded with them and little
else, had escaped across the nearby Uzbek border.

Operation Mercy wanted to send a rapid response team of
Uzbek speakers to the refugee camps springing up inside Uzbekistan
to provide trauma counselling – something it had done well in
the aftermath of previous disasters, such as the Izmit earthquake
in Turkey. I couldn't go because – as far as I knew – I was still
blacklisted from Uzbekistan. But then Uzbek refugees returned to
Kyrgyzstan in droves to vote in a key referendum.

And so, I found myself on a plane heading to Kyrgyzstan to
lead the response team, full of anticipation and trepidation.

4. THE TENT DWELLERS

'Come up here!' shouted a young, topless, rifle-toting man in Kyrgyz. The rifle in question was trained on me from the top of the steps that led up Solomon's Mount in the centre of Osh, the epicentre of the violence that had brought me here.

I thought for a moment and decided that being a friendly but ignorant tourist was my best policy. 'Hiya!' I called back cheerily, ignoring the rifle. 'Is this the way up? Can I come?'

'Yes,' he shouted back uncertainly in English, thrown by my bonhomie. I started up the steps. It was July and I was soon sweating. Off to one side of me were the worst-affected, burnt-out Uzbek neighbourhoods, which is why I wanted to climb up, hoping to get a sense of the devastation. Usually, this holy mount was a popular place of pilgrimage, as well as the best viewpoint of the city. Uzbeks and Kyrgyz alike would climb the steps, often affixing votive rags to the nearby bushes and tree branches. At the top was the tomb of a saint, where people prayed for blessing. Then, as they skirted the upper reaches of the mount, there was a large rock, polished smooth with use, which, if you slid down it, would reputedly cure you of backache. Further along was a cave in which barren women could place their hand in a hole and their wombs would open. Further round still was a Soviet-era museum built into the rock face, which looked very much like a Roger Moore-era Bond villain's lair.

'Hiya!' I said again with a breathless grin, holding out my sweaty hand to shake, once I'd arrived at the top. The Kyrgyz man had lowered his gun by this time and gripped my hand hard.

'Journalist?' He asked. It's the same word in English or Russian.

'No,' I shook my head for emphasis. 'Tourist.' Another of those international words.

He visibly relaxed. 'You like Kyrgyzstan?'

I put both thumbs up. 'Jakhshi!' I said, meaning good. Then he and his rifle-toting friend wanted to know which football team I supported. We were friends in no time, and they insisted on slinging their arms around my shoulder and posing with their guns for a picture. I was then allowed to proceed, as long as I kept away from the other side of the mount which gave the best views of the burnt-out Uzbek neighbourhoods. I nodded, but later, after they'd gone, I went back to take in the sea of UNHCR tents and the remains of prosperous courtyards that now looked like scenes from war-ravaged Warsaw. In some places, rather than camp in their courtyards, families had clustered their tents together on their street, like a circle of wagons, to provide some sort of protection. With a bitter sense of irony, I realised that now it was the traditionally sedentary population who were the tent-dwellers.

I was still shaken up by my walk to get to Solomon's Mount. It was the afternoon of the second day of our three-day training, conducted in English and Russian, and I was feeling sceptical. Tens of thousands had fled with nothing but the clothes on their backs and returned to find their homes looted and burned. They hardly needed me, with a packet of Kleenex and a messiah complex, helping them with their feelings when they barely had food, shelter or safety.

'When a whole community experiences trauma, no one can really listen. It's like everyone's in the water. You can't save others from drowning because you're too busy keeping your own head above water. That's why outsiders who are on dry ground are so important and can help pull people out,' we were told during the first training session. Pam, who had led the trauma-counselling project in Izmit, assured me that people's mental and emotional health and well-being were just as important as their material well-being.

We learnt about active listening: allowing people to tell their stories without challenging their feelings at all. Only once we'd listened properly could we gently challenge some of the beliefs people now held, such as the Kyrgyz coming back to finish what they'd started, or thinking that they would never feel safe again.

One of the Kyrgyz volunteers at the training looked ethnically ambiguous and could have passed for Uzbek. He told me how he had been driving home to Osh on the first of four days of carnage when he had encountered a checkpoint set up by an armed mob from the Kyrgyz villages in the Chong Alai mountains to the south. They thought he must be Uzbek and dragged him from his car. He pleaded with them, explaining that he was Kyrgyz and even sang the national anthem. Unconvinced, they turned to his Kyrgyz-looking wife who sat terrified on the back seat.

'Is this your husband?' they barked.

'Yes, yes,' she stammered, wide-eyed.

'And is he Uzbek?'

'Yes, yes,' she cried, not even listening to what they'd asked. They were about to shoot him when his father arrived and intervened.

'And now you're willing to go into Uzbek neighbourhoods?' I asked. 'Are you sure you'll be welcomed?'

'Of course, I won't be. But we need peace, and that begins by telling the truth and asking for forgiveness.'

This attitude was impressive and extremely rare.

I still felt that we should be doing something more useful. So, I'd taken the free afternoon to walk to Solomon's Mount and to clear my head a bit. I attempted a shortcut and got lost, asking for directions from a middle-aged Uzbek man squatting outside his house, smoking.

I was a foreigner speaking Uzbek, and that made me someone safe. His face crumpled and he began to weep. 'Come, come and sit with me, little brother.'

I'd rarely seen Uzbek men cry. At funerals, women wail inside the house around the body of the deceased, but outside, men simply sit on benches tutting their tongues or shaking their heads.

'We've been forgotten,' the man wept. 'No one cares if we live or die. The Kyrgyz just want to wipe us out. Karimov doesn't care. He doesn't really want us in Uzbekistan because he thinks we're all Islamic fundamentalists, and Putin isn't interested. Even God has forgotten us.'

I sat with him and let him weep. We were joined by several other men who also cried. 'We have no future in our own country,' they said.

'I came from England because I saw your suffering on TV. The world does know, and look, they've bought tents and they want to help you rebuild your homes. Would this have happened if God had truly forgotten you?' I asked.

The man nodded and held my hand, wiping his eyes with the other. Then they started asking questions. What would happen next? What about winter? How would those in tents survive then? What were they supposed to do, as they were all taxi drivers but too afraid to leave their neighbourhood because Uzbek men were getting kidnapped and tortured for ransom? I didn't have many answers but was able to help them with some information. None of them had lost their homes or their loved ones and yet their world and their way of life had been completely upended. After they sent me on my way towards Solomon's Mount, my attitude towards the trauma-counselling course shifted and I started to understand that mental wounds may not be visible but were no less real.

How had all of this happened?

When Stalin started carving Soviet Turkestan into nation states, he recognised that the largest concentration of population was in the Fergana Valley. Ringed on three sides by mountain ranges, the valley is around 300 kilometres long and 70 kilometres wide. It's well watered and probably the most fertile place in Central Asia. Consequently, it's been settled for centuries. The sedentary people who lived there were mainly Uzbek and Tajik speakers, with a few Kyrgyz villages in the foothills. Stalin was keen to parcel out the valley between three of the new nation states. Although Uzbekistan got most of it, the mountainous republics of Kyrgyzstan and Tajikistan demanded arable land, too, so the mouth of the valley went to Tajikistan. The eastern rim was incorporated into Kyrgyzstan, including the urban centres of Osh, Uzgen, Jalal-Abad and Bazar Kurgan. The border with the Uzbek Socialist Republic was largely symbolic – people regularly lived on one side but worked on the other, and families married across this new line, just as they always had done.

In the 1970s and 1980s, as the population grew, more Kyrgyz started to come down from the higher regions, where they'd been effectively banished to as their sheltered winter pastureland was appropriated by Russian settlers, and moved into the big cities. Kyrgyz pride themselves on their straightforwardness and consequently found the charming but duplicitous ways of city life repellent. Most were treated with a blend of patronising acceptance and disdain by Uzbek city-dwellers. In Osh, as long as the Kyrgyz lived in the newly built apartment blocks with the Russians, all was generally well. It was when they tried moving into Uzbek neighbourhoods that their kids would be pelted with stones and told to 'fuck off back to the mountains where they belonged'. Kyrgyz would shake their heads in disgust at how untrustworthy and double-crossing Uzbeks were, while Uzbeks were constantly offended at the blunt, hot-headed coarseness of their Kyrgyz brothers.

'Do you know how the Kyrgyz people came about?' an Uzbek woman in Osh once asked me. I shook my head, interested to hear what she'd say. 'There was a wild girl. No one could tame or control her and eventually she was cast out of her village and roamed alone amongst the mountains. Then, one day she met a wolf and she mated with him and bore children. They were the Kyrgyz. Ask anyone if you don't believe me.'

When the Soviet Union collapsed, states that had been deliberately created to be co-dependent and to fail if attempting to secede from the Union were now cast adrift from the socialist experiment. The second-largest city in each of these new nation-states was populated by an ethnic majority from a neighbouring nation. Osh in Kyrgyzstan was majority Uzbek. As for Uzbekistan, the second most important city was Samarkand, which was majority Tajik. In each case, these second cities struggled to find their place as a process of cultural homogenisation took place.

Russians also felt exposed without the protection of Moscow. In the north of Kyrgyzstan, thousands of Russians nervously began selling up and moving 'back home', even though their culture and accents marked them out as different in Russia, and some families had lived in Kyrgyzstan for four generations.

In the south, Uzbeks started to adapt to their new minority status. Although it was still possible for Uzbeks to work in certain state jobs, such as teaching in Uzbek-speaking schools, there were almost no Uzbeks in Kyrgyzstan's police force, army or regional government. Instead, Uzbeks focussed on trade, dominating the bazaar, and opened teahouses and restaurants. Even the most nationalistic Kyrgyz would generally opt to eat at an Uzbek restaurant over a Kyrgyz one, unless they wanted a whole boiled sheep.

Uzbeks were particularly known for their Islamic piety, which included avoiding alcohol. They would often view Kyrgyz as lazy, godless, entitled drunks, and that sense of entitlement grew strong after independence. 'Why are Kyrgyz the poorest people in our own country?' was a regular question Kyrgyz would ask. Rather than explore the roots of colonial exploitation and the resulting borders that had cut through existing communities, it was much easier to simply demand, 'When will the Uzbeks show some gratitude for the hospitality we give them? They should pay higher taxes.' It didn't matter that Uzbeks had been living in Osh, Jalal-Abad, Uzgen and Bazar Kurgan long before they were incorporated into the Kyrgyz SSR. By 2010, the populations of both Osh and Jalal-Abad were fairly evenly split between Uzbeks and Kyrgyz, with a smattering of Russians and Tartars thrown in, along with a colourful list of minorities who'd been exiled to Central Asia by Stalin, including Koreans, Chechens, Kurds, Gypsies and Germans.

The country was ruled by President Kurmanbek Bakiyev. He had come to power after the Tulip Revolution of 2005 and was a Kyrgyz from the south of the country, which was often under-represented in politics. Despite the Tulip Revolution's aim to overthrow a clannish president whose family had interests everywhere and were growing increasingly corrupt and authoritarian, Bakiyev and his family soon superseded their predecessors by a long shot. While Uzbeks would generally express disgust at governmental corruption and then shrug helplessly, the Kyrgyz began planning another revolution. In April 2010, there was an attack on the Presidential Palace in Bishkek and Bakiyev was chased out.

He fled to the south, shaking his fists and promising a bloodbath. The interim government were still trying to find their feet and garner international legitimacy, given how they'd come to power. Roza Otunbayeva, a former ambassador to America, became Central Asia's first female president, promising to step down after a year, by which time the country would be ready for elections. Meanwhile, an Uzbek politician from Jalal-Abad, Kadirjon Batirov, used the moment to urge for greater Uzbek autonomy in the south, for Uzbek to be recognised as an official language and for Uzbeks to have more say in local government.

This was misrepresented as a call for separatism. Tensions were stoked by nationalist local Kyrgyz leaders, particularly the Mayor of Osh, and then, on the twentieth anniversary of the ethnic violence that had taken place in Uzgen in June 1990, the fighting started.

There was a phone text of unknown origin which was widely shared, calling on Kyrgyz to come and fight because female students were being raped by Uzbeks at the medical college dorm. They hadn't been, but it achieved its objective. Then there were rumours of a clash in a local casino between the two rival mafia gangs who controlled most of the trafficking of heroin coming from Tajikistan to Russia. The head of the Kyrgyz mafia was said to be the son of the recently ousted president. The Uzbek mafia lost.

Disaffected young men from these poor mountainous villages were collected on local football pitches and given speeches about the importance of taking back control of their own country and teaching the Uzbek freeloaders a lesson. They were armed, and then set out for Osh.

Mobs stormed the main police station and army barracks, unimpeded, and helped themselves to weapons. They used these to systematically attack, loot and destroy Uzbek neighbourhoods in Osh, before moving on to Jalal-Abad and Bazar Kurgan. Huge army trucks were soon full of electronic goods and anything else worth looting. Later, President Roza Otunbayeva commissioned an international independent investigation into the events. On its release, the investigation raised serious questions about the complicity of local government, police and the army in providing free access to weaponry, concluding that they either participated or enabled the violence which ensued.

That these events were premeditated was evident from the number of Kyrgyz in Osh messaging their Uzbek or Russian friends, warning them that something was about to happen and that they should leave the city until it was over. Eyewitnesses spoke of looters and rapists with strangely red, swollen skin and unfocussed eyes. Uzbeks who had defended their neighbourhoods noted that the Kyrgyz looters all drank out of bottles which they were careful to collect each time before moving on. Similar symptoms had been observed among some of the violent protestors in the April revolt to oust the former president in Bishkek. One theory was that they had been given some sort of drug – possibly horse Viagra. A week or so after the violence, middle-aged women came to Osh to protest outside the local government building. They were from villages in the Chong Alai, and it was their sons who had done the raping and looting. Now, these men were experiencing chronic liver failure, and all had the same symptoms. What poison had they been given?

I spoke to one Uzbek woman who was too old to flee. She described how first they would loot and rape, then they would throw military-grade incendiary devices into the courtyards which burnt fiercely. Most courtyard roofs were made from corrugated asbestos and disintegrated in the heat.

The mob grew and now included urban Kyrgyz men as well. They moved on to Jalal-Abad, where the murder rate was lower because most Uzbeks had already fled. Then they headed towards Bazar Kurgan. On the way, some wanted to attack the predominantly Uzbek town of Suzak, but the men from the town, warned of what was to come, had placed a barricade across the road and armed themselves with rifles. The looters and rapists weren't expecting resistance, and some were killed in the skirmish before heading on to destroy large sections of Bazar Kurgan. The following year a special roadside statue was erected to commemorate these fallen Kyrgyz. There have been no such statues for their victims.

By the time order was restored, official records show that almost 500 people had been killed, around 70 per cent of them Uzbek. Thousands had been injured and 400,000 people had been displaced. Almost 3,000 courtyard homes for extended families were destroyed, the vast majority of them owned by Uzbeks.

By the time I arrived in Osh, there were still signs of the violence everywhere. Whole neighbourhoods, bazaars, shopping centres, universities and restaurants had been burnt down. Spray-painted on the charred walls were either a simple 'C' or the word 'sart' (spelt 'CAPT' in Cyrillic), dooming them to destruction. This was a term used by Russian colonists to describe the sedentary population of Central Asia, and it was now being used as a racial slur by those of nomadic origin. Other homes or businesses with a K for Kyrgyz, or R for Russian, remained untouched.

'There were military helicopters flying overhead the entire four days,' explained another Uzbek woman. 'At first, we actually thought they'd come to help us, not just to watch, so we sprayed S.O.S. on the roads, but they did nothing.' While I was in Osh, the coverup began, and S.O.S. signs were scrubbed off roads, where possible, or turned into 888. After all, they did not fit with the narrative that was now forcefully repeated on local television: the Uzbeks did this to themselves to make us look bad.

I heard more about this from an old Uzbek couple as we sat in a small backroom which hadn't been considered worthy of burning, in the charred remains of their courtyard. The main walls facing the street still stood, but they had filled the gaping window frames with rocks to prevent any more intruders.

'They took all seventeen flat-screen TVs that we had brought back from Korea to sell,' explained the husband.

'The looting I could understand,' his wife interrupted. 'But then they smashed all my jars of homemade jam and winter salad and smeared them everywhere and – I'm ashamed to say this – did their business on our guest-room carpet. Why do that? What did we do to them?'

'They didn't go down to our basement where we still had our old Soviet TV, so we set it up here, and now we just watch it all day and get even more depressed, wondering what's happened to our country,' the husband continued.

'Every day they show the same two Kyrgyz houses that were burnt down, and that was only because they were in Uzbek neighbourhoods,' said the wife. 'And they never show any of the hundreds of burnt Uzbek houses. Then, the other day they showed the outside of our house from the street. We were so shocked, weren't we, because it was the first Uzbek house they were showing, and we wondered why they hadn't knocked on the gate, so we could let them come and film from inside. Then some Kyrgyz actress started wailing, standing in front of my own front gate, saying that this was her house and that the Uzbeks had burnt it down. Can you believe it? I know what my own house looks like, there was no mistaking it was ours. Everything they're saying is just lies.'

I met some seasoned aid workers from Human Rights Watch International who had come to Osh to investigate and had already worked extensively in Rwanda. I wanted to get their take on things. 'You've come here a month after the violence and yet already there are two completely different versions of events,' I said. 'How do you know who to believe?'

'Oh, it's easy,' a Norwegian woman replied. 'One group have their stories. They're not completely accurate, as people don't remember accurately, so they'll get some of the times or dates wrong, but they'll add in the little details and talk about how their own lives were interrupted. They're the ones telling the truth. The other side has a script.'

'The Uzbeks did this to themselves to make us look bad,' I stated.

'Exactly.'

On my first day, I braced myself to hear horrible things, wondering how it would be to pick my way through the rubble and misery of wrecked lives. I wanted to document what I heard and had purchased an inappropriately colourful homework book from the bazaar, but wasn't sure if people would feel comfortable with me taking notes. The retired teacher who I spoke to first, inside her refugee tent, demanded to know why I didn't have a notebook with me. As I rummaged for it, she stated, 'I want people to know what happened here; what happened to me and to the rest of us.'

She took me on a tour of her rubble, sighing as she remembered the expensive Turkish carpet that had been in the guest room, and wiped away a tear when she pointed to the scorched wall niches where her documents, family photo albums and safe with savings had been.

'I just don't understand it. What did we do to them? What did I do? I taught Uzbeks and Kyrgyz and Russians and Tartars. I always told them that we are all God's people and to respect one another. I never showed favour to one group. I worked hard and was finally enjoying my pension, but now it's all gone. I still don't understand why. And they say we did this to ourselves to make them feel ashamed. Why would I destroy everything I worked so hard for? Then, after they kill us and steal from us, they blame us and start arresting and torturing the young men. We have no future, and nobody cares.'

Visits developed a strange pattern. Our little ragtag team were just a drop in the ocean, so we prioritised those who had lost family members. 'Who died here?' I'd ask, as we entered an Uzbek neighbourhood. There were usually three or four grannies drinking tea outside at the entrance to the larger streets. We discovered later that they were acting as sentries, with mobile phones tucked away in their baggy pants, ready to warn of any Kyrgyz incursion. Then a child would be dispatched to take us through the rubble of a burnt courtyard, still topped with charred vines and blackened fruit trees.

Inside the tent, or sometimes a surviving room at the back of the courtyard, there would be apologies for the lack of hospitality from the host. 'All our teapots were smashed. I'm sorry we only have this thermos.' This would be followed by protests from me that I wasn't thirsty. I'd give small soft toys to any children and a few household items to the family.

'I'm so sorry,' said one woman, frantically climbing onto the rubble of her courtyard wall to pick some apricots from the branch of a tree that hadn't charred, 'But this is all I have.' She insisted that I eat some, as I was a guest in her tent. Of course, I found this very difficult, but to deny her the opportunity to practise hospitality – something so deeply ingrained in all Uzbeks – was to make her feel even less human than she did already. Stories of wounding by snipers or witnessing the murder of family members were interspersed with sobs but also admonishments: 'Please, have another slice of melon. More tea?'

Regularly, I would leave the tent to find that someone had quietly rotated my sandals around so that they'd be easier to put on. It was these small gestures of kindness and hospitality that threatened to unravel something in me that I knew needed to stay tightly wound until all this was over and I had enough emotional distance to unpack my own feelings.

One young man, who had been shot in the armpit (his hands raised in surrender) had lost several family members and spent an hour shouting, swearing and jabbing his finger at me. I considered it a profound privilege to simply listen, my face sprayed occasionally with saliva as he finally found a way of releasing some of the pent-up rage and anger he was feeling. At the end of it, spent, he thanked me and said that we were brothers.

Our listening and bearing witness, our paltry gifts and our attempts to encourage, all felt woefully inadequate but were greeted with enormous appreciation. 'Why are you apologising?' asked one of the neighbourhood elders. 'It's a miracle to us that you foreigners have come here to help us. It means that we're not forgotten. It means that God hasn't forgotten us. Do you understand how important that is to us? You're the first foreigners to not just send help but to send yourselves and come and help us rebuild our lives. Maybe it's a small step, but it's an important one.' She then promptly began to weep, kissed my forehead and then prayed a blessing over me as I silently wiped my eyes.

I learnt that the ransom for Uzbek men taken to basements had gone up from a couple of hundred dollars when I first arrived, to several thousand dollars or the deeds of a house. I interviewed two brothers in Jalal-Abad whose burnt courtyard was situated behind the torched remains of the University of Friendship.

'We spent a week with relatives in the village and then we came back,' explained Yunus. 'Our house was burnt down except for this back room. All we had were the clothes on our back and my little car. We started trying to clear the rubble when twenty Kyrgyz men showed up and said that they'd take me to the mayor's office to help me get compensation. Well, we drove straight past the mayor's office to the KGB building. They demanded to know where the weapons cache was in the University. I told them that I didn't know anything about that. They beat me with rifle-butts and injected me with something to make me tell the truth. Then they said that I should give them my car, but I refused because it's my brother's. They pretended to shoot me in the head after that. When they finally released me, my family had to take me to Uzbekistan for treatment because no Kyrgyz doctor would help. I would have stayed in Uzbekistan, but they wouldn't let us. Now that all the men are being rounded up and tortured, we're heading to Russia. I don't know if we'll come back. What's left for us here?'

Those in Jalal-Abad were warned of what was happening in Osh, which usually gave them time to flee. But there were some exceptions.

'We heard from relatives what was happening,' said one old woman I spoke with. 'Everyone panicked and many people fled to the Uzbek border. My son, daughter-in-law and their children live here with me. Then another of my daughters-in-law arrived with her children and then another. Their husbands are working in Russia. So, with ten children in the house, and only one man, there was no way we could flee.

'We heard the armed vehicles outside on the street and screaming and shouting. I sent my daughters-in-law with the children to the back room and they hid behind a mattress. We told them to keep quiet because otherwise they'd find us and kill us. I'm an old woman, so I didn't think they'd attack me. Then incendiary devices started raining down into our courtyard. I went out with my son and we tried to douse the flames as quietly as we could.

'They must have heard us, though, because someone raked the front gate with bullets and then stuck their gun under the gate and let off a round. One of the bullets clipped my son's ankle and he shrieked in pain. Then we heard voices telling us that if we didn't open the gate, they'd burn the whole courtyard down. What could I do? I opened the gate, with my son lying in a pool of his own blood. They looted us and took the TV and DVD player and anything else they thought was valuable. They didn't even bother about wearing masks or hiding their identity. Then they went into the back room and found the children. I rushed in front of them and they started to hit me and call me awful things. They wanted to know if I was working with Batirov, or if he was my relative. I told them that I'm just a retired schoolteacher and that they could take me outside and rape me or shoot me if they wanted, as I'm old anyway, as long as they didn't harm the children.

'They hit me again and then they left us. I went out to help my son, but it wasn't safe to take him to a hospital. We all just shivered and wept for the rest of the night. None of us have slept properly since then. If we hear gunfire, we panic. Even the scuffle of a mouse is enough to terrify us. My son is in hospital now, so we have no income. Was it such a crime that I was born Uzbek? What is to become of us?'

since then. If we hear gunfire, we panic. Even the scuffle of a mouse is enough to terrify us. My son is in hospital now, so we have no income. Was it such a crime that I was born Uzbek? What is to become of us?'

The Kyrgyz media campaign was working. One Uzbek man drew out a three-litre jar full of ashen lumps as we sat in his tent. 'That's all we could find of my mother, my auntie and my sister,' he said grimly. 'They hid in the basement and burnt to death there. After it happened, my Kyrgyz friends were all calling me and putting credit on my phone. They wanted me to know that this wasn't them, but Kyrgyz from the Chong Alai. They all promised to bring their largest rams to slaughter on the 40th day of remembrance, but none of them came. Now they just blame us for what happened.'

Soon, the only men left to interview were the old. Some wept as they described sons or grandsons who'd been killed. One particularly pious man with a white flowing beard had only his son's passport photo, as they considered taking photos *haram*. He sobbed as he described his son to me, and silent tears splashed my notebook as I wrote down what he said. I was served tea by his impassive daughter-in-law, who'd been married for three months, pregnant for two months and a widow for one.

I heard many awful stories that I won't repeat here, and they began to take their toll on me. I found myself hating Kyrgyz and had to remind myself of all my Kyrgyz friends in the Pamirs. Outside the local government offices in Osh, Kyrgyz who had lost family members were holding vigil in a yurt and demanding justice. I had mainly been listening to Uzbeks and felt I should listen to their side as well.

I knocked on the door frame and asked tentatively if I could come in. Slipping off my sandals and apologising for speaking Uzbek and not Kyrgyz, I sat down. There were mainly stout middle-aged women inside, and they were angry. One waved print-outs of her son's dead and mutilated body. Another declared that they should finish what was started and chase all the Uzbeks back into Uzbekistan where they belonged. I tried to reason with them, pointing out that they were all Muslim brothers, and telling them stories I'd heard from Rwanda, of forgiveness and reconciliation.

'Forgive?' one woman spat, 'After what they did to my son? Never.'

'But I've spoken to so many Uzbeks who also lost their sons or their grandsons, and they tell me that all they want is to live in peace with you as they always have done.'

I was dismissed as the largest woman clambered to her feet and declared that it was lunch time. We filed out of the yurt and a mild-mannered man took me aside. In a gentle voice he presented his son to me. 'Look, he's just seven years old,' he explained, 'and I have to think about his future. I know he doesn't have one unless we wipe out all the Uzbeks. We have to. We have to just get rid of all of them.'

His mild manner, so at odds with this statement, shocked me more than anything else had. '*Adamsizbe*?' I asked, which literally means, 'Are you a man?' but translates better as, 'Where is your humanity?'

'Yes, I'm a man, but first I'm a Kyrgyz,' he stated.

I spent the rest of the afternoon trying to encourage terrified groups of Uzbek women who wanted to know if the violence would restart, and my previous assurances now sounded hollow in my own ears.

A consortium of local development organisations and international aid agencies were working on a re-housing scheme. Luckily the international agencies listened to local wisdom, otherwise they were going to commission hundreds of yurts to be made, which would have rubbed salt in the wound of those who had lost their houses at the hands of the previously nomadic Kyrgyz. Instead, they offered to rebuild one small room in each courtyard, which would see families through winter. After that, they would have to rebuild the rest themselves.

After a while it became clear that no one wanted to talk about the past anymore, as their thoughts turned constantly to the future, and particularly to winter. 'It's fine now, as everything's cheap. We can even skip a meal and just eat a cheap melon from the bazaar. But we haven't bottled or pickled anything. What are we going to be eating in January?' asked women as I visited their tents. Tomatoes, for example, were practically free in August. They'd steadily climb in price as we entered September, and by the end of October they'd be unavailable until the following May or June. So, this was the time when homemade tomato and vegetable sauces were made, along with huge quantities of jam. As I'd walked through charred courtyards, I'd seen the remains of jars which were always kept and reused, now melted into fantastical shapes.

So, I gathered some of the smaller, local organisations and proposed that we work together to buy cauldrons and gas burners, hundreds of empty jars, sealable lids, sugar, vinegar and fresh produce and that we start our own winter-food project. We could work with neighbourhood committees so that one woman from each tent could come and work for the day, and her family would get the fruits of their labours to keep for winter.

An Australian/British couple offered the use of their large garden and liaised with a Romanian businessman who imported second-hand clothes from Europe. We raised funds to purchase the clothes and made them available. We bought sacks of sugar, jar sealers and everything else we'd need. Eventually, we were ready for our first group of 30 or 40 women. We learnt after the first day to specify that only young women need come, as the older women, having issued orders to the younger ones, promptly began to nap on the outdoor picnic platform.

Gleaming two- and three-litre jars of produce, still steaming with heat, were then taken home by each woman, including savoury mixes of cabbage, tomatoes, garlic and peppers, which helped relieve the winter monotony of onions, potatoes and carrots. We found that the women who came each day saw it as something to relieve the stress and boredom of sitting in their overcrowded tents all day, but also as a taste of normality.

I started another canning station in Jalal-Abad with local development organisations there. It was Ramadan and most of the women were fasting from food and water until nightfall, as well as wearing heavy modesty garb, and working in outside temperatures close to 40 degrees. We never heard one complaint. We hired a widow who had worked particularly hard on the first day, and she helped oversee the daily running of the chopping, cooking and stirring, leaving me with more time to search the bazaars for more jars and wholesale prices for all the fresh produce we were ordering. I was also trying to fundraise despite ropey internet connections. The money came in, though, as many Westerners had been moved by what they'd seen on their TV screens.

'This lid-sealer is rubbish,' I overheard one woman say to another as she tried using the one we'd purchased. 'I wish I'd brought mine from home, it's one of the old-style ones ...' she tailed off, having forgotten for a moment that her better, Soviet-era lid-sealer had burnt along with everything else she owned.

The trauma-counselling training I had undertaken earlier had laboured the point that we should also look after ourselves in this process. Consequently, I made two trips up to Arslanbob, the most popular tourist destination in the region. It was wonderful to escape the heat of the dusty valleys and enjoy the beauty and tranquillity of this traditional Uzbek village nestled in the world's largest walnut forest, with a backdrop of 3,000-metre mountains, and boasting the longest waterfall in Central Asia. Even here, Uzbeks were terrified about the future, and a number had received abuse from Kyrgyz holidaymakers. I went hiking in the mountains and in the forest, but learnt that there was a large problem with deforestation, with trees felled for winter fuel. I rummaged through some of the woodpiles in Arslanbob and found beautiful, seasoned walnut wood destined for burning, but with so much wood-carving potential. There was just one woodcarver I spoke to, and he, too, lamented the quality of wood being shoved into stoves.

By the time my visa was about to expire, I left with an unexpected sense of purpose, knowing that I would try to return to Arslanbob and start a school for woodcarving.

The following spring, I did return, but based myself in Jalal-Abad until I could recruit enough colleagues to move up to Arslanbob with me. I still found myself resenting Kyrgyz there, so I moved in with a Kyrgyz family, hoping that this would keep any prejudice at bay. I'd only been living with them for a little while when the UN international report on the previous year's violence was finally published.

'What do you think, Aslan? It's all lies! What do these foreigners know?' said my host.

'Which part is a lie?' I asked.

'All of it.'

'The Uzbeks did this to themselves to make us look bad,' his wife added.

I had generally tried to be diplomatic and avoid confrontation with my hosts, but I had my limits.

'Really?' I asked, holding her gaze. 'They burned down everything they'd worked for, they destroyed their passports, land deeds, wedding pictures, pets and even their family members, all just to make you look bad? Is that really what you believe?' My voice had raised at this point.

She looked away. 'Well, we helped our Uzbek neighbour escape,' she replied, and that was all that was said on the matter.

What does any of this have to do with the Wool Road?

Well, more than you might think.

Most of the rural Kyrgyz men caught up in the violence came from villages clustered in the mountains of the Chong Alai, south of Osh. They eke out a living growing onions and potatoes, raising a couple of cows or a small herd of sheep or goats. Winters are bitterly cold, and fuel is expensive. It's not an obvious place to settle nor did they do so willingly. They lived there because their land had been stolen. As recently as the 1930s, Kyrgyz hordes had migrated across this region with huge herds of cattle, camels and horses, and enormous flocks of sheep and goats.

How had a way of life which had remained unchanged for millennia been wiped out so rapidly, taking with it much of the glorious textile heritage it had spawned? How did the Wool Road unravel, and who unravelled it?

5. NOMADS NO MORE

The enmity between pastoralist and agriculturist is as old as time itself. In the Book of Genesis, Cain is an agriculturalist and Abel tends his flocks. Both brothers make offerings to the Lord. Cain offers his first fruits, but they are rejected. Abel's sacrificial lamb is pleasing to the Lord and is accepted. In a fit of jealousy, Cain then kills his brother; the first recorded murder. The relationship between nomad and settler has been a conflicted one ever since.

However, the topography of Central Asia meant that by the early 19th century, nomadic and sedentary people lived a fairly harmonious existence – the obvious exception being the sedentary Shia Muslims of North-western Iran, who were preyed upon by Turkmen marauders and taken off to the slave bazaar in Khiva. The total human population of this vast region was only around 8 million, and most were concentrated in the oases made possible with irrigation. Only 3 per cent of this vast region was irrigated and cultivated. The rest was too mountainous or too dry to support anything other than grazing flocks and herds. This was where the nomads roamed.

Sedentary communities depended heavily on water irrigation as there was so little rainfall, and a network of irrigation channels was dug. These were open for a certain number of hours per week, and then closed off again to allow a larger number of farmers to make use of the water. This process took place day and night, which meant that some farmers had to wake at three in the morning if that was their allotted time-slot, to ensure that they weren't denied water.

I spent seven years living on the edge of the Khorezm Oasis. In one direction, you could drive for over an hour through lush orchards and fields of wheat, cotton and even rice paddies. In the other direction, you barely left Khiva behind before arriving in the scrub and dunes of the desert. The Khorezm Oasis gets no more rainfall than the desert around it, but relies on a network of canals supplied by the Amu River.

Under Islamic law, only land that had 'been brought to life' through irrigation could be considered owned. This principle worked well for agriculture and resulted in famously sweet peaches and grapes from Samarkand and world-class rice and melons from Khiva. For nomads, though, this left them with little written legal framework that recognised their own land ownership. Generally, this wasn't a problem, as sedentary people had no intention of farming the arid steppes or the rolling hills, and nomads themselves generally respected and recognised each other's pasturage. However, this balance shifted in the latter half of the nineteenth century, with the arrival of Russian colonisers.

Tashkent was the first city to fall, and the others soon followed. Khiva and Bukhara managed to retain their rulers and a degree of sovereignty, but only as vassal states. While the Russian forces experienced little armed opposition from the sedentary people, the nomads – in particular the Turkmen – put up more of a fight. Turkmen had originally proved a useful pretext for colonial expansion, as Russia could claim that it was merely liberating the unfortunate sailors from the Caspian, or peasants who'd lived near Orenburg, who had been captured in raids and then sold as slaves. In 1871, the Russians began a fully fledged military offensive against the Turkmen, but struggled to fight an enemy that could attack and then melt away into the desert. They needed a clear target, somewhere with population density and nowhere to run.

There was one particular oasis, known as Akhal, which had a high concentration of yurts, clustered within the ruins of the old fortress of Geok Tepe, or Green Hill. In 1881, this is where Mikhail Skobelev – a ruthless Russian general said to court danger as passionately as he courted women – chose to mount his attack. By then, thousands more Turkmen from the surrounding area were also seeking safety behind the fortress walls. They watched and jeered as the Russian army seemed to do nothing but snuffle in the mud, like pigs. The Turkmen understood nothing of mines. When the walls came down, the slaughter was indiscriminate, with over 30,000 killed. Neither women nor children were spared.

British Captain Frederick Burnaby, no stranger to a bit of bayonetting himself, wrote with revulsion how 'hell was let loose on Turkomania. And this, the Russians would have us believe, was done to further Christianity and civilisation ... they had no chance against the breech-loaders of their foes and were repulsed with great slaughter.'*

Skobelev maintained that the harder his enemy was hit, the longer they would stay down. He certainly succeeded in subjugating the Turkmen, although many chose to flee across the new frontiers of Imperial Russia into Northern Afghanistan, where their descendants remain to this day.

While the Turkmen had been taught a lesson, few Russians actually wanted to settle in their desert. Far more attractive were the steppes

---

* Burnaby, F., *A Ride to Khiva: Travels and Adventures in Central Asia* (1876), p. 422

of Northern Kazakhstan, which weren't far from the Russian border. The alpine valleys of Kazakhstan and Kyrgyzstan, with their familiar climate, were also desirable. So, from 1875, Russian peasants were given tax incentives and encouraged to migrate southwards into these lands. Over the next twenty years, a staggering 1.5 million Slavs emigrated into the region that is now Kazakhstan. It was getting crowded.

As well as peasants, educated classes came to Turkestan to make their fortune. They were helped in this endeavour by a policy that usually favoured Russians and other Slavs when it came to employment opportunities. Those Turkestanis who did manage to get employment in a Russian-run cotton gin or on the railway lines were paid less than their Russian counterparts and rarely got the top jobs.

As demand for land grew, Russia declared nomadic land as having no fixed ownership and therefore belonging to the Russian state. Nomads were still allowed to utilise some of that land, but 'surplus' land, which the state had decided that nomads didn't need, could now be used for Russian immigrants. Of course, the nomads had no say in what parts of their land would be considered 'surplus', and the most fertile areas were usually stolen first. There were even cases of arable land taken from settled Kyrgyz and Kazakhs who were already farming it.

It wasn't uncommon for a Kyrgyz family to return from their summer pasture up in the hills to discover that their winter pasture in a sheltered valley now contained a hastily built Russian log cabin and tilled fields. When this happened, a confrontation with the settlers would often result in nomads being shot, or if a nomad was to harm a settler, they would be hunted down by Russian forces. Petitioning the Russian administration for justice was generally a waste of time, and the nomads' own tribal leaders also wanted to stay on the right side of their new colonial masters and rarely helped. Then there was the Forestry Commission, which tried to stop Kyrgyz living in mountainous regions of 'forests' even when there wasn't a single tree for miles around.

As a result, most Kyrgyz got moved from their attractive and fertile lowlands and had to eke out an existence living in their summer pastures, which were generally too cold and too exposed during the winter months. As their land got smaller, so too did their flocks and herds.

With Russian colonisation came vodka, cigarettes and syphilis. There were credit schemes to swindle trusting nomads out of their livestock. The lack of guile, cunning or literacy simply confirmed notions that nomads were backward and stupid. Landless Kyrgyz resorted to hiring themselves out to the very people who had stolen their land. First the numbers of livestock and then the numbers of surviving Kyrgyz children dropped.

Russian authorities were baffled when nomadic Kazakhs persisted in their 'backward' nomadic ways and incentivised them to settle with an offer of 100 roubles per family. Only the most destitute did so.

The perks of colonisation were broadcast loudly, such as the new railways and telegraph system. However, budgets for colonial development of Turkestan dried up when Russia joined the First World War. Taxes were raised as Turkestanis were expected to contribute financially towards the war effort. At first, only Russians and other Slavic peoples were deemed trustworthy enough for conscription. However, with resources stretched, the Russian administration decided to enlist Central Asians as well. They weren't trusted to fight, but could do the grunt work of porters, trench-diggers and other menial tasks.

The actual conscription was outsourced to the upper classes of Turkestan, who were told that they and their families would be exempt if they drew up lists and managed any resistance. There would be exemptions made for those sedentary men working in the cotton fields, but for nomads there were no such options.

Wild rumours circulated around Turkestan that soon everyone would be forced to dig trenches in between Russian and German troops as shells rained down on them. These sparks landed on dry tinder, and it wasn't long before rumours of revolt led to terrified Russians fleeing to the cities, demanding arms to defend themselves.

The revolt began in the summer of 1916, and it started among the settled peoples. They attacked places of conscription, destroying lists that had been drawn up, and killing those who were conspiring with the Russians. Protests broke out in Samarkand, Jizzakh, Andijan and Kokand, and were violently suppressed by Cossack forces at the behest of Russia.

Soon furious mobs began attacking symbols of Russian colonisation, such as the railways and telegraph lines, and even Russian settlers. Jizzakh – a city between Tashkent and Samarkand – was one of the epicentres of the violence. The Russian colonel sent to respond decided to make an example of the local people, ordering his men to murder, rape, and then burn entire villages.

Unlike their sedentary neighbours, the nomads were mobile and many upped sticks and fled in order to avoid conscription. Hearing of the uprisings in the towns and cities, Kazakhs and Kyrgyz were emboldened. Not only had they experienced systematic injustice, but many of the Russian men of fighting age were away at the front, leaving Russian settlements largely unprotected. They sent threatening messages to those remaining, telling them to leave, or else. Some made good on their promises and tortured and killed whole families of Russians. Generally, though, when a Russian settlement was successfully overpowered, the men were killed and the women and children taken into captivity. Peasants' fields of grain were trampled and locals refused to help bring in the harvest. Anyone attempting to draw up new lists for conscription was attacked and often killed.

One enterprising group of Kyrgyz managed to capture a military convoy of ammunition, and others took weapons from those they'd killed. However, Cossack regiments sent in to quell the uprising were then equipped with machine guns and subsequently mowed down anyone who attacked them. This was but one example of the incredible cruelty meted out by Russian forces as they exacted reprisals. These soldiers were largely reservists and conscripts who lacked military discipline and were often Slavic colonists themselves with scores to settle. Hundreds of nomads who'd played no part in the uprising were slaughtered and their land and livestock stolen. Indiscriminate shooting of men, women and children was the norm, as yurt camps and entire native villages were burned. So much livestock was requisitioned that the Russian authorities had no way of feeding all the cattle, which began to die. Many Kyrgyz now faced a winter of starvation, with no livestock to depend upon and their yurts destroyed.

Recognising that they had no future in Russian Turkestan, nomads began to flee, trekking over the Tian Shan mountain range into Chinese-administered Turkestan where they hoped to start afresh. First to go were the Dungan, who were Muslim but ethnically Chinese, speaking an ancient dialect of Mandarin. The Kyrgyz followed, with 100,000 to 120,000 leading their livestock in an exodus, pursued by Russians. The hurried pace and the onset of winter meant that thousands of livestock perished. Even for those who managed to cross successfully, many were mistreated by Chinese authorities and some even attempted to return the way they had come. Turkmen nomads also fled, but their escape route was over gentler mountains into Persia.

By the time the dust had settled, just over 2,000 Russians had been killed in the uprising, which was more than had died in the original conquest of the region, and hundreds of thousands of Turkestanis had been killed or died of starvation or exposure. By the end of the reprisals, over 300,000 Kazakhs and Kyrgyz had fled to Chinese-administered Turkestan. This exodus, along with the many deaths from famine and violence within Turkestan, meant that the overall nomadic population shrank by 2 million.

The first time I visited Kyrgyzstan properly, I went trekking in the mountains in the north of the country, luxuriated in the hot springs and swam in Issyk Kul – one of the largest alpine lakes in the world, ringed with soaring snowy peaks. I thought nothing of the wooden Russian houses clustered along the roadside or dominating towns such as Karakul. I enjoyed their chocolate-box charm, with carved eggshell-blue window shutters. I'd heard about the steady exodus of Russians since independence, but hadn't fully appreciated that this beautiful and fertile region was not virgin territory – it had been stolen. A statue in Karakul's main park depicts and commemorates the events of 1916, often referred to simply as *Urkun,* or exodus.

What is staggering is how few Kyrgyz know about the uprising – an event that halved the population through famine, flight and murder. This is partly due to the burying of the uprising during Soviet times, as even more nomadic misery took place under Stalin's rule. It's also partly because the present-day government is keen to keep the Russians who live in Northern Kyrgyzstan from leaving, as they benefit the economy. So, locals around Issyk Kul today complain about the loud and wealthy Kazakh tourists who come over from nearby Almaty, but have largely forgotten the atrocities that happened over a century ago. In the south, ire has been directed towards the Uzbeks. The centenary of the 1916 uprising did prompt more publicising of the events, but you'd be forgiven for making the same assumptions that I had: that Kyrgyz like living up in the mountains or have always lived there, rather than the reality, which is that it was the only place left to them that wasn't taken by sedentary colonisers.

A lack of understanding about how nomadic Kyrgyz had been dispossessed from their own land, combined with populist politicians pointing at the relative affluence of hard-working urban Uzbek entrepreneurs, caused many of the inhabitants of the Chong Alai mountains to turn to violence and worse.

While there are very few nomads left in post-Soviet Central Asia, raising livestock is still common practice, even in some surprisingly urban settings. I've seen cows cramped onto balconies in Afghanistan. In Uzbekistan, urban sheep-rearing is often the preserve of retired men. It gets them out of the house, and their two or three sheep graze on laybys, in parks, and by eating the organic household waste that in Britain would typically end up in the compost bin, such as melon rind or potato peelings. I once endured an hour-long ride from Arslanbob in a shared taxi, buffeted on the back seat as three protesting rams, wedged like woolly Tetris pieces into the boot of the car, kicked hard against my seat in a failed bid for freedom.

In the villages around Khorog, sheep and cows are pooled. Teenage boys take it in turns to lead the whole neighbourhood's livestock up the mountainsides to graze. In late spring, these neighbourhood herds join thousands of sheep from other villages to be herded by professional shepherds up the steep valleys to remote high pastures, inaccessible in winter. Meanwhile, the meadow ground around the villages is left untouched until August, when it is cut, dried and speared onto wooden poles. These poles are then strapped onto the backs of young men, who trudge back to their farmstead looking like walking haystacks with winter fodder for when their livestock return.

There are still shepherds with much larger flocks in the desert. Spring is so short and the summer heat so intense that spring fodder simply dries on the stalk, providing sustenance for hardy flocks of fat-rump Karakul sheep, famous for their pelts.

While relatively large flocks of Karakul sheep still roam the desert, they are nothing compared to the enormous flocks that existed throughout Central Asia until the 1920s. Such large flocks could support larger numbers of humans, and nomadic communities up to a hundred people strong would shepherd flocks of over 10,000. Ninety per cent of these animals were to die due to Soviet policies. Their owners often fared just as badly.

One year after the 1916 uprising, the largest contiguous empire the world has ever seen was under new management. The Bolshevik Revolution may have taken place thousands of miles away in Moscow and Petrograd, but its effects reverberated throughout Turkestan.

A civil war ensued, which led to the halting of trains that brought grain from Siberia to Central Asia. Most agricultural land had been forcibly given over to growing cotton, and so began the first wave of famine that was to devastate Soviet Turkestan.

Making the most of the chaos, Khiva and Bukhara declared themselves sovereign states, hoping to throw off colonial rule. Independent republics were declared and flourished briefly in the early 1920s, but eventually the Bolsheviks won control of the entire Tsarist Empire. Russians and Slavs made up just 5 per cent of the total population of Turkestan but dominated the top ranks of the new rulers in this corner of the Russian Empire.

This was problematic for socialists, as colonialism was supposed to be the preserve of capitalist countries, and now all people were meant to be equal. However, no one wanted to give up conquered territories; after all, the whole world would soon embrace the communist cause, so they might as well start with the non-Slavic peoples of the Russian Empire. The delicate dance of colonising but not officially colonising became known as 'the nationality issue'.

Lenin decided that the creation of nation-states was an important stepping-stone to the eventual union of socialist republics. So, former-Tsarist ethnographers set about creating national identities and national borders out of the mishmash of ethnicities, languages and lifestyles of Turkestan. Each new nation state was equipped with an alphabet (which often differed from alphabets of neighbouring countries to foster a sense that Russian was the only language for inter-ethnic communication), a pantheon of national heroes and a literary canon. Young Stalin – a non-Slavic Georgian himself – was put in charge of all this nation-building and set out to create countries 'national in form, socialist in content'.[*]

The new republic of Kazakhstan was the ninth-largest country in the world. The vast steppes which had been eyed up previously by Russian settlers now spurred a renewal of interest to grow something the Soviets had in short supply: cotton.

---

[*] Thomas, A., *Nomads and Soviet Rule* (2019), p. 10

First, though, the Bolshevik government set about righting some of the wrongs permitted during Imperial Russian colonisation. In 1920–1 they expelled more than 30,000 Slavic settlers and returned some of the stolen land to Kazakhs and Kyrgyz. Much of this land was now cultivated and it was assumed that nomads would choose to settle and farm it. Instead, most simply rented the land back out to the remaining Slavs, used the money to buy more livestock, and continued in their itinerant ways.

The vastness of the steppe made communicating the message of socialism a challenge. So, some members of the largely Slavic regional Communist Party became temporary nomads themselves, as founders of the Red Yurt campaign. Groups largely composed of Russian men set out to visit remote yurt settlements, offering a mobile court for legal disputes, veterinarian and medical support and lively classes on the joys of socialism, which included plenty of songs and the chanting of slogans. There were training sessions on the evils of the bride-price, polygamy and bride-stealing, and the benefits of personal hygiene, as well as pregnancy consultations. These secular missionaries roamed the steppes with a red flag fluttering from their yurts, declaring their intent, staying in each *aul* for a week or so before moving on.

If nothing else, these endeavours demonstrated the Soviet state's ability to interact with nomads if it wanted to, taxing them differently and recruiting from them to fill their party ranks. However, as Soviet rule became more established, nomadism was seen as an impediment to socialist statecraft, with its tribalism, illiteracy and the difficulty of controlling nomadic people or demarcating their geographical limits. Soon the 'problem' of nomadism became a useful scapegoat for when government quotas hadn't been reached, and nomadism became associated with backwardness.

Ongoing attempts to entice nomads to settle bore little fruit. Visiting in the 1920s, the adventurer Gustav Krist recounted how Kyrgyz clan leaders had free, generous quarters built for them, in the hopes that if they decided to settle, their clans would follow. Instead, they used the buildings for their horses and happily lived in their yurts next to these palatial stables. English traveller Ethel Mannin witnessed similar attempts near Samarkand, where villages of circular concrete structures were connected with electricity, hoping to induce nomads to settle. Being concrete and not wool, these imitation yurts were stifling in summer and freezing in winter.

There was talk of 'liberating' the land that was perceived as unproductive because it was only used for grazing. Soon 'ideologically correct' reports were commissioned to back this claim up, despite evidence from scientists that pastoral nomadism was the most efficient use of land with low and sporadic rainfall. Then, in 1926, the Land Settlement Administration abruptly declared that all land suitable for agricultural development was to be prioritised for sedentary cultivation. Two years later, 500,000 Slavic immigrant peasants were brought in.

Soviet authorities seemed certain that the steppe was big enough to accommodate the nomads' needs as well as their own desire to settle and cultivate much of the land. They hadn't grasped the precariousness of weather conditions, where some years rain fell late or not at all. Winter conditions were generally cold and dry, allowing cattle to find enough winter grazing. However, once every five years or so, there would be an early thaw, heavy rain, and then a freeze again. With pasture trapped under ice, this phenomenon, known as *jut*, was particularly catastrophic for nomads and usually resulted in a huge loss of livestock.

The nomads' bewildering unwillingness to settle was then blamed on nomadic leaders, so a new policy was introduced. It was called Little October and aimed to divide and conquer by requisitioning livestock from wealthier nomadic leaders, known as *bais*, who were now branded as class traitors and rural elites. This livestock, so the theory went, could then be used as the initial stock for new collective farms. A *bai* was defined vaguely as anyone whose 'social or economic influence hinders the Sovietization of the *aul*'.[*] This was then replaced with a more concrete definition of anyone who owned over 400 cattle. Economies of scale meant that larger herds could support proportionately more people than smaller herds; the herds of each *bai* represented large numbers of dependents. None of this was taken into account as the requisitions began.

The small Kazakh minority within the Communist Party were mainly urban; they often used the requisition to settle old scores and to appropriate livestock for themselves. Once stripped of their assets, the impoverished *bais* were internally exiled from kinship ties or anyone who might have helped them survive. In an assault on the family unit, wives could be spared exile and destitution only by divorcing their husbands. Cattle that weren't simply stolen by Bolshevik Kazakhs were rounded up and penned. However, the Bolsheviks did not understand the economics of transhumance, which dictated that four times as many livestock could be kept on land, provided they rotated with the seasons to four different areas of pasture. Once too many cattle were kept in one place, the land was soon exhausted and the cattle began to starve.

When nomads heard that their cattle were to be stolen, some slaughtered them, both in protest and to gain some benefit by feasting on them. Leftover carcasses began to rot, leading to outbreaks of disease. Survivors recall the eerie silence of the *auls* where once there had been the lowing of cattle and the bleating of sheep. Others redistributed their cattle among relatives or bartered them for grain which they were obliged to give as a tax of sorts, to fulfil Soviet grain quotas.

The scene was set for catastrophe, but the axe really fell when Stalin launched his first five-year plan in 1929. Forced collectivisation of agriculture was at the heart of the plan: it had no place for nomadism. Now all Kazakhs, regardless of their number of livestock, were expected to settle in collective farms. There was

----

* Cameron, S., *The Hungry Steppe* (2018), p. 89

to be no leniency shown towards those who stubbornly remained nomadic. Non-compliance was dealt with by confiscation of property, internal exile, ten years in prison or the firing squad.

Stalin insisted on rapidity, even though the region wasn't ready for collectivisation. The locations for these new farms were planned from Moscow using unreliable maps, which meant that Kazakhs often discovered their new utopian collective farms were located in the middle of a swamp, ravine or desert. Although experts on the ground estimated that the cost of establishing collectivisation would be over 300 million roubles, they were given a budget of just 4 per cent of this from Moscow and told to get on with it.

Nomads had traditionally migrated according to water availability. Now, as they were forcibly collectivised and settled on the steppes, it became apparent how little irrigation infrastructure had been put in place. It was also clear that large herds could not be kept in one place without swiftly exhausting the nearby pasturage. These struggling collectivised farms – under-resourced, badly planned and often without adequate housing for workers – far from receiving encouragement from Moscow, were burdened with ridiculous quotas which they were then expected to over-fulfil. And no matter how hard the desperate overseers whipped and beat the Kazakhs beneath them, livestock died, crops failed and everyone began to starve.

Kazakhs who still had the means fled. Some crossed to Siberia, others to Kyrgyzstan, Uzbekistan and Turkmenistan, but the most popular destination was over the Tien Shan Mountains and into China. The optics of this exodus displeased Stalin; it was impossible to patrol such a long and remote border. However, significant numbers of Soviet troops were sent to the main crossing points to apprehend as many fleeing refugees as possible. Unarmed families were shot, their remaining livestock taken and their bodies left in the snow for wolves.

Meanwhile, the famine raged on, exacerbated by a failed harvest. From 1930 to 1933, the famine spread from the countryside to the cities. In the early days, when people still had energy, they held demonstrations all over the country. Then a new form of nomadism emerged, as desperate Kazakhs stumbled on foot from one urban centre or train depot to the next, clothed in nothing but rags, destitute and desperate for food. By 1932, the streets of the Kazakh capital, Alma-Ata (now Almaty), were littered with corpses and orphanages overflowed with children. Slavs treated Kazakhs with horror, worried about catching diseases from them. Many itinerant Kazakhs were lynched by Russian peasants as a result.

There are survivor accounts which make for grim reading. Mekemtas Mirzahmetov was a young child during the famine. After his family's house was destroyed and his father arrested for being a *bai,* Mekemtas fled on foot with his mother and eight-month-old sister. 'On the way, we came across a pack of wolves. I was still a child, but I saw how the eyes of the wolves were burning, approaching the villages because of hunger. I remember how I grabbed my mother's hem out of fear. If we started to run, the wolves would attack all three of us at once. Realizing this, my mother put my eight-month-old sister on the ground, grabbed my hand and ran. We heard my sister cry for the last time. When my mother came back to look, all that was left of my sister was her hair.'*

In the last three months of 1931, as the republic's herds had dwindled to a third of their previous levels and famine raged, Stalin still demanded 59,500 tons of meat for Moscow and Leningrad – more than twice what was expected from any other republic or region. Collectivisation was now taking place in Russia with similarly disastrous consequences. The wealthier peasants, or *kulaks,* were often exiled to Kazakhstan, creating more mouths to feed at an enormous Gulag complex called Karlag, which held hundreds of thousands of prisoners.

By 1934, 300,000 Kazakhs had escaped to China, Mongolia, Afghanistan, Iran or Turkey, never to return. A quarter of those who remained died of starvation. By the end of the famine, of the

---

* https://www.aa.com.tr/en/world/kazakhstan-honors-millions-who-died-in-great-famine/2260046

1.5 million who died, 1.3 million of them were Kazakhs. Ninety per cent of all livestock perished during the famine, and it wasn't until the 1960s that their numbers reached pre-collectivisation levels.

When Scottish traveller Fitzroy Maclean visited Alma-Ata in the 1950s, he discovered that only a third of Kazakhstan's capital was made up of Kazakhs. It wasn't until 1989 that Kazakhs outnumbered Russians again in a nationwide census of Kazakhstan, and not until 1999 that they made up the majority of the country, which has a sizeable Uzbek population as well as Uighurs and other ethnic minorities.

The Wool Road had truly unravelled, and nomadism in Central Asia was never to recover.

Today, there's a statue commemorating the famine beside a busy road in Nur Sultan, Kazakhstan's new capital, and several others in Almaty and Shymkent. But there are still unmarked mounds outside many villages, full of the bones of adults, children and their livestock who perished together in an entirely avoidable famine.

So, as nomadism disappeared, taking much of its rich woollen textile heritage with it, we're left with ghosts, bones and the echoes of cultures built on wool. These echoes can be clearly heard, though, if you know where to look.

6. A CARPET TO BABA LENIN

Although nomadism has been largely wiped out, there are still traces of its culture, particularly in the woollen textiles found even in contemporary urban settings.

A year after the violence of 2010, I moved to Jalal-Abad in Southern Kyrgyzstan, preparing for another move to the mountain village of Arslanbob. Jalal-Abad was the third-largest city in Kyrgyzstan – not to be confused with Jalalabad in Afghanistan. Its bazaar was plentiful, but foreign restaurants, Turkish bakeries and fancy supermarkets were still only available in Bishkek, the capital. Like Almaty in Kazakhstan during Soviet times, the grid-like city was largely populated by Slavs. Now, though, it was full of 'asphalt Kyrgyz' – as rural Kyrgyz referred witheringly to urban Kyrgyz – who dressed in cheap Western-stye clothing from China and often spoke Russian better than they did Kyrgyz.

There were still plenty of semi-nomadic rural Kyrgyz who left their village each summer to take flocks and herds to the summer pasture. Many 'asphalt Kyrgyz' also headed to the high pastures for a yurt-stay, but in their case it was for a cleanse. Traditional Kyrgyz food is heavy on meat, fat and starch, with little in the way of vegetables or fibre, which can have undesirable effects. The traditional remedy for uncorking is to drink fresh mare's milk. It's a powerful laxative and apparently does the job.

For the asphalt Kyrgyz, though, however proud they felt of their nomadic past, their main interaction with yurts was to sit in one at a Kyrgyz-themed restaurant or at a funeral. Any woman in traditional embroidered-velvet tunics or man wearing a *kalpak* – the national peaked white felt hat – marked themselves out as visitors to the big city.

The only time most Bishkek Kyrgyz wore the traditional *kalpak* was for a wedding, funeral or sauna. By contrast, the hat is still widely worn in rural areas. The traditional version has a black velvet brim and black embroidery on white felt. The more contemporary version, favoured by urban Kyrgyz, is white felt with white embroidery. The government even introduced 'National Kalpak Day' to encourage more urban appreciation of this distinctive headwear.

The lack of *kalpaks* in urban areas made it all the more unexpected to find so many men wearing them – and nothing else – while sweating in the saunas of Russian-style public baths or *banyas*. My first experience of these hats and of a Russian *banya* set the bar high during my initial trip along the Silk Road.

I was in Almaty, the capital of Kazakhstan at the time, which was less polluted in the nineties and still had plenty of Russian wooden houses fenced with tidy vegetable plots and flanked by enormous bushes of cannabis. I'd spent most of my time there shuttling between embassies, waiting for my China and Pakistan visas. In the meantime, I visited the world's tallest wooden church, built entirely without nails, and noted how Russian the city was.

I visited the Arasan Baths with an English guy around my age and his older Australian brother-in-law, who was something of a *banya* expert. Built in the 1980s, the baths managed a rare architectural feat, combining Soviet brutalism with luxury. We arrived at steps leading up to an imposing concrete structure topped with a large green dome that gave the place a religious feel.

'Have you got everything you need?' the brother-in-law checked as we passed a stall selling felt hats, loofahs, scrubbing mitts, plastic sandals, shampoo and fans of dried birch leaves.

I nodded. 'Sandals, shampoo, trunks.'

'Well, you won't be needing the trunks,' he said, and I blinked, quietly digesting this information.

Inside, we paid for our tickets and climbed a sweeping staircase to the changing rooms. I'd done plenty of sports and had no problem with locker rooms. However, getting changed in public was quite different from spending several hours wandering around wearing nothing but sandals. Having stripped, I began the self-conscious shuffle into the actual baths. We showered briefly and approached the door to the Russian sauna, being slapped by a wall of heat as we opened it and entered.

Men glistened in rows, heads bowed in silence, most wearing felt hats. Within a minute or so my hair felt crinkly, dry and hot, and I wasn't even sitting on one of the higher rows. I cupped my hands in a bucket of water and sprinkled it over myself.

'Now you see why they wear the hats,' said the brother-in-law. It hadn't occurred to me until then how effectively felt could insulate the wearer from heat as well as from cold.

We stayed in the *banya* for the pathetically short period of a few minutes before wandering dazed through an invigorating sluice of water to a large circular plunge pool with the green dome above it. All was gleaming marble and Soviet opulence, and I leapt in, enjoying the vastly superior experience of swimming entirely uninhibited by textiles of any sort. This process was repeated several times, alternating with the Turkish steam room, and then we got flicked with a birch-leaf fan, which is said to draw blood to the surface of the skin – apparently a good thing. By the time we left, I had removed all the grime from my travels as well as my British inhibitions. Or so I thought, until we passed a party of naked and corpulent middle-aged men in the changing rooms seated at a table and drinking bowls of green tea and shots of vodka, tucking into rounds of Kazakh bread and a bloated horse sausage. 'No thank you,' I thought to myself, lips pursing in disapproval. Most activities, I felt, were still best done ensconced in at least some form of textile.

A love of horses remains very much part of Kyrgyz and Kazakh cultures. They play *Ulaq*, also popular with mountain Tajiks and Afghans and known as *buzkashi*. It's more interactive than any other sport I know of, with spectators perched on a steep hill, ready to flee up it should they need to escape the thundering of approaching hooves. The game has been described as rugby on horseback, but with a headless goat carcass rather than a ball. The manliest of men ride into a huge scrum, wearing Soviet-issue pilot helmets to protect their ears, and then tussle with each other for possession of the goat. One manages to grab it from the others and then gallops towards the goal, chased by the rest. The goat inevitably ends up torn to pieces but whoever manages to get the most goat into the goal section is the winner. I watched the game in winter in Kyrgyzstan, and the scrum was almost obscured in a fog of breath from the horses.

Some traditional practices of the nomadic past might best have been forgotten. One legacy of nomadism has a much darker side. While living in Jalal-Abad I worked at the Jalal-Abad Education Development Institute, or JEDI for short; the best-named language centre ever. Our German director made an off-hand comment about our administrator, Cholponai, bemoaning her youth and prettiness. 'She won't last long,' he stated. 'And I can't seem to find older, married women to take the job.'

I looked confused, and he explained how Cholponai was just the latest in a string of administrators. The previous ones had all been bride-napped. Traditionally, Kyrgyz men were expected to pay a hefty bride-price, usually in the form of livestock. Sometimes young men from poorer backgrounds would circumvent this by galloping into a girl's village, throwing her over his horse and then making off with her. If it was a love-match then the girl might even collude with him, but if not, so it was said, if she hadn't put up a decent fight, then she had effectively given her consent. Once the girl had been raped, her parents usually resigned themselves to the situation and agreed to a marriage, typically reducing the bride-price by a third, making bride-napping an economically attractive prospect for young men.

If there was ever cultural romanticism attached to this tradition in the past, there can be absolutely no justification for the way in which it has morphed in modern, urban cities into something truly predatory. A young man finds a girl he likes and starts to follow her, marking out her daily routine and her route to work, waiting for the right opportunity to strike. When he does, often with help from his friends, the girl is grabbed by the hair, kicking and screaming, and dragged into a car. She rarely manages to get away.

One of JEDI's previous administrators was followed a few times by a strange man in a car. He wasn't breaking any laws and there was nothing she could do other than be vigilant. Then one day he gave chase and managed to grab her, drive off with her and rape her. Her parents were told and prepared for a wedding, but the administrator wanted nothing to do with this man and refused to marry him. Although she was the victim, she was blamed and shamed by both his parents and hers for refusing to marry. She ended up having to move to Bishkek for a new start.

The next administrator realised she was being followed by a young student and his friends. She called on her brothers to talk with them and explain that she had no interest in marriage with anyone and wanted to focus on her career. They were undeterred, and when she realised that bride-napping was inevitable, she quit her job and moved to a different town.

The problem is endemic. On average there are 32 bride-napping attempts a day, with almost 12,000 young women bride-napped a year. It's estimated that around half of Kyrgyz marriages begin in this way, although at least 60 per cent of them end fairly quickly in divorce. Very few women report their rapists to the police as there is huge social pressure for them not to. A growing number resort to suicide, some doing so before they can be raped. The practice of bride-napping was only properly criminalised in 2013, but conviction rates are still low and the penalty for stealing and raping a woman is still less than for stealing someone else's cow.

Many of the incredible textiles produced by the nomads now exist only in Soviet-era museums. The irony of Soviets preserving and celebrating the rich nomadic cultures they so violently eradicated was lost on me when I went to see the world's largest handwoven carpet in Ashgabat. After all, I was just grateful to have actually made it to the Turkmen capital. I almost didn't.

It was during my first trip along the Silk Road, and I had taken an overnight ferry across the Caspian Sea from Baku to the port of Krasnovodsk – later renamed Turkmenbashi. The ferry was over-crowded with both traders and their wares. Bazaar bags full of merchandise were stacked to create walled enclaves behind which women brewed samovars and cooked meals on portable gas stoves. I was sure this was breaking a fairly long list of maritime regula-tions, so chose to sleep up on deck under some metal steps, watch-ing the silhouettes of oil rigs that we passed by in the moonlight.

Ruslan, my Tartar contact in Ashgabat, had arranged for an extremely kind Russian lady from the local Russian Baptist church to meet me at the port and provide me with somewhere to wash and rest during the afternoon. This was a welcome surprise, as the morn-ing summer temperatures were already into the 40s when the ferry finally disembarked. We had no shared language, but she accepted my gratitude and financial remuneration, and purchased a ticket for me on the night train through the desert to Ashgabat. I insisted that she keep the change, which meant I had no local currency, but could always exchange more in the capital.

That evening, my host helped me find the right wagon and compartment, which was furnished with four bunks and a fold-out table between them. She entrusted me into the care of a middle-aged Turkmen man who was in the bunk below me, and a mother and her daughter who had the other bunks. Once the train had lurched to a start, I showed them photos from home, which they enjoyed, particularly one of me in a kilt. They, in turn, unpacked parcels of food and insisted on sharing them with me. I felt ashamed for coming to the carriage empty-handed, and learnt that in Central Asia, it's impossible to eat in front of others without sharing your food with them.

'Turkmen will give you their last crust if you're a guest in their house, even if they have to go hungry,' explained Ruslan later. As the sun set and the train jolted and shuddered its way through the desert, I learnt how to squat on the toilet – a raised platform with a hole onto the tracks – without falling over, and to fill a teapot with boiling water from the samovar situated in the corridor of our carriage without scalding myself too badly. I slept well and had to be roused the following morning by the man in the bottom bunk.

'Aslan, Ashgabat!' he said as I looked up blearily. He motioned for me to get up and fold the cotton bedsheets into neat stacks at the end of my bunk as the others had done. The train began to slow, and I panicked, hurriedly bundling them and then grabbing my rucksack from under his bunk. As the train slowed to a halt, I looked out of the window and saw a giant mosque. We had arrived and I hadn't even brushed my teeth.

The older woman and her daughter motioned for me to sit down, but I didn't have time to find my phrase book for us to attempt a conversation, and nor was I willing to have local people carry my bags for me, as the Russian Baptist lady had attempted. I heaved my rucksack into the corridor and down the steep metal stairs to the ground just as the whistle blew and the train lurched forward. Three faces stared back at me in consternation as the train moved away. Soviet trains are large and the carriages are high. It wasn't until the last carriage left that I realised that – other than the enormous new mosque behind me – there was little else here in this village.

This wasn't Ashgabat.

I had no local currency and no way to inform Ruslan that I would be late. I fumbled for my phrase book and managed to ask what time the next train to Ashgabat would arrive. Something twisted in my stomach as the conductor told me, 'Same time tomorrow.'

I tried not to panic and asked where I could make a phone call. There was only one phone in the village, and it was situated in the post office. So, I shouldered my rucksack and went in search of it. I queued and then tried to pay in dollars, which were refused, and eventually a free call was put through to Ashgabat. Ruslan's mother answered, speaking rapidly in Russian, clearly aware of who I was. When she realised that I couldn't understand she eventually resorted to, 'Ruslan, nieto!'

I understood: Ruslan wasn't there.

I made my way back to the train station, unsure what to do next, and then discovered that beside it was a small bus depot. I made enquiries with the help of my phrase book and a student offered to pay for my ticket, assuring me that I could change money and repay him when we arrived in the city. It was only a 40-minute journey, and we were soon passing generic concrete Soviet apartment blocks that gave way to opulent civic buildings clad in flashing-white Italian marble. Eighty per cent of buildings in the capital today are covered in this imported stone, just one of many vanity projects, white elephants and Potemkin villages that have been used by two megalomaniac presidents to fritter away the world's sixth-largest gas reserves and impoverish its population.

My new student friend asked for $100 to change, which even I wasn't naïve enough to agree to. I gave him $10, and then waited in a park full of furtive men with bulging pockets while he approached one and a small bundle of notes changed hands. He flagged down a taxi to take me to the train station, paying the driver with one of the notes and keeping the rest.

'Aleksandr?' called a woman expectantly at the railway information desk as I approached. I nodded, and she breathed a sigh of relief and then phoned Ruslan. Foreign student backpackers were still a rarity, and it transpired that when my train had arrived, Ruslan had asked disembarking passengers where the foreigner was and they had explained how, despite their best attempts, he had got off at the wrong stop. Ruslan had then left his number at the information desk. Even in a capital city, the bonds of community and hospitality towards incompetent foreign visitors were still strong. The rules of hospitality among nomadic Turkmen in the 19th century were such that if a guest in your yurt stole something, he could do so with impunity until he had ridden a certain distance away, at which point he was no longer considered a guest and could be duly chased down and punished.

And so it was that I approached everything I saw in Ashgabat with a sense of gratitude. I visited the Sunday market on the outskirts of the city, where stalls in the desert had mushroomed overnight. The camel bazaar was the most photogenic spot, and nearby were stalls selling men's robes made from one-ply camel wool, tightly woven to make them incredibly warm, despite their lightness, and extremely popular for winter if you could afford them. Their quality was such that they were among the only robes in Central Asia to retain their natural colour. Not only is camel wool warm, it is purported to provide magical protection against the evil eye. Even Turkmen robes made of cotton or silk would be edged with camel wool, offering extra protection. There were also knitted slippers made of camel wool and large camel-wool belts worn against the skin to keep the kidneys warm.

Nearby, carpets hung for sale, all in the deep blood red that has always predominated in Turkmen weavings. I knew very little about carpets at that point in my life, but I could still appreciate how finely knotted they were, although there was something bland, standardised and commercial about them. They lacked the vitality of older pieces that had been woven by girls and their mothers for dowries, gracing their own marital yurts.

I saw examples of these older carpets in Ashgabat's carpet museum. At first, the designs of the carpets all seemed fairly similar, with larger octagonal motifs repeated in the field, interspersed with smaller cruciform motifs. However, as I looked more closely, I started seeing variations in these motifs and noticed how each one was unique. Each of the five main Turkmen tribes had their own *gul* motifs. There were octagonal lozenges for the Tekke, sometimes referred to as elephant footprints. For the Yomut tribe, who roamed along the banks of the Oxus River, a flotilla of squashed diamond shapes filled with anchors created boats that floated across their rugs. Even when two carpets were made by the same tribe, there were subtle differences and variations. The carpets also featured symbols of magical protection, either the typical ram's horn motif used across the tribes, or the very thing which you wanted protection from, such as a thorn bush or a scorpion.

The Turkmen didn't simply weave rectangular pile floor coverings. There were beautiful *chuvals*: wide rectangular bags that would hang on the yurt walls, used for storing clothing or tools. Some were flatweave and others pile; the more you had, the richer you were considered to be. Then there were deeper sack-shaped bags for storing wheat, or small ones with woven bottlenecks for salt. Most had an asymmetrical addition along their bottom dotted with stylised vegetal and floral motifs, a sort of woven garden known as *alem*.

Then there were beautifully woven yurt-pole protectors, to stop you taking an eye out during migration. There were semi-circular rugs designed to fit around the hearth in the middle of a yurt, lighter *kilim*-weave pieces (usually encrusted with flour) on which bread was kneaded, and embroidered envelopes for wrapping rounds of bread to keep them fresh.

Not all items were utilitarian. Some were simply to show off a bride's skill as she was transported in a tent-like covering, sat atop a camel, leaving behind her mother's yurt and arriving at her marital yurt, now full of the textiles she had spent her childhood weaving. These included freestanding patchwork drapes that initially hung from the bridal camel's neck, and pile carpets in the shape of open envelopes that hung from the flanks of the camel. The camel even wore woven knee- and ankle-decorations. These procession textiles were repurposed and used as decoration within the new marital yurt.

Covering the front door of the new yurt for the first 40 days after a wedding was a specially woven *ensi* rug, its field design mimicking the panelling of wooden doors, with a front garden *alem* along its bottom. This could be rolled up during the day and draped over the yurt door at night. They're now highly collectible. There were also prayer rugs which contained a *mihrab* and could be rolled out to face Mecca. Dividing the middle of the yurt interior between men and women was the *kiz gilam*, or virgin carpet, which was always a flatweave.

While sedentary girls embroidered dowries that were often more decorative than practical, nomadic girls created textiles that were both, such that the word dowry in Karakalpak translates as, 'full set of yurt bands'. Newborn babies would be rocked to sleep in hanging carpet cradles, and the deceased would be wrapped in carpets. They were an essential part of life.

In the 19th century, as Turkmen pieces were sold in the bazaars of Bukhara (which is why they are sometimes erroneously referred to as Bukhara rugs), Cairo and Istanbul, commercial demand grew. However, traders lacking a nomadic imagination simply ripped the *kilim* backs from *chuval* bags along with their decorative tassels and sold them as small rugs. Further vandalism took place in English stately homes, where pieces were butchered for use as upholstery on chairs and sofas. Ironically, this destructive practice has actually preserved some of the oldest pieces which might otherwise have frayed under wear and tear and then been discarded.

As Turkmen women began to weave commercially, carpet designs became less about about tribal affiliations and inherited stories whispered from mother to daughter and more about what would sell. There is a marked shift in the designs of many carpets from that era, not helped by the cheaper synthetic dyes that became readily available.

By the time the Soviets took over Imperial Russia and scrambled to industrialise everything, carpet-weaving was seen as backward and feudal. There was also something inherently capitalist about handwoven commercial carpets, requiring someone poor enough to weave them and someone else rich enough to buy them. Women needed to be freed from the yurt to head boldly into shiny new factories where machines could churn out ugly but cheap standardised carpets for the toiling masses. In the midst of all this emancipation, no one seemed too concerned with the wishes of Turkmen women or how they felt about the denigration of their art form, representing countless generations of knowledge carefully passed down the female line.

One proud and enterprising weaver, desperate to retain her livelihood, wove 'To Baba Lenin' in Persian script into a large carpet. Suddenly, rather than symbolising backwardness and feudalism, the carpet was transformed into a regional cultural expression of Socialist devotion and became a ticket for at least a few hand-weavers to continue their craft. Turkmenkover, a new textile factory opening in Ashgabat in 1929, specialised in handwoven carpet propaganda, turning common visual Soviet tropes into a series of tiny knots. Many were traditional Turkmen carpet frames, with portraits of Stalin, Lenin or Castro woven into the field, while others celebrated the first cosmonaut and other Soviet achievements.

After the collapse of the Soviet Union, these carpets had been removed from the carpet museum, replaced with new portrait carpets that were inevitably of the president. One was based on a popular portrait that was hung in virtually every municipal building in the land. Thankfully it had been woven after the president began to dye his hair, otherwise it would have been thrown out along with all the silver-haired portraits that were no longer acceptable. Another portrait carpet with an incredibly high knot-count detailed the president as a boy with his parents and siblings, before his father went off to war, never to return, and his mother and other siblings died in an earthquake. Has ever such skill and artistry been devoted to something so kitsch? The museum also boasted the largest handwoven carpet in the world, its main attraction. It was impressively large but bland in style and did nothing for me.

Far more gratifying were the large weft-faced brocade woollen flatweaves produced in the 1950s and 1960s in the villages of Turkmenistan and Southern Uzbekistan. Unlike a regular *kilim*, which looks the same on both sides, these were a tangle of loose ends on their underside, while their topside contained a repetition of predominantly red lozenges with ram's horn motifs woven into the borders along with the weaver's name in Cyrillic. These were sold in Bukhara to tourists, who generally avoided them due to their weight. Then wily Bukharan merchants offered shipping, and within a year or two they were all gone. I bought several and treasure them.

The main woollen headgear still popular today throughout Central Asia is the Karakul fur hat. I purchased one during my first winter in Khiva. My hope had been that it might help me blend in. It was partially successful. Now, instead of cries of 'tourist' from passing schoolchildren, it was assumed I must be Tartar. I didn't look very Tartar, but I was blonde, as many Tartars are, and I spoke Uzbek, as do many local Tartars given the similarity with their own language, so it was the only category they had for me. I considered it an upgrade.

If I'd known more about Karakul pelts, I would never have made the purchase. Karakul sheep are fat-bottomed and live in the desert scrub of Southern Uzbekistan. They thrive on adversity, and when Russians attempted to breed their own stock on far better Russian fodder, the resulting pelts were dull and had no sheen. Karakul has the lowest crimp-factor of any sheep wool, making it unsuitable for spinning, but the loose curls of newborn lambs make the actual pelts highly desirable. This requires the slaughter of the lamb at just a week old, after which its pelt is cured in salt and barley. Sometimes the lamb is even younger, and for particularly soft pelts, it is cut from its mother's womb, killing both the lamb and the ewe.

Like Bukharan rugs which are in fact Turkmen, Karakul is often misnamed 'Astrakhan' after the bazaar where it was most frequently traded. It was particularly fashionable in Europe as lapels for jackets or as warm winter hats, and before the Soviet Revolution, all the major fur-houses of London, Geneva and Moscow had agents in Bukhara who bought up Karakul. Today the industry is coming under increasing criticism for the inhumane way in which lambs are slaughtered.

While so much of the wool heritage of Central Asia has been lost, there are glimmers of hope for the future. A business in Bishkek now has its first dehairing facility up and running, scouring and dehairing cashmere. The project purchases from small-scale farmers, who own seven or eight goats, paying them a fair price for good quality, and reinvesting in local schools. The resulting dehaired cashmere is of exceptional quality and is exported to be used by luxury brands.

Kyrgyzstan is seeking new ways to capitalise on its mountainous landscape that favours livestock over crop cultivation. There's an ambitious project in Osh to build a whole new suburb of textile factories producing high-end yarn and working with leather. There will be homes, shops and a mosque on the new site.

Tourism, more than anything else, is driving a revival of textile traditions and innovation with new products. Visit a handicraft shop in Kyrgyzstan and alongside felt *shyrdaks* and traditional felt hats, you'll find nativity sets with a yurt instead of a stable, Aladdin-style slippers with curled toes, felt laptop cases, figurines in traditional dress, wall calendars, mobile-phone holders and much more. Artisans are selling on Etsy and other online handicraft platforms, and even as I've been writing this chapter, I've participated in an online forum to help Turkmen artisans sell online, so that their work can leave the country even if it's increasingly difficult for Turkmen themselves to get an exit visa.

Despite these green shoots, Russian and then Soviet colonisation dealt nomadism a deathblow it's unlikely to recover from, killing off the Wool Road. This makes me all the more grateful for the time I spent with the semi-nomadic Kyrgyz of the Pamirs, with those glimpses into a way of life that is so challenging and yet so beloved by many determined Kyrgyz.

And yet, in its heyday, the Wool Road populated Central Asia with nomads who wielded so much power that they acted as a blockade of sorts between the sedentary civilisations of the Mediterranean and China. It would take a fabulous and mysterious new textile, worth enough to risk traversing the treacherous deserts, mountains and steppes of Central Asia, to break the blockade and carve a network of trading routes that would usher in the first era of globalisation. Today, we call these trading routes the Silk Road.

PART TWO

The Silk Road

warp

/wɔːp/

noun

a twist or distortion.

the threads on a loom over and under which other threads (the weft) are passed to make cloth.

7. THE HEAVENLY VEGETABLE

'Are we sure about this?' I ask Tobias and Mary.
Because I'm really not, even though it was my idea in the first place.

I should also know better, being older but clearly not wiser, and the repercussions if we get caught are greater for me as I actually live in Khorog, while Tobias and Mary are short-term volunteers – the remnants of a team who came to help us run a summer camp at the orphanage. We've just waded through fast-flowing, knee-deep water which is colder than I'd expected, even in late August. We clamber onto a rocky island with a little scrub growing on it. Now, on the edge of the island, we face the main body of the Panj River, the border between Afghanistan and Tajikistan. At this point, Afghanistan doesn't seem quite so close.

Two weeks before, we had driven our team of volunteers from Dushanbe to Khorog. In places where the river narrowed into foaming rapids, Afghanistan was a literal stone's throw away. On the other side, hair-raising paths carved into the mountainsides were interspersed with small villages with neat terraces of orchards and flat-roofed mudbrick houses covered with drying fruit. It was all so incredibly close. That was when I'd mentioned how one day I wanted to swim across. Now, with most of the volunteers gone, this fanciful idea had become a plan, and not a very good one.

'I think we should turn back,' I continue.

'Come on, Chris, we can't stop now,' says Tobias, a tall, confident, young German with legs like tree-trunks from competitive cycling.

Tobias and I are in swim shorts. 'We won't be able to wear more, even though the water's cold, in case someone stops us in either country and thinks we're drug-smugglers,' I'd explained earlier, during the preparation stage. 'If that happens, then we'll just have to look helpless and say that we were swimming in the river on the Tajikistan side but got swept over by the current to Afghanistan. We'll try our crossing on Sunday afternoon when there's very little traffic along the main road and it'll be a long walk upstream to get enough distance away from the town.'

'I'm not wearing anything revealing,' Mary had said.

'I don't think women are involved in smuggling, so that's fine,' I said. Now she stands in a cheap Tajik kurta she picked up in Dushanbe. It's definitely not ideal for swimming but at least she'll arrive in Afghanistan modestly dressed.

I look up at the sandy bay we're aiming for. The water between us seems to be flowing much faster than a few moments ago, but that's probably just my imagination.

'Right, on the count of three,' says Tobias, impatiently. We nod at each other, count, and then dash into the water, diving as soon as we can. I'm a strong swimmer and feel myself propelling forward after the first few strokes. I'm just beginning to think this will be easy when I hit the main current and am tugged under. I come up spluttering brown water out of my mouth and flailing wildly in the direction of Afghanistan. I'm moving incredibly fast, but not forwards. The current is bearing me rapidly downstream towards Khorog.

I glance over and see Tobias, wild-eyed with panic. 'Mary, where's …' he starts and then gets tugged under as well. I thrash my head around but can't see her. I'm far enough across now that the only way is forwards, so I give it everything I've got. I'm not fast enough, though, and I realise that I'm almost past the sandy bay. After that there are cliffs all the way to the bridge with its border guards and patrols. I'm not sure if I'm more afraid of drowning or of being caught crossing illegally into Afghanistan. I'm about to give up hope when I see Tobias clambering to his feet near me, and I realise I can touch the bottom. We both drag ourselves, coughing and spluttering, onto the last stretch of the sandy bay.

'Where's Mary?' I gasp and look back. My stomach floods with relief as I see her wading back out to the little island where we started. 'She's safe!' I punch Tobias's shoulder. 'We made it!'

Tobias nods, shivering, and says nothing. We sit there, both exhausted, cold, and coughing up river water. I have a craving for a hot cup of tea with three sugars. Neither of us is willing to acknowledge the obvious: we may have successfully swum to Afghanistan, but now we need to swim back again. Tobias looks close to tears and I'm worried he might be going into shock. I put my arm around him to try and keep him warm.

'We're actually in Afghanistan! Come on, Tobias, this is amazing,' I say with bravado I don't feel.

'I thought Mary had drowned,' he says flatly. 'How are we going to get back?'

'Well, we'll have to walk further upstream than before. I hadn't realised how strong the current would be, so we should find a spot where the water flows fastest on our side, that way we get the hard bit over with first.' He nods. I clamber to my feet, aware that the sun will be setting soon. 'Come on, let's get going.'

We pick our way along the rocks. The Afghanistan side of the river is deserted and there are only a few cars passing on the Tajikistan side. Most don't spot us, or if they do, none slow down. We gesture to Mary that we'll have to go further upstream and she stays with our stuff.

We go slowly, as the rocks are difficult to navigate in bare feet. The shadows lengthen. 'How about here?' I ask, after about 45 minutes. We've stopped at a point where we can dive straight into the water, which flows really fast on our side but then seems to slow down. We've had as much rest as we're going to get, and the air temperature is cooling as, somewhere beyond the steep mountains, the sun is setting.

Tobias looks at me. 'How are we going to do this?'

'The same way we did before. If the current sweeps us downstream, it doesn't matter as long as we get across. Come on, we'll be fine.'

We crouch, nod to each other and then dive in. Once again, I've underestimated just how fast the river moves. We push through the fastest-flowing part, but even so, the current tugs at me as if it were alive. I think of all the women I've heard about who've drowned in these waters, gone to fetch water and then been yanked in by a bucket and swept into the current. I feel a wave of cold and exhaustion and slow for a moment. Tobias yells my name as I'm swept downstream, so I flail on. I'm almost at the steep riverbank, which is a blur of dried grass sweeping past me. I try standing up, but sink under, come up spluttering, and with one last push manage to claw onto some dried grass and then a boulder.

I've made it. I pause, shivering and coughing up water. Then I drag myself up and onto the bank. I hear Tobias whooping for joy further upstream. Then I hear applause. I glance around. Up on top of a cliff, invisible to us when we were on the other side, are three young Afghans in *shalwar kameez*, who've been watching our stupidity with amusement. I wave at them, and then Tobias barrels into me.

'We did it! We did it!'

We head triumphantly towards Mary, who has not had an enjoyable time, wondering if we'd bobbed past without her realising it, and imagining how she would break the news of our demise. We're all happy to see each other alive.

I offer up a prayer of gratitude, feeling elated and stupidly reckless. Only later do I get into serious trouble with Andrea, the director of Operation Mercy, who warns me than if I ever do something like that again, she'll put me straight on the next flight back to England.

We were lucky. Very lucky. Our badly chosen crossing spot and the timing of it meant that we hadn't run into any problems with border authorities or with the scrawny Tajik conscripts from the lowlands who are billeted here, swallowed up by their ill-fitting uniforms. The main swimmers across the Panj do so after the river has passed the bridge, where the valley widens out and the river becomes slower and shallower, dotted with islets making it far easier to cross. On the Tajikistan side is the sprawling village of Porchinev, where I visited the felt-making workshop. On the Afghanistan side, across the bridge, is the small town of Dimurgan.

Its inhabitants are also Pamiri and Ismaili and would once have intermarried with communities on our side. Now they're a country apart. They have their own small bazaar which might have been lifted from the pages of black-and-white photos taken in Samarkand or Bukhara a century earlier. Traditional merchant houses are built above their shops on the main street which then peter out into smaller wooden stalls that, when shuttered, look like beach-huts. On one of my subsequent legal visits, this time across the bridge with a visa, I discovered in one of these stalls a trove of Pakistani marmalade – a jam unheard of in Tajikistan – and bought several jars back with me.

The river seems to divide two different eras. In Khorog, which can be easily seen from Dimurgan, there are Soviet-built blocks of flats, wide roads and overpopulation. Men wear cheap Western-style clothes from China, with plenty of lazily branded Nikee and Adadidas. Young women style out their skinny jeans with Pamiri socks worn like legwarmers. In Dimurgan, on the other hand, the houses are made from mud, stone and wood, and most people depend on the land for the majority of their food. Men wear *shalwar kameez* and turbans. Women wear headscarves and long kurtas. At the time of writing, they probably have to wear burkas again after Western forces abandoned Afghanistan.

At passport control on my return to Tajikistan, no one checked my small backpack which could have been full of heroin instead of marmalade. Perhaps they didn't think I'd be stupid enough to smuggle heroin into a town where a gram sold for less than a bar of chocolate. The village of Porchinev was the epicentre of this drug smuggling. Young men would wait for a moonless night and then strap crates of vodka to inflated lorry inner-tubes and paddle across the Panj, avoiding the border guards and roving spotlights, and exchange the vodka for heroin on the other side before paddling back again. As a result, Porchinev boasted a better gym and sauna than any found in Khorog, and luxury sports cars were a common sight, despite the potholes on the village roads.

Given that this was one of the main export routes for Afghanistan's heroin, both poppy cultivation and heroin-cooking were widespread in Afghan Badakhshan, particularly as the mountains provided a plentiful source of water for crop irrigation.

Three months after planting, the poppies bloom in pinks and mauves, and then the petals drop and the seed-heads swell silvery-blue, giving them their Afghan name: *blue pomegranate*. At this point they can be cut and bled. The white sap which oozes from the heads is collected and dried to make sticky, fragrant bricks of opium. However, it's worth a lot more if heated to the right temperature and with the correct types and quantities of acid added, which turns it into heroin. Once this is packaged and bartered for vodka, most of it makes its way through Khorog and along the Pamir Highway to Osh, in Kyrgyzstan. From there it's dispersed mainly to Russia, and sometimes then to Europe.

An estimated quarter of the population of Khorog have been involved in trafficking at some point. It's an open secret and not hard to work out who the key players are, given their sports cars and flashy clothes. Key government and army officials are most likely involved or paid to look the other way.

Khorog is remote and getting to and from there is a challenge. In winter there are avalanches and the possibility of the roads simply becoming impassable due to heavy snow. More than once, I've been in a shared van stuck in a snowstorm as all the passengers are handed shovels so we can help dig our way through. In early spring, flooding and river crossings are the main problem as they swell with water. As spring progresses, snowmelt also causes mudslides and rock-fall. I witnessed enormous car-flattening boulders bounding down the mountainside as we drove at speed below, attempting to get away. Beyond Khorog to the east are treacherous roads that lead to the Roof of the World, littered with the remains of Chinese lorries in ditches or shattered in ravines on river rocks. Beyond the High Pamirs is the Tian Shan mountain range, today's natural great wall with China. If you manage to travel over that, then there is brief respite in one of the oasis cities that ring the huge expanse of the Taklamakan Desert, but to travel through it was unheard of until vehicles and tarmac roads were introduced. At this point you haven't even reached the Gobi Desert.

These vast expanses of treacherous shifting dunes are bitterly cold in winter and searingly hot in summer and have claimed many a traveller. In the opposite direction, once you've navigated the mountains, there's the Kyzylkum and then Karakum, or the Red Desert and the Black Desert. Until the past century, all it took was one dry well or a wrong turn to spell disaster.

It's unsurprising, then, that China knew little about the lands beyond its western frontier, and that's just the physical terrain. This vast region was the preserve of nomads, many with marauding tendencies. Similarly, those living in the Mediterranean were only vaguely aware of great civilisations to the east. It would take something more valuable than gold, highly desired, but only available from one place, that would make the challenges and dangers of traversing this part of the world worth it. Long before heroin (with its cheap production costs and huge mark-ups) was smuggled along the Pamir Highway, another discovery made the opening of trade routes across the middle of Asia an appealing prospect.

And that discovery was, of course, silk.

Before Chinese silks were sold in the Roman Empire, the only place where silk was spun was the small Greek island of Kos, using wild silk moths. Although the resulting fabric was diaphanous and highly sought-after, it was of vastly inferior quality to the bolts of silk which would eventually arrive from China. When it did, the Romans were entranced, but they knew very little about the Chinese, referring to them simply as the people of *Seres*, from the Latin word for silk, from which we get our English word for raising silkworms: sericulture.

According to legend, the Yellow Empress discovered the secret of silk around 4,500 years ago. She was enjoying a quiet bowl of tea in the shade of a mulberry tree when a stray cocoon plopped into her bowl from a branch overhead, and as she tried to fish it out, it began to unwind. In that moment, she realised she was on to something. Today, she has morphed from royal inventor to Silk Goddess, and statues of her are venerated. Following in her sacred footsteps, the rearing of silkworms has always been a predominantly female occupation.**

We know from ancient burial sites in China that knowledge of sericulture probably predates the Yellow Empress, with ceramic images of silkworms dating back at least 6,000 years. However, for millennia, as China developed sophisticated methods of weaving silk, including satins, velvets, brocades, crepes, taffetas and gauzes, the harsh landscape and wild nomadic peoples to the west prevented this knowledge from expanding beyond China's western borders.

....

* In pre-Soviet times, tending silkworms was one of the few money-making opportunities women had. Annette Meakin, a Russian-speaking Englishwoman who spent time in Uzbekistan at the end of the 19th century, noted how young girls would keep their silkworms nestled in the folds of their robes, hand-feeding them. When feckless or lazy fathers or husbands neglected to provide their wives and daughters with mulberry leaves, the women would often threaten to visit the bazaar themselves and barter the man's best robes in return for leaves. This approach usually did the trick, and even young girls were allowed to keep the profits they made from their enterprise.

There were two nomadic peoples who were particularly troublesome; they were known by the Chinese as the Xiongnu and Yuezhi. One of these tribes may have been the Hun. Chinese scribes described them as homeless, unproductive barbarians, eating raw meat, drinking the blood of their livestock, abandoned by heaven and good for nothing.

This certainly wasn't true when it came to raiding. They were adept at loosing arrows from a moving horse and were fierce in battle. They could attack a town or city and yet retreat over vast distances, sleeping in the saddle. If the Chinese gave chase, their local short-legged and shaggy *taki* ponies with unshod hooves didn't get them far. So, the nomads continued to raid while the Chinese attempted various strategies to deal with them. One was to build a wall to keep the nomads out. Eventually, different sections were joined to form the Great Wall.

Although impressive to look upon, the wall proved both costly and ineffective, as nomadic intruders simply bribed or fought their way through the wall, making it as far as Xian, China's capital at the time. An alternative strategy was the annual tribute paid by China to the nomadic rulers in the hope of placating them. In one year alone, 20,000 pounds of silk floss were sent as tribute, and the drain on the royal purse was significant.

Finally, Emperor Wu of the Han Dynasty decided on a new course of action, capitalising on grievances between the Xiongnu and the Yuezhi. The Yuezhi had been chased out of their lands and moved westwards, and their fallen leader's skull was now used by the Xiongnu king as a drinking vessel. If the aggrieved Yuezhi could be found, so the emperor reasoned, perhaps they would ally themselves with China against a common enemy. He commissioned an army of 100 men, led by a young and strapping palace guard named Zhang Qian.

They set off in 138 BC from Xian, but got lost and were then captured by the Xiongnu. Attempts to claim diplomatic immunity were ignored and Zhang Qian was enslaved by a wealthy family and put to work as their shepherd. He was given a slave girl to marry and they had a son. Eleven years later he managed to escape with his family and a few men. They skirted around the Taklamakan Desert and eventually got as far as the Fergana Valley. Here they discovered unknown and exotic foods, such as sesame, garlic, carrots and grapes.

Even more important for the fortunes of China was another food discovery, but not one fit for humans. Alfalfa, or lucerne, grew in abundance and was a superior and nutritious forage for Fergana horses. The Greeks had discovered alfalfa from the Persians in the 5th century BC and referred to it as Persian grass. It had been a game-changer in creating a much stronger cavalry. By contrast, alfalfa was unknown in China, where there was little pasturage and the soil lacked calcium. The horses of Fergana, which fed on the abundant alfalfa, were nothing like the second-rate steeds of China and were so fleet of foot that when they galloped they were said to sweat blood. Poems written about them later (and there were a lot of them) described them as celestial horses sired by water dragons, and Emperor Wu was convinced that they could gallop over mountains and leap over gorges with such prowess that one day they would bear him up to the celestial gates.

The rest of Zhang Qian's mission was a failure. When he eventually spoke to the new leader of the Yuezhi, who were now living along the banks of the Amu River, he showed no interest in becoming anyone's drinking cup. Dejected, Zhang Qian and his wife chose an alternative route home and were captured yet again by the Xiongnu. Their escape was only possible during the power struggle for succession after the Xiongnu king died.

Thirteen years after his departure, Zhang Qian and his wife returned to Xian. The emperor, who had long given Zhang Qian up for dead, was thrilled, particularly by the news of the heavenly Fergana horses. Not only would they give the Chinese cavalry a chance against the nomads in battle, but they would also speed up communication throughout the vast territories of China.

The emperor sent an envoy to Fergana bearing gold pieces and even a gold horse statue, requesting the best of their steeds. After some diplomatic misunderstanding and several resulting skirmishes, the people of Fergana eventually sent 3,000 horses and alfalfa seed.

This was enough for a breeding programme, but the calcium-poor soil meant that it was never very successful, so China continued to barter for horses.

There were three main currencies used for trade within China during the Han Dynasty: copper coins, grain and silk. The problem with copper coins was that they weren't particularly valuable and therefore larger quantities were needed, which made them heavy to transport. Grain was good, in case travellers lost their way and needed to eat into their supplies, but it also spoilt easily, particularly in rainy weather. Silk, on the other hand, was a divisible currency, as you could always halve or quarter a bolt of fabric. It also maintained its value better than the fluctuations of other currencies. Soon, bolts of silk and silken robes were being traded for horses.

Zhang Qian was granted the title of 'Great Messenger' and led several more epic expeditions to the wild west, establishing trade routes and alliances, before he eventually died in 113 BC. As an improved Chinese cavalry kept the Xiongnu at bay, trade increased past this former impediment and soon Chinese silks were dazzling Parthia – present-day Iran – commanding such incredible prices that it made the arduous journey worthwhile.

The Silk Road was born.

Silk remained relatively unknown among the Romans until 53 BC, when Marcus Crassus led his army along the Euphrates and the Parthians struck. The Parthian helmets, made from superior Chinese iron, glittered in the sunlight far brighter than any helmets the Romans had ever seen. After a gruelling battle in which the Romans lost thousands of soldiers, the Parthian silk standards were unfurled, writhing in the wind as if alive. It was all too much for the Romans, who thought the war a vanity project anyway. They turned and fled.

When Rome itself finally discovered silk, it caused scandal. Anyone who could afford it now dressed themselves in 'glass togas' leaving very little to the imagination. Cleopatra's white breasts covered in just a wisp of silk became famous. Pliny the Elder complained at the ridiculous prices of silk, and all for reducing a woman to near nakedness. He estimated that 10 per cent of the entire treasury was being frittered away on eastern luxuries. Seneca harrumphed further, stating, 'Wretched flocks of maidens labour so that the adulteress may be visible through her thin garment, meaning her husband has no more acquaintance with his wife's body than any outsider or foreigner.'[*]

Nor were women the only ones to receive such censure. Petronius described seeing 'everywhere, these frail-limbed and mincing effeminates, flowing of locks, bedecked with an infinite number of silken garments whose names ever change'.[†] Soon, silk became so closely associated with debauchery and effeminacy that Emperor Tiberius banned all Roman men from wearing this corrupting and enfeebling fabric, and a later decree also banned all but female royalty from wearing purple-dyed silk.

While silk caused an enormous stir and sold for similar prices to gold and pearls, the Romans were still largely mystified as to the origins of this 'heavenly vegetable'. Pliny the Elder posited that silk was gleaned from the white downy secretion of a certain kind of leaf, doing a better job of inadvertently describing cotton. Virgil also opted for the leaf theory, while Strabo thought that silk came from tree bark. As China realised that no one else knew how to produce silk, they were very keen to keep it that way. Secrets, though, have a habit of spilling, as we will discover.

Along the first silk-trading routes, what began as simple yurt settlements for merchants to seek food and shelter were gradually replaced by caravanserais. A typical caravanserai consisted of a large courtyard with a well, surrounded by a ground floor of stalls and storage, and an upper level where merchants could find

....

[*] Wood, F., *The Silk Road* (2002), p. 30

[†] St Clair, K., *The Golden Thread* (2018), p. 90

lodgings. These eventually became villages, then towns and cities, all thanks to trade.

One reason for the growth of a network of trading routes rather than one single, continuous road was that there were significant natural obstacles, such as the Caspian Sea, or seas of dunes such as the Taklamakan Desert, which had to be skirted north or south. Referring to 'the Silk Road' can be misleading: it was a network not only for trade east to west, but also north to south. In fact, the term 'Silk Road' is a relatively modern one, only coined in the 1880s by Baron von Richthofen, a prominent German geographer and cartographer working in China to map coal deposits. Having been commissioned to create the best route for a railway line which might transport coal from China to Germany, and drawing on his knowledge of history, von Richthofen dubbed it *die Seidenstrasse*, or the Silk Road.

There have been challengers to this moniker, with some arguing for the term 'Paper Road', given that the journey of papermaking from China to Samarkand and later to Europe arguably impacted our society far more than luxury clothing, enabling the spread of thoughts and ideas. There are even proponents for 'Rhubarb Road', as Chinese rhubarb was extremely precious to medieval Europeans, who paid even more for it than they did for saffron. It wasn't the red stalks that interested them, but the roots, which were thought to increase semen production and act as a powerful purgative – and medieval Europeans loved a good purge. Marco Polo's own rhubarb stash was considered valuable enough to be itemised and included in his will.

However, it was silk that really kickstarted trade between the civilisations of East and West. This wide-ranging exchange of unknown foods, clothing, medicines, technology, art, fashion, religion and inventions has been so successful that many on both sides are now unaware of what was once foreign to them. The Silk Road ushered in the first age of globalisation.

And it all began with a pale, greedy caterpillar.

8. WORMS THAT CHANGED
THE WORLD

During my first trip along the Silk Road in 1996, I planned to make the 24-hour bus journey from Urumchi down to Kashgar, and from there to Pakistan. However, while in Urumchi, an English teacher I met told me about another English teacher – a Swiss lady – who was the only Westerner living in Khotan, an isolated city further east from Kashgar. It would mean an extra eight-hour journey, but Khotan was unspoilt and of historical importance, and this English teacher often missed Western company and would value my visit.

So, I found myself on a 36-hour bus journey across the Taklamakan Desert, which felt considerably longer. I'd ended up on a top bunk in the middle aisle on a sleeper bus. The bunk was most definitely designed for someone a third shorter than I was, and my legs dangled off the end, becoming a poking hazard for passengers lurching past. My view from this vantage point was largely of the road and the sand beside it. It was hot and uncomfortable, but the pee-stops offered views of beautiful dunes that undulated far more pleasingly than the scrubby wastelands of desert I'd seen in western Central Asia. There were stands of mature saxoul trees, hundreds of years old, that thrive on little water and grow so slowly that their dense wood sinks in water and is highly prized for the aromatic flavour its smoke gives to skewers of mutton *shashlik*.

Eventually we left the desert behind and entered the oasis city of Khotan. It was very Uighur, and the only Han Chinese I saw worked in the bank and the hotel. There was just one hotel, with a dusty collection of jade for sale. Outside the hotel were more jade shops. For centuries, the White Jade River has washed up lumps of green or creamy-white 'mutton-fat' jade. This was so valued by the Chinese that during the Han Dynasty, emperors often gave their daughters to jade princes from Khotan, ensuring that trade ties continued smoothly. It was one of these bridal exchanges that would lead to the secret of sericulture escaping from China.

The Han jealously guarded their silkworms, and all merchants were thoroughly searched on departing through the Jade Gates at the Yumenguan Pass to ensure that no silkworm eggs or cocoons travelled with them. Towards the end of the 1st century AD, a Han princess betrothed to a jade prince was approached by the prince's emissary with another proposition. His prince, her future husband, was fearful of what might happen to his people if the river ever stopped bringing them lumps of jade. The prince had begged her father to sell him silkworm eggs and mulberry seeds so that Khotan might also benefit from the lucrative silk-weaving industry, but all requests had been rebuffed. She would win the unwavering love and devotion of her future people in her new home if she could help them somehow with this matter.

The princess told the emissary that she would consider his proposal, but said nothing more about it as she left her homeland forever, passing through the Jade Gates towards Khotan. As royalty, the frisking she'd received was largely cursory. It was only after their entire party had been duly searched and waved through that the princess approached the emissary and let him know that she had concealed mulberry seeds in her medicine chest and had hidden silkworms in her elaborate coiffure.

A painted wooden panel discovered in the desert by British archaeologist Aurel Stein depicts the princess with another woman – possibly her servant girl – standing nearby and pointing, pantomime-style, at the princess's elaborate hair-ornamentation. There's also a depiction of a four-armed sericulture deity, holding the tools of his trade in each of his hands.

The people of Khotan were indeed grateful to the princess and today over 150 million metres of silk are spun there annually. The princess, though, felt compassion for the industrious silkworms, busy spinning cocoons from which few would emerge. So, she set up a monastery where moths would hatch and mate. There's no evidence of the monastery today, but I visited the Khotan silk factory which produced atlas silk, for which all of Turkestan is famous. I didn't know how to ask for directions, but had purchased some silk in the Sunday bazaar earlier in the day and held it up to kids playing on the street and looked questioningly. They understood and led me further down several dirt streets until I could hear the whirr and clatter of machinery.

We had no common language, but I was mimed a welcome at the factory gates and then left to wander. There was the distinct, slightly sour tang in the air of cocoons being softened in hot water before unravelling. I'd later come to know that smell well as I worked with silk in Khiva. Large metal looms clacked loudly, churning out metres of brightly coloured silk. My ears were soon ringing, but none of the Uighur women, who looked indistinguishable from Uzbek women, had any kind of ear protection. In the sorting room, I picked up a silk cocoon. It rattled with the pupa inside. I mimed putting the cocoon in my pocket and looked at the nearest factory worker. She shrugged her assent, so I took two. Back in the UK, I kept them beside my bed, waiting for them to hatch out. I wasn't sure how many weeks or months it would take. They never hatched, because by the stage I picked them up in the sorting room, the pupae inside had already been killed by heating or steaming, to prevent a moth hatching out and ruining the cocoon.

I really knew very little about silk, and still hadn't seen an actual silkworm. That wouldn't happen until five years later, when

I started researching the sericulture process for the silk carpet workshop I had just opened in Khiva.

Over 10 billion cocoons are spun every year to keep us in silks. China produces 80 per cent of them, and Uzbekistan (ranking third) produces just 5 per cent, which still adds up to around 2,600 tonnes a year. Uzbekistan has the highest percentage of its population working in sericulture and even has its own origins myth, which I discovered during a visit to Job's Well in Bukhara. This conical-domed building was transformed from a place of Sufi pilgrimage into a Soviet-era museum about water management. It's where the Biblical prophet Job is said to have drawn water, although this is fairly unlikely.

In the Islamic version of the story, Job is plagued by worms, his body riddled with them. Eventually, after God permits his time of testing to finish, the worms are so ashamed at the pain they've caused Job that they hide themselves by spinning cocoons, which is how we have silk today. Stories about worms resonated with Bukharans, who relied on a network of stagnant pools for drinking and often ended up with metre-long guinea worms, which were extracted by barbers. They made an incision where the worm's head came near the skin surface, and then wound out an inch of the worm each day, careful not to let it break, as this would cause blood poisoning. Eventually, the entire worm was removed and was then thrown, still alive, back into the water pools, thus keeping the barbers in business.

Outside Bukhara and alongside most rural roads, it's impossible to ignore the annual feeding of silkworms. Throughout late April and into May, village women in brightly coloured clothing hack at mulberry trees, loading the branches onto donkey-carts. In winter, these pollarded trees, grown for their leaves rather than their fruit, look a little like rows of severed hands, their squat trunks ending abruptly at chest height and then fanning into spindly branches which represent a year's growth.**

When I started the silk carpet workshop in Khiva, I was aware of how little I knew about the actual process of making silk, so I decided to find out more. My host mum, Zulhamar, suggested that I meet her brother-in-law, Nuraddin, in nearby Yangi Arik, as he was responsible for hatching silkworms for the whole village. Nuraddin was lean, dark, with a prominent nose and eyes that quickly crinkled when he smiled. I liked him. He was soft-spoken, which it turned out made him the perfect man for the job. Silkworms are extremely finicky when they first hatch and need a lot of coddling. Nuraddin's were three days old and were kept in the comfort of his bedroom.

'When we go inside, you'll need to whisper,' he explained. 'They don't like music or loud talking.' He leaned forward to sniff me and then nodded, satisfied. 'Good, you're not wearing aftershave. They don't like that, or the smell of perfume or tobacco or menstruating women.'

I wondered how he knew all this, but didn't doubt him. Since then, I've learnt that during egg-hatching season, silkworm-rearing villages in China used to station teenage boys at the village perimeter to chase away wandering travellers lest they walk through the village and inadvertently make noise. In Italy, it was the spring storms that caused the main worry for silkworm farmers, with their propensity for thunder. Not only do newly hatched silkworms require a quiet and unscented environment, they also need the air temperature and humidity to be just right, with no draughts. Nuraddin uses a plant mister to prevent the room getting too dry.

....

* While silkworms can survive on leaves from the dark mulberry, these are tougher and the resulting cocoons are of inferior quality. This important distinction was lost on King James, who was determined to rival Lyon in production of silk and ordered all the noblemen of England to plant mulberry trees in their gardens. Instead of white mulberry trees, they planted dark mulberries and while that was disastrous for sericulture, it resulted in enormous trees with far nicer fruit, now gracing many a British stately home.

Millennia ago, when silkworms were still wild, female moths laid eggs on the underside of mulberry twigs and branches. There, they remained dormant over winter until spring warmed them, just as the new leaves were budding. Once sericulture took off, eggs from the previous year would be stored in a cellar through the winter and then placed in a pouch and warmed between the bosoms of the larger female farmers. Today, less excitingly, they simply keep the little grey eggs in a fridge until the first signs of mulberry budding, at which point they're placed on a bed in a heated room so they can hatch around ten days later. These hatchlings are just two millimetres in length, but within five weeks and four skin moults, they'll end up 60 times longer and 10,000 times heavier.

We tiptoed into the bedroom. Under a mosquito net, the bed writhed, covered with the tiny newly hatched caterpillars of *Bombyx mori*.

'I didn't think they'd be so small,' I whispered.

'They won't stay that way for long,' Nuraddin whispered back with a grin. 'At least now, they're easy to feed, although we have to chop up the new leaf buds for them. I'll keep them here until they're ten days old and then we'll weigh them out and distribute them. Typically, a matchbox of ten-day-old worms will eventually translate into 50 or 60 kilos of cocoons.'

Their potential was huge.

'Do all the worms hatch out at the same time?' I asked.

'These ones all hatched out together, but on the other side of the village they have older worms that hatched out several days earlier. Would you like to see?'

I nodded, and we walked along a dusty path accompanied by whispered speculation from neighbours, as foreigners were a rare sight. We arrived at another flat-roofed, mudbrick house and were greeted by a toothless old woman. She took one look at me and spoke in broken Russian.

'Auntie, he's English, but you can speak to him in Uzbek, or even in our dialect,' Nuraddin explained, as she looked at me, unconvinced. 'He's come to see the worms.'

Once we'd removed our shoes, we were led inside, where, instead of the usual carpet and low table framed by seating mattresses, there were trestle tables covered with piles of chopped mulberry leaves, flecked by cream-coloured silkworms that were a week older than the hatchlings we'd just seen. Her daughter-in-law was chopping up leaves and scattering them over the existing pile.

'Why do you have to chop up their food for them?' I asked.

'It's only for two more days,' the old woman replied. 'Then they'll be big enough for us to just lay the whole mulberry branches down, and they'll make short work of them. They won't eat dried leaves and they don't all sleep at the same time, so we have to feed them non-stop, starting before sunrise and finishing around eleven at night. At this stage, it's still easy but within a week, I won't have time for anything except cutting and collecting mulberry branches. We'll have to sleep outside, because all the rooms in the house will be taken up by the worms. I won't even have time for the nine o'clock *kino*.'

I smiled. The daily dubbed telenovela from Mexico, Brazil, Korea or Turkey was the highlight of the day for most women and generally considered unmissable, each episode discussed at length with neighbours on the street the following morning.

I asked how much they got paid, and the woman looked at Nuraddin uncertainly. He nodded. 'Go ahead, you can speak openly with him.'

'We don't always get paid. The government have their quotas and they put pressure on the local administrators who then put pressure on the head of our farming cooperative. After last year, we told Nuraddin that we wouldn't be doing worms again because it's just too much work, but others dropped out and the cooperative chairman had to fulfil his quotas and turned up here complaining, so ...' She shrugged helplessly.

The system of government quotas and collective farms with one specialist hatcher is a legacy from the Soviet times. However, back then, farmers were actually paid and usually on time. One kilo of cocoons sold for the price of a kilo of red meat, which was a decent amount. Despite the hard work, farmers liked rearing worms because the turnaround was much faster than with soil-based crops. After independence, under the Karimov regime, sericulture was effectively indentured labour.

Farmers were coerced easily because technically, all agricultural land belonged to the state. Given that no farmer could live off the meagre profits they received for their commercial cotton crops, which were purchased below market prices by the government, most farmers used a portion of their land to grow fruit and vegetables for their own consumption and to sell any excess. This infraction gave petty officials the leverage they needed to force villagers into sericulture, threatening fines or land confiscation to those who did not comply. Where threats didn't work, beatings generally did. In a 2015 study, none of the 50 villagers interviewed from various parts of Uzbekistan had been paid the measly $2 per kilo of cocoons they'd been promised.

'We work like slaves for a month and they say they'll pay us $80 for all our cocoons,' snapped the old woman, fuming as she flung clusters of leaves at the indifferent silkworms. 'Well, I'd be grateful even for that. Usually, if they pay us anything, it's with something that fell off the back of a truck somewhere. Last year they gave us crates of vodka. I don't want my sons turning into drunkards! We tried to sell it, but everyone else in the village also got vodka so there were no buyers. You tell me, is that fair?'

Most of the silk produced in Uzbekistan is exported, and although conditions have improved since Karimov's death, it's still the villagers who work hardest and bear most of the risk, yet see just a tiny fraction of the profits. And there are risks. This intensive farming of silkworms in confined spaces can lead to outbreaks of disease that spread swiftly. There's scarlet disease, where the worms take on a rose-coloured hue and then die during skin moulting, or the yellow disease where silkworms almost appear to glow, before their heads swell and pus starts oozing from their mouths. In fact, it was Louis Pasteur's attempts to prevent pandemics within sericulture in 19th-century France that gave him his guiding principles for epidemiology, which are still used in modern medicine today.

A week later, I returned to the village to see how the worms were faring. Along the roadsides, villagers were hacking at leafy mulberry branches, stacking great piles of them on donkey-carts. Nuraddin took us back to the same house and we knocked on the front door but no one answered. We waited tentatively and then a side door opened.

'We can't use the front door anymore,' explained the old woman apologetically. 'The worms have taken over the main hallway.' The cavernous hallway and main living room were now filled with trestle tables covered in an eddying sea of cream as the silkworms gently undulated. Within minutes of a fresh branch being laid over them, it was covered and began to disappear. The air was thick with the pitter-patter sound of munching caterpillars, like milk on Rice Krispies, and felt humid and smelt of mown grass and bird droppings.

I picked up a fallen worm and it reared back at me aggressively. As soon as I placed it on a leaf, it began to eat. Silkworms have now become so accustomed to pampering that they seldom roam in search for food as their wild cousins would. Worms that fall from the trestle table simply wait, confused, for more leaves to be brought to them.

'Where are the silkworms you had before?' I asked, pointing in the direction of the room where they'd been kept.

The daughter-in-law grinned. 'These are them. Or at least some of them. They keep taking up more space and soon we'll have to move some of them to the stable.'

We returned just a few days later and the worms had grown again noticeably and had almost reached their full size. Nuraddin pointed out black markings on them that differentiated males and females.

The following week, Nuraddin called to say that there was no need for me to come to Yangi Arik. The worms had stopped eating. For the next week, they would simply rest as their bodies prepared for their metamorphosis. He could hear the disappointment in my voice. 'Don't worry, next week will be really interesting. Then, you'll see them spinning.'

A week later, we drove past denuded mulberry stumps and lorries stacked high with scrubby desert bushes. These, I discovered, were used as nesting sites for the silkworms to then spin their cocoons. Nuraddin greeted us with bad news. 'Our' worms had started spinning early and had finished already, but there were others in the village still spinning.

First, we visited the old woman and her daughter-in-law. Both looked exhausted. Where before there'd been a frenzy of activity, there was silence. Although it was late May and hot, it seemed as if winter had fallen inside the house. All over the clumps of desert scrub were white gossamer strands of silk, softening this landscape, like snow. Nuraddin tugged free a cocoon from the anchor threads around it and gave it a rattle.

'That's the pupa inside,' he said, and handed it to me. 'Keep it, it can be your souvenir.'

The grandmother and daughter-in-law resumed their work, which was disentangling cocoons from the bushes, removing any snagged twigs and then tossing the cocoons into sacks at their feet.

'Are you looking forward to having your house back?' I asked, with a grin.

The old woman didn't smile back. 'Let's just hope we actually get paid something this time,' she said, and continued her work.

'Even after scrubbing the floors for hours, it's hard to get rid of the smell,' the daughter-in-law added.

At a house further down the street we found silkworms spinning.

'You know they're ready to spin when their bodies turn translucent,' Nuraddin explained. 'Then they get restless and start looking for a good nesting site. That's why the desert bushes are so important. They choose somewhere with plenty of twigs around, but not too close to other worms. Once a worm has selected its spot, it makes a sort of nest with anchor threads around the twigs, so that the cocoon won't fall. After that, it begins to spin.'

We watched as the worms used a figure-of-eight motion with their heads to entomb themselves. Females spun slightly larger cocoons.

'What happens if they spin too close together?'

'Sometimes two worms create a double cocoon. It's twice the size, but the silk gets tangled up so it's not a good thing. As for the shape of the single cocoons, it depends on the weather. If it's been a hot spring then they're shorter and fatter, and if it's been a cooler spring, they're longer and thinner. It doesn't make any difference to the quality of silk, though.'

'How long is one if you unravel it?' I asked.

'Between a kilometre and one and a half kilometres.'

I nodded, impressed.

Silk may well be a byword for luxury, but it is essentially just dried caterpillar spit. It is secreted in liquid form from two spinnerets located just below the mouthparts, and is coated with a sticky substance called sericin, which helps the cocoon stick together. This coating makes unwound silk feel slightly stiff and more like horsehair. In the silk carpet workshop, the first thing we'd do is to get rid of the stiffness by immersing skeins of silk into cauldrons of hot water, to which we would add caustic *ishkor*, an ash made from the roots of a certain desert bush. After much dunking, this mixture strips away the sericin and, once washed in a soap bath, leaves the skein glossy and dazzlingly white.

I watched the dim silhouette of a worm inside the beginnings of its cocoon. Its continual silken strand is 30 microns in width, around half that of a human hair. One estimate is that, over a period of several days, the silkworm makes 150,000 figure-of-eight moves to complete its cocoon. I was distracted by another worm, a slower starter, which was just completing the nesting bed of threads which looked a little like the kind of spider's web found in room corners. It was about to embark on its cocoon.

'They're amazing,' I said quietly.

'Most of them will be heated to kill them,' Nuraddin stated matter-of-factly. 'If the moth hatches out, then the cocoon is destroyed in the process and the silk is useless. So, just a few are allowed to hatch and lay eggs for the following year.'

This is the dark side of sericulture. That said, silk moths have no mouthparts, so were never destined for a particularly long life.

I took photos and just before I left, Nuraddin presented me with a bouquet of sorts. It was two desert bushes twisted together and studded with cocoons, 'So you can show the tourists who visit your workshop.'

I placed the bouquet in the corner cell of the old madrassah we'd renovated into a workshop. A few weeks later, I watched as the tips of each cocoon turned an unattractive brown. This was acid released by the silk moth inside, which dissolves the silk fibres. The moths could then force their way out. They were fat and surprisingly fluffy, as soft, white and silky as their cocoons. Some had bushy antennae, which marked them out as males, equipping them to locate females and mate. The females themselves were larger, with abdomens already swollen with eggs. Millennia of pampering have left the silk moth refusing to fly, which means that male moths are manually placed beside females. It also means that the silk moth is locked into a system of symbiosis with us for its continued survival.

After mating, the females lay between 300 and 500 bright yellow eggs that then fade to a nondescript grey. These eggs need to go through a cold spell and then be warmed in order to wake them a year later.

Although I was fascinated by the lifecycle of the silkworm, it was still hard to grasp fully the impact these pale caterpillars had on the world.

Once Rome got a taste for silk and trade routes became established, just one bolt of silk was worth around 60 kilos of rice.

Several bolts made up a bale, and a large camel could carry up to 50 such bales, netting a tidy profit for those willing to risk the journey. The best camels for transporting this silk were also a product themselves of the Silk Road. One-humped Arabian dromedaries from the west and two-humped Bactrians from the east were interbred by the Parthians, resulting in a one-and-a-half humped camel still common in Central Asia today. These hybrids can withstand cold, thanks to their Bactrian influence, yet produce larger quantities of milk, as Arabian camels do. They're particularly suited to heavy loads, able to carry 400 kilograms over short distances and 250 kilograms on longer journeys.

Transported from west to east by these camels were goods including ivory, exotic bird feathers, Arabian pearls, Babylonian glass beads, Baltic amber, purple cloth from Tyre, Sassanian metalwork, tortoiseshell, saffron, pistachio, oak gall, narcissus, pomegranates, walnuts, wine, olive oil, sesame oil, frankincense, coriander, gold, silver, indigo, dates, Alexandrian glassware, grapevines, almonds, linen and lapis lazuli.

Headed the other way from China, as well as silk, were ginger, rhubarb, lacquer-ware, mirrors and chrysanthemums. From the Indian subcontinent came cotton, indigo, spices and various jewels. One of Central Asia's main contributions was flower bulbs. These included wild tulips, which became popular in Turkey and, from there, the Netherlands. Today, roads through Central Asian mountains are lined in spring with boys selling bunches of wild tulips, and the mountainsides are studded with wild irises and narcissus. Hollyhocks, those supposedly English cottage-garden staples, are actually from Central Asia and grow in wild abundance in Kyrgyzstan.

Silk Road trade affected fashion and architecture. The first chairs to arrive in China were fold-up backless ones, immediately dubbed 'barbarian beds'. However, they took off, meaning that clothing style had to adapt for chair-sitting, and rooms became larger to accommodate this new furniture, and windows and tables were raised to waist height. Nomadic clothing became popular everywhere as togas and robes were set aside in favour of trousers with short tunics worn on top, with side slits to allow for ease of movement, particularly while riding.

Apples originate along the foothills of the Tien Shan Mountains, where they evolved from being hard fruits with soft seeds to sweet, soft fruits with indigestible seeds. Their sweetness made them popular with bears and wild horses, and their hard seeds exited from the gut intact, helping the trees to spread in dung and scat. The largest city in Kazakhstan was once called Alma Ata, meaning the Father or Grandfather of Apples. There were also local legends about it being the site of the Garden of Eden, as the word for apple also means 'don't take', and the word for man is Adam. Apples soon traversed east and west, as did the famous peaches from Samarkand and the melons of the Khorezm desert oases, which were considered such delicacies that for many centuries they were placed in ice-filled lead cases and transported by camel all the way to the Emperor of Peking's table. Camphor, musk, ammonium chloride (useful for working leather) and pepper also traversed this road. A dangerous textile, even more mysterious and expensive than silk, was occasionally traded. This was fire-cloth. It could be cleaned by simply throwing it into a raging fire where it wouldn't burn but would return to its pure white colouring. In Europe its origins were the subject of much speculation, and it was thought to be the skin of a salamander or fire-newt. It was in fact asbestos. The fibres, once mined, were pounded to separate them and then cleaned and spun into thread and woven.

One Chinese export that would more profoundly impact the West than silk was gunpowder. This would revolutionise the way in which wars were fought, and lead to far greater numbers of casualties.

Transported along with these goods were ideas and religions. Nestorian Christians, persecuted in the Mediterranean, spread eastwards, establishing churches and cathedrals in both Central Asia and China. Similarly, Buddhism spread northwards out of India and eastwards (where it still dominates today). As for the Buddha himself, the Silk Road gave him a face – one of the most recognised faces on the planet, whether the serene spa/garden-centre iteration, or the fat, golden, jolly Buddha.

Of course, we have no idea what the Buddha looked like because his early followers didn't consider that important and made no attempt to depict his likeness except symbolically as a footprint in the sand or a lotus flower or an empty throne. But, as Buddhism hit the slipstream of the Silk Road, it was influenced by Greco-Roman aesthetics, and they gave their gods faces – and usually abs. As a result of this fusion of artistic influences, Gandharan art emerged, along with the first visual depictions of the Buddha.

Other fusions took place in silk designs. The Parthians of Persia may not have known how silk was made, but they soon rivalled China in their quality of weaving. Some Parthian designs made from unravelled and reworked Chinese silk found their way back to China where weavers attempted to copy these new Western designs or motifs, integrating them into their own existing patterns. Soon, Chinese dragons writhed around Greek goddesses. It's likely that the Parthians were also the first inventors of the drawloom, which is so complex it requires one person to weave and a second to sit above the loom and manipulate the warps. This then allowed for heavier fabrics and more complex patterns. The Chinese weren't to be outdone and also began using drawlooms themselves.

The Parthians had become excellent silk-weavers, but had also realised that the main silk-trading routes all passed through their own territory. They were able to control this flow, taxing it heavily, much to the irritation of those west of them, who paid a premium and felt that they were being overcharged.

Particularly peeved by this over-charging was Justinian, ruler of the Byzantine Empire, which relied heavily on silk to maintain its social hierarchy. The only people who could afford to buy it were priests, bishops, royalty and the fabulously wealthy. Justinian grew tired of this monopoly and set in motion a plan to steal the secrets of sericulture from China. Nestorian missionary monks were some of the few non-traders who could be found up and down the trading routes, and were unlikely to arouse suspicion, so Justinian hired them for his own mission.

The monks had already spent time in China and understood the process of sericulture, but this was of no use unless they could actually procure some silkworms, cocoons or eggs. They were dispatched from Constantinople with promises of riches should their mission succeed. They visited Khotan, to where the secret of silk had first escaped from China. A monk's tonsured pate was hardly a good hiding spot for silkworm eggs, but the monks managed to hollow out the tips of their walking staffs and hide the eggs there, bringing them back to Constantinople, where they hatched.

Justinian might then have revolutionised his kingdom by rolling out mass sericulture. Instead, he opened a small workshop for the royal production of silk for palace usage only, and left the rest of his empire to continue their haggling with Persians over Chinese silk. It was not until much later that sericulture became widespread around the Mediterranean basin.

Once large-scale production of silk took place in the West, and with a quicker and more economical maritime route, the Silk Road no longer teemed with trade and so fell into decline.

Sericulture, though, is still innovating and changing today.

In Japan, silkworms can be raised throughout the year, fed with pellets of dried and powdered mulberry leaves. China has developed new mulberry trees which produce several crops of leaves, which also means sericulture can take place all year. Uzbekistan is innovating, and now most villages grow a new type of Chinese silkworm.

'Here they are,' explained Farida breathlessly. Her smart, knee-length black skirt and jacket were at odds with a mouth full of gold teeth. I was leading a tour group in late April 2019 and we were hoping to find sericulture taking place in one of the villages near Khiva. We'd stopped the bus and by good fortune were introduced to Farida who was overseeing the process.

Our interest excited her, and she spoke so fast that I struggled to understand everything. She walked fast, too, and I scurried alongside her as she marched us to her pride and joy. 'It's completely new. We just had to wait for the paint to dry,' she announced, waving expansively at the worm-house. 'The worms don't like the smell of fresh paint,' she added. Of course they don't.

We came to an abrupt halt at the entrance, and she raised her hand. The tour group who hurried behind us were silenced. We were then instructed in hushed tones to keep our voices down and to stay near the entrance, which was well ventilated, in case any of our group were perfumed.

Inside were racks stacking up to two metres. The ones nearest to us contained trays of newly hatched silkworms. All the rest were empty. Some of the group seemed underwhelmed until I explained that soon, these tiny worms would fill every tray in the cavernous barn of a building.

'These new silkworms are smaller than the old ones, so they eat less,' explained Farida. 'The cocoons are also smaller as the silk is finer, but their length is consistently 1,200 metres.' She spoke with obvious pride. 'We've planted these new imported mulberries that will give us several harvests once they're bigger. They already have two harvests a year in the villages near Tashkent.'

President Mirziyoyev has decreed that Uzbekistan must increase its silk production, particularly as it tries to wean itself off cotton-dependency, but as I looked around at the women working there, my main concern was how much they were getting paid. As sericulture becomes more industrialised and less of a cottage industry, would the grandmother and her daughter-in-law in Yangi Arik greet the news with disappointment not to earn a little extra spring cash, or relief that never again would their house be taken over by silkworms, the odour of their droppings lingering long after each room had been scrubbed and aired?

9. AT THE HEART OF
THE SILK ROAD

Who actually traversed these trading routes, through inhospitable terrain, risking natural disasters or bandit attack? Apart from a few missionaries or emissaries, the majority of travellers along the Silk Road were merchants, and most of these were Sogdians, an ancient Iranian people. They would generally specialise in one particular stretch, learning local languages, bartering with nomads or other settlements they passed through, and always aware of alternative routes when a landslide or dried-up water source forced their hand.

Samarkand was the Sogdian capital and is more or less in the middle of the east–west routes as well as the north–south trade between India and Russia. It was the perfect location for a cosmopolitan people who were consummate traders, and bearers not only of new goods but also new gods, disseminating novel ideas, inventions and religions. It was the Sogdians, for example, who taught the Chinese how to make wine. Significant numbers of them settled in China, where they became so associated with trade that the terms Sogdian and merchant were interchangeable. Wherever their community grew larger than 40, they would erect a fire temple and appoint a Zoroastrian priest. Those who traded in India and settled in what is now Mumbai were the ancestors of the Parsee community; their fire temple still stands.

Sogdians were considered wily and avaricious. Xuanzang, a Chinese traveller who made his way west to Central Asia in the 7th century, described them as charming but untrustworthy, particularly when it came to haggling. Such was their commitment to their profession that newborn sons were initiated in a ceremony where honey was placed on their tongues to make them sweet-talkers, and gum on their hands so that money would always stick to them. Visit Samarkand today and you'll find the same blend of charm and bullshit from souvenir sellers. Unusually for the time, most of the Sogdian population were both literate and numerate – vital skills for those in the business of trade.

This trade brought wealth, which meant that Sogdian houses, such as those found in the ruins of Panjakent in modern-day Tajikistan, were often spacious pillared courtyards, with wall-to-ceiling frescoes including scenes from daily life, and large depictions of their local deities. One deity, depicted astride a camel, is thought to be the god of commerce – a forerunner of today's Santa.

A particularly impressive Sogdian fresco was unearthed accidentally in the 1960s in Afrosiyab, the site of ancient Samarkand, in the process of road construction. A bulldozer broke through a buried Sogdian living room, destroying the top half of the fresco in the process. The rest is now the star attraction of the Afrosiyab museum. It depicts a traditional positioning of ambassadors before the throne of a great ruler. They come bearing gifts from different regions and all have distinctively different clothing, hairstyles and skin tones, the group including Koreans, Chinese and Turks. The Sogdians themselves wear dazzling white and blue robes of silk, featuring geese, which were part of Zoroastrian sacrificial practice.

The first time I saw the fresco, I was charmed by the details on one of the walls depicting a royal pleasure boat. Fish spiral around a dropped morsel of bread and a frog is chased by a water snake. It was only on subsequent visits that I examined the remarkable intricacy of the Sogdian silk robes. Flowing within the robe of one of the ambassadors is a blizzard of Sogdian script describing the greatness of their ruler.

So, Samarkand was cosmopolitan, with religious tolerance and pluralism and a Babel of languages spoken in the bustling bazaars until the arrival of Islam. When the Arabs invaded, many Sogdians fled, sometimes to remote mountainous areas. Those who stayed in Samarkand would eventually lose their religion and indeed their language, which now exists only in these distant mountain communities.

An Australian friend, Jeff, lives in Tajikistan and speaks Sogdian, so I decided to contact him to see what else he could tell me about the Sogdians and their language.

Jeff is an agriculturalist and lives in Zafarobod – situated in a finger of Tajikistan which juts out into Uzbekistan, not far from Tashkent. There on the dusty plains live a hodgepodge of different mountain-people groups, including the Yaghnobi, who are the linguistic heirs of the Sogdian. During Soviet times, all these people were moved from their isolated mountain villages to pick cotton. Some left their mountain eyries voluntarily, with promises of agricultural land and an easier way of life. The Yaghnobis, though, had no intention of leaving the mountains where their Sogdian ancestors had once sought refuge. Instead, they were moved forcibly. When some attempted to return to their mountain homes, the Soviets destroyed their houses, and whole villages were officially removed from Soviet maps. The shock of forced relocation and the heat and dust of the plains killed off many of the very young and very old, but the survivors and their descendants still live there today, as we'll explore in more detail later.

Their descendants may be proud of their Yaghnobi heritage, but many have assimilated and tend to speak Tajik better than the language of their forbears.

'I've visited some of the isolated villages scattered around Tajikistan where people still speak Yaghnobi,' Jeff explains, on a ropey internet call which keeps cutting out. 'They laugh when I use certain Yaghnobi words, as they've stopped using them now, and use a Tajik or Russian word instead. It's hard to have hope for the language surviving.'

I had similar concerns when living in Khorog and working on a textbook preserving the Shugni language, also known as Pamiri. Like Sogdian, Pamiri is part of the East Persian language family and is in danger of disappearing.

'And are the Yaghnobi born traders, like their ancestors?' I ask Jeff.

Jeff pauses in thought for a moment. 'If they consider themselves anything, it's shepherds. Centuries of remaining in the mountains has changed them. The irony is that they fled Islam, but now they're Muslim, or sort of. They still practise some of the old ways, hanging ibex horns above their graveyards for protection. Many are stopping this now because Tajiks have told them it's un-Islamic. After all those centuries of isolation, it's just been in the past 50 or so years that they've been moved and forced to mix with others and are now losing their language and culture. They probably couldn't be more different from their Sogdian ancestors.'

While the Arab invasion and conquest of Samarkand in AD 712 may have been news for many Sogdians, those who stayed and converted reaped the benefits of further invasions eastwards, as the Arab army went on to fight the Chinese. They clashed at Talas in modern-day Kyrgyzstan and thousands of Chinese were taken captive and dragged back to Samarkand. There, they bargained for their lives by spilling their secrets. Some revealed their techniques for weaving the very finest of silks. Others revealed secrets that were to transform Samarkand and would impact the Western world far more than silk ever would. They explained the art of papermaking.

We're not entirely sure who first invented paper in China, but in AD 105 a palace eunuch demonstrated to the emperor the various stages of soaking, mashing, spreading and drying wood pulp. In the early days of its invention, it wasn't actually used for writing but rather for packaging, in particular the wrapping of precious medicines. In places such as Khotan, it still is.

On my first trip along the Silk Road, I visited Erna, the Swiss English teacher in Khotan mentioned earlier, who offered me a bowl of the most delicious tea. Golden liquid swirled small bits of dried spices around my bowl. 'What's in this?' I asked, as my mouth filled with the taste of Christmas.

'Locals call it *dari chai*,' she said. 'It means medicine tea.'

The previous day I'd settled into the only hotel available for foreigners, fished out the crumpled scrap of paper in my pocket with her number on it and called her from the reception phone. The line crackled, but I could hear her. She invited me for breakfast the following morning.

I arrived to meet a tidy, short-haired and bespectacled lady who asked me to remove my shoes before leading me across a carpet to the low table and seating mattresses I'd become familiar with in Uzbekistan. She explained that Uzbek and Uighur cultures were very similar in terms of history, language and culture.

'Wouldn't Uighurs like to have their own country, like the Uzbeks do?' I asked in the course of our conversation.

Erna looked uncomfortable and then cleared her throat and announced matter-of-factly that her flat was bugged and that our conversation was being recorded, so I should just be aware of that.

'What – now?' I mouthed as she poured me a bowl of steaming tea and nodded, smiling.

'Don't talk about Uighur independence,' she mouthed silently. I hoped I hadn't got her into trouble.

Early the following morning, I headed for the famous Sunday bazaar, surrounded by the clank of horse-bells from carts full of people and merchandise. Amid the clamour I found the apothecary section of the bazaar, a stall full of all manner of strangeness.

'*Dari chai*?' I asked the seller uncertainly, my eyes drawn to the sacks and metal tubs filled with dried seahorses, snakes and insects of indeterminate origin. He pointed at a row of weights and looked at me enquiringly. I selected one in the middle, and he nodded and began scooping up ingredients. Pretty star anise, curls of cinnamon bark, and lumps of root ginger were scooped and tossed into the waiting scales. His hand hovered briefly over a sack of dried frogs but thankfully passed over them to scoop up some peppercorns, dried mint leaves, cloves and other ingredients I didn't recognise but could tell were reassuringly plant-based.

It turned out that the weight I'd chosen would give me far more tea than I wanted, but it was too late to change my mind. His selection was tipped into the funnel of a motorised mill which ground it all down into fine sawdust-consistency, exuding a wonderful aroma. This was then poured into manilla paper envelopes. Each envelope had a red block-print stamped on it with what I assumed was a list of ingredients, or possibly health claims. After all, in Kashgar I later found a bottled elixir from Pakistan with a label in English boldly claiming: 'Cures all ailments but death'. Once filled, each envelope was stapled shut and, despite drinking my medicine tea regularly and giving away many of the brown paper packets, it kept me going for at least two years.

Although paper continues to be used for wrapping medicine, more and more people in China discovered that its mildly absorbent surface was better to write on than bamboo strips or pieces of bark, so this became its primary usage. Paper would also pave the way for the invention of printing, as it was cheap to produce and could absorb ink better than papyrus or vellum.

My envelopes of tea had been block-printed with Chinese characters extolling the health-giving benefits of its contents. The Chinese invented block printing around 2,000 years ago, and it was the Uighurs who took the concept and then invented moveable type printing in the tenth century, long before a similar invention was introduced in 1450s Europe by Johannes Gutenberg, ushering in the dissemination of ideas and, ultimately, the Reformation and the Enlightenment.

Once Sogdians discovered the secret of papermaking, workshops proliferated all over Samarkand. Samarkand paper then traversed the silk-trading routes and was used all over the Islamic world. Europeans first purchased paper from the Muslims, and when they finally started making paper themselves, it was made

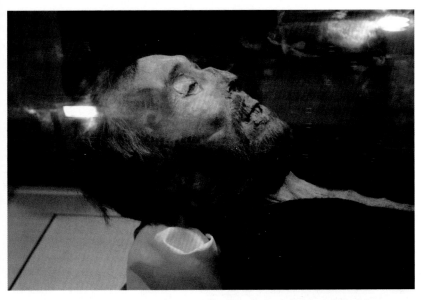

Above: Cherchen man – his ochre burial markings are still clearly visible.

Below: An Uzbek woman in her burnt-out courtyard in Osh, with Solomon's Mount behind.

Our first attempt to get down from a yak.

The *jailo* is the summer pasture for semi-nomadic High Pamiri Kyrgyz.

Horsand, one of the yak herders we befriended, with a newborn yaklet in his arms.

Above: The colourful interior of a yurt, with storage bags hung from the walls and *palas* and *shyrduks* around the dome.

Below: A Kyrgyz girl weaving *palas* on a strip loom.

Above: Women trialling the American and Mongolian combs, moments before the mobile bazaar arrived.

Below: Pamiri women making felt by rolling it up and down for over an hour.

Suzani embroidering in the village of Shofirkhon, near Bukhara.

Royal nomadic architecture, with embroidered silk yurts in red and blue.

'Together we will end the paranja!' A Soviet poster from the Hujum campaign.

Whole living rooms get taken over by silkworms as they reach maturity.

Reassembling atlas silk warp threads that have been dyed teal, in Margilan.

Left: Atlas silk warp threads drying after their first dye-bath.

Below: The last Emir of Bukhara, photographed by Prokudin Gorsky around 1908.

A crowd of men in Samarkand wearing an array of striped locally produced cotton robes, and floral Russian chintz. Photographed by Prokudin Gorsky around 1908.

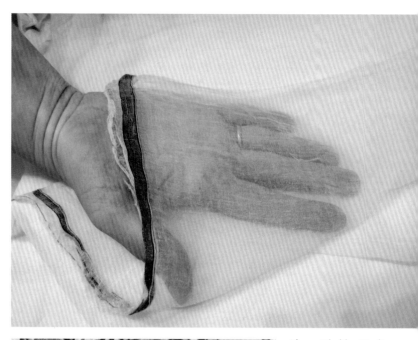

Above: Dhakka Muslin, a fabric that is now extinct.

Left: Detail from a *suzani*, including a triangular tumar.

A bride, wearing seven veils, is led up the steps to her husband's new home in Khorog.

Above: The author with local boys on the prow of *The Karakalpakia*, a beached fishing vessel in Moynaq.

Below: A cotton boll.

from pulped rags for a long time; only much later did they learn how to utilise wood pulp.

The art of papermaking in Samarkand was destroyed, along with most craft industries, by the Soviets. Paper would now be mass-produced in factories.

Located on the edge of the city beside a fast-flowing water channel, the first workshop in Samarkand to revive the art of handmade paper is a definite tourist trap. Here, branches of mulberry trees left over from sericulture are steeped in water for several days. Then the bark is peeled away, and the inner part of it is scraped off and kept. The rest – once dried – can be used as firewood.

The strips of inner bark are boiled in a large vat and left to simmer, softening the fibres within, which exude a sharp and unpleasant smell. This pulp is then slopped into wooden buckets and beaten with wooden hammers powered by a waterwheel. Once thoroughly pulverised, the pulp is mixed with water in a rectangular basin. The paper-maker then stirs the water and submerges a framed wire mesh. As it is lifted out, the water drains away, leaving behind an even coating of pulp over the mesh. The frame is then removed and the neat wet rectangle of pulp is upended onto a clean dry sheet of cloth, which is part of a stack of up to a hundred. A flat piece of wood is then placed like a lid over this stack and a huge stone heaved on top of it to help press any liquid out.

After 24 hours in the press, each damp sheet of paper is carefully peeled off and brushed onto the wall, like wallpaper, where it will dry for another day. Then, each sheet is laid on a marble slab and burnished with an agate stone, or a piece of horn or seashell, flattened and polished with use. Now, the paper is ready and can be written on double-sided without ink seeping through. The paper-makers boast that it will last centuries longer than commercial paper because it contains no chemical bleaching agents, which weaken paper over time.

One of the main clients for handmade paper are the miniature painters of Bukhara. Originally these illuminators worked in royal workshops where each stage of book creation, from papermaking through to book-binding, calligraphy and illumination, took place.

Wherever you have art you have ego, and wherever you have ego you have art. And it was ego which allowed these workshops to flourish despite the Islamic prohibition on the depiction of living beings, because great rulers wanted their deeds preserved in written and visual form.

Similarly, although most miniaturists viewed themselves as simple cogs within the mechanisms of these royal workshops, there were some who couldn't resist signing their illuminations, perhaps hiding their name within the leaf of a tree, painted with the finest of brushes. A few miniaturists did become famous, for example Behzad, whose miniatures from the 15th century often depicted carpets which we wove back to life in the Khiva carpet workshop.

Illuminated manuscripts from the 15th and 16th centuries may be filled with mythical dragons, jinn and simurghs, but they also portray palace life, fashions of that time in silks and cottons, carpets, and an incredible textile architecture which has been completely lost. In one miniature by Behzad, a prince sits on a carpet, surrounded by musicians, flirting with a young boy to whom he offers a carnation. Above him is the upper dome of a yurt covered in indigo blue felt and embroidered with gold and multicoloured silks. Above this, a large canopy of gold brocade silk had been erected to provide additional shade. Nor is this set-up unusual. We see similar opulent soft furnishings in many other miniatures, indicating a blurring between indoor and outdoor architecture.

Sadly, none of this incredible textile heritage has survived except in the illuminations of manuscripts and in the writings of visitors to the region. The most famous of these Western visitors was Gonzalez de Clavijo, a diplomat from Spain who travelled to the court of Amir Timur in the early 1400s.

Clavijo and the other ambassadors with him had originally intended to meet Timur in present-day Georgia, which had just been conquered, but ended up trailing the tyrant all the way to Samarkand, where they were treated to lavish hospitality. As they first approached the city, officials presented each ambassador with a beautiful silk robe as a gift. Before meeting any important visitors, Timur left them for at least a week of leisure, to be awed by the opulence of his city and to recover on a gentle diet of whole boiled sheep and whole roasted horse, served on enormous gold and silver platters which took several servants to lift, along with copious amounts of wine and jugs of sweetened cream.

When the ambassadors were finally carried under the armpits into Timur's presence, they found him 'seated cross-legged on silken embroidered carpets amongst round pillows. He was dressed in a robe of silk with a high white turban on his head, on the top of which there was a ruby-red spinel with pearls and precious stones around it.'*

Most entertaining took place outdoors in the beautiful palace gardens, each equipped with 'many tents, and awnings of red cloth and of various coloured silks, some embroidered in various ways, and others plain'. Timur himself was seated in a shaded pavilion, with the breeze wafting through drapes of fine silk, studded with jewel-encrusted silver. Clavijo was entranced by the awnings, set up on two high poles above each yurt to allow for the crown to remain open, letting in light and air, but shading from direct sunlight. Some were plain linen or cotton, while others were elaborately embroidered silks.

Islamic prohibitions on alcohol consumption were completely ignored, with Muslim guests cajoled into drinking each cup down to the dregs. Whoever drank the most was hailed *Bahadur* or hero. Timur even had wine sent to the ambassadors' residence so that they might arrive at his palace already in a jovial mood. It was prudent not to be too relaxed, though. When a translator arrived late, the peeved monarch ordered that his nose be bored and a rope put through it. Timur only conceded after the translator had fallen at his feet and wept, begging for mercy.

Amir Timur pooled the expertise of captured architects from all over his new empire. They were given virtually unlimited budgets and commissioned to cover Samarkand in fabulously opulent

....

* de Clavijo, G., *Narrative of the Embassy of Ruy Gonzalez de Clavijo to the Court of Timur at Samarkand* (1403–6), p. 132

palaces, mosques and mausoleums, some of which have survived. Never known for his patience, Timur would harry builders of these new projects, tossing gold coins or pieces of choice meat to them as liberally as threats of torture or execution if he thought they were slacking. Clavijo was extremely impressed by these monuments and described them in his account. However, far more remarkable to Clavijo was a city of 14,000 dwellings he witnessed spring up in a matter of just a few days, large enough to accommodate 30,000 guests who had come to celebrate several marriages of Timur's grandchildren. It was a city made from silk. Clavijo marvelled as streets sprang up between the textile structures. Larger tents and yurts became shops, restaurants and even bathhouses equipped with heated hot water and wooden baths. In the centre of the city was an enormous silken palace, covered in long strips of black, yellow and white silk. The main hall was square but employed the textile equivalent of a squinch, as it boasted a domed roof held aloft by twelve enormous poles, each the width of a man. It could accommodate 10,000 people, dwarfing many modern circus tents.

Hanging from the vaulted ceiling were silk drapes, and on the floor was a gigantic silk carpet. Fabric corridors led off the exits to other meeting tents, also lavishly decorated and carpeted. The whole structure was topped with silken turrets and towers that from a distance gave the impression of a great castle.

Stuck with his sedentary language and paucity of words to describe nomadic dwellings, Clavijo refers to everything as a tent, although he clearly describes yurts with their lattice walls and lack of tent-poles within to keep them aloft. These yurts also received the royal treatment and might be embroidered with silk and gold, or studded with gemstones. One was covered in sable, the costliest of furs, at a time when just one pelt was worth several plots of land.

When eating and drinking proved insufficient entertainment, Timur ordered the craftspeople and merchants of Samarkand to come out to the plain and to sell their wares. He also set up a gallows to add to the festive cheer, hanging bureaucrats who had displeased him. When he tired of executions, there were always wrestlers, trapeze artists, jugglers or races and mock battles between mounted elephants and horses.

The ambassadors did not sleep in the silken city, but one day, on their return to it, they discovered that new silk-walled enclosures the height of a man on horseback had been erected, containing tents even more extravagant. One had silk walls of crimson, embroidered with gold lace, topped with turrets made from cloth-of-gold, which had been further embroidered. Another large enclosure was dazzling in its simplicity, consisting of pure white silk satin.

One of Timur's wives offered to show the ambassadors her mobile quarters, and they were astonished by a huge yurt of crimson silk covered in silver gilt. The crimson interior was embroidered with blue and gold knots. Its doors had been taken from Byzantine churches in recently captured Bursa and were still decorated with the images of St Peter and St Paul.

Yurts continued to be used by Central Asian royalty until the late 19th century, when plate glass became available. Before then, brick and stone buildings were inevitably cold and draughty. In Khiva, the palaces of the Khan still have the circular podiums where royal yurts once stood. Royal yurts could be easily transported, so that princes and princesses could escape the simmering summertime temperatures of the city and enjoy a life of leisure and fresh mountain air, glamping beside a bubbling brook. Summer tents were also popular, and wealthy Bukharans and Samarkandis would retire to these beautifully embroidered and patchworked tents, situated beside rivers or in the foothills of mountains.

Sadly, Timur's fabulous brick structures were built in a seismic zone and experienced several severe shakes, the most recent causing a lot of damage in the late 19th century. When Arthur Koestler visited in the 1930s, he 'just wanted to sit down in the shade of the decaying turquoise columns and cry. For the arches were crumbling, the tiles peeling off, and the broken fragments were strewn amongst the rubble smelling of dog's urine.'*

Annette Meakin's first impressions of the city in 1896 were more favourable. 'Keats could not have chosen a more appropriate epithet for that city than "Silken Samarkand"; almost every other man we met was clothed in silk. A gentle breeze filled their long wide sleeves till they looked like silken pillows and spread out on the folds of their ample garments, while the silk embroidery on the boys' caps shone in the direct rays of the midday sun.'[†]

Even since my first visit, Samarkand has changed a lot. Back then, I walked along a teeming road from the Registan – three breath-taking madrassahs which form three sides of a square – towards the Bibi Khanum Friday Mosque. The main bazaar spilled out into it and the street was thronged with stalls and hawkers. I found a pillared teahouse with good views of the mosque and the opportunity for some people-watching as well. It was built before the 1930s, which meant that it had most likely been co-opted by the Soviets and equipped with loudspeakers, portraits of Lenin and copies of *Pravda* and transformed into one of their many Red Teahouses. The city may not have had an old quarter with winding alleyways like Khiva or Bukhara, but it looked very different from today. Now, the teahouse and the stalls are all gone, bulldozed to create a wide and featureless pedestrian pavement for tourists, plied by golf buggies full of local visitors. Beside it is a shadeless park, full of browning conifers. Samarkand had become Samar-bland.

---

* Koestler, A, *The Invisible Writing* (1954), p. 136

† Meakin, A., *In Russian Turkestan* (1903), p. 40

Can we combine silk and papermaking today? That's what we're hoping to achieve at the Khiva silk carpet workshop. The carpets are all pure silk and hand-knotted. After each row is completed, it is trimmed, and we've never found a good use for these silk trimmings other than as pillow stuffing, which seems a waste of such an expensive resource. However, an artist friend of mine based in Frankfurt thinks she might be able to make paper from this waste.

'You can use anything for papermaking,' Sarah assures me. 'One of my favourite materials to use is the fluff that collects in the tumble-dryer drawer. It makes a really nice, soft paper. Egg cartons, cardboard, it can all be used.'

I tell her about the papermaking process in Samarkand with the waterwheel and hammers.

'A hand-blender also works really well for creating the pulp,' Sarah replies. 'I sometimes add beetroot or onion skins, or a handful of blueberries. They all create different colours.' I smile at Sarah's foray into colours, given that her surname is Dye.

At the time of writing, we've sent Sarah a selection of silk trimmings from the workshop and she's experimenting with them. She's made some beautiful paper with half silk trimmings and half egg cartons, which has a wonderfully soft, supple feel to it. Sarah is hoping to come and visit Khiva to give us training. The Silk Road continues to innovate and transform.

Samarkand may be the historical and geographical heart of the Silk Road, but for actual silk weaving in Central Asia, one city remains unrivalled. In the middle of the Fergana Valley is the silk capital: Margilan.

10. FROM MOTH TO CLOTH

It's spring of 2022 and I'm in Tashkent, where I feel like a relic. When I first visited the city in 1998, I was oppressed by the concrete brutalist architecture everywhere, but now that lies behind shiny glass exteriors or has been knocked down and replaced with lavish new buildings clad in sandstone. I find myself seeking out the brutalist buildings I've come to feel fondly nostalgic towards, and also the Soviet statues, and the mosaics that often adorn Soviet-era blocks of flats, many of which are now obscured by electronic billboards.

In 1998, the city's Slavic population was declining as Russians were uncertain of their future in an independent nation where many still resented the Russification of their country and culture during the Soviet years and before. Now, though, there is a new wave of Slavs who don't need visas to live here, as they're part of the Commonwealth of Independent States. They are here because of the war in Ukraine. Some are Ukrainian refugees; others are mobile Russians tired of Putin and, now, the war he's started, or are simply pragmatic IT workers who can use Uzbekistan's banking system for business as it doesn't have sanctions against it like their own. They soon discover other perks, such as warmer weather, a cheaper cost of living, and the fact that they can continue speaking Russian and be understood without having to learn a foreign language. Some Tashkent residents benefit from this influx, particularly owners of coffee shops with good Wi-Fi. Most simply complain about how the Russians have driven up rental prices throughout the city.

In today's Tashkent, people order taxis via an app, but I don't have a local SIM card, so the girl at the hotel reception desk kindly orders me a car and I wait outside for it. When it fails to materialise, I head back to the street and try the old-fashioned method of sticking my hand out. Reassuringly, seconds later a battered white Lada with a cracked windscreen careens towards me and we start to negotiate. I'm taken to the depot where cars depart for the Fergana Valley and get mobbed by several drivers all waiting for customers. Usually you pay for one seat, but I end up with just the driver and a backseat filled with boxes of ketchup sachets which need delivering to a restaurant in Fergana City. We cup our hands in a prayer for the journey and then he thoughtfully turns the radio to a Russian station that plays only eighties power ballads in English, because he thinks this is what I'll like, and so we depart to the strains of Michael Bolton and Chris de Burgh.

There are two ways to get to the Fergana Valley from Tashkent by road. The easier but longer route, popular in Soviet days, takes you round to Khojand, at the mouth of the valley, and then to Fergana from there. However, Khojand is in Tajikistan, which is now a separate country, so everyone takes the harder route over the mountain pass.

Today, there's possible danger from avalanches in winter, but generally the road is kept clear. However, as recently as the early 20th century, caravans of camels crossing this mountainous terrain ran the risk of all sorts of dangers, as Gustav Krist discovered while taking refuge for the night with a gnarled old forester in his hut. By the light of the fire, the forester told Krist about the *rabat,* or inn, which before the revolution had once stood on the same ground. Caravans of camels laden with bales of cotton, bolts of silk, chased copper, atlas robes, carpets, jewellery and other high-value goods would overnight at this spot, and the merchants would enjoy shelter and a hearty meal.

But then whole caravans began to disappear. They would depart from Bukhara but never arrive in Kokand, or leave from Andijan but never make it to Tashkent. Neither the Emir of Bukhara – then a vassal state – nor the Russian authorities in Fergana could solve this mystery. It was only in the 1920s as Bukhara fell to the Bolsheviks that they captured a rebel who – knowing he would be executed anyway – boasted of murdering over 400 merchants who had innocently visited his inn.

The innkeeper would collect poisonous spiders from the mountainside which he stored in a glass jar. After several days of starvation, he would toss pieces of dried fruit into the jar and the ravenous spiders would sink their venomous fangs into them. These pieces of fruit were then added to wine, which was served to the unsuspecting caravan merchants. Within minutes of drinking the venom-laced beverage, madness set in, swiftly followed by convulsions and then paralysis. The innkeeper then dragged each merchant to a staircase leading down to the cellar and toppled them down to a waiting bear, who had been similarly starved until he acquired a taste for human flesh. The bear did the rest.

The Soviet authorities sent a contingent of troops to the old *rabat,* and sure enough, down in the cellar was the carcass of a large bear surrounded by hundreds of bones. When news of this reached the local population, they were enraged, and, unconvinced that the Soviet authorities would punish the innkeeper harshly enough, they broke him out of prison and then tied him to two different camels, stuffing raw chillies up their backsides. The enraged camels galloped off into the desert, not always in the same direction, and the remains of part of the innkeeper trailed behind one of the returning camels a week or so later.

As for the treasures carried by the caravan? The forester would search for them every day, but they were never found.[*]

Luckily, the teahouse where we stop for lunch has no bear or poisoned tea, and we continue down into the valley, passing a long row of electric pylons, each topped with a stork's nest. Drawing

---

[*] XXXXXX

closer to Margilan, I see villagers cutting down mulberry branches. The season of sericulture has begun.

Margilan itself was founded by Alexander the Great. According to legend, Iskandar, as he was known locally, had a lunch-stop here, not far from his most eastern Alexandria (present-day Khojand) and enjoyed chicken and bread, or *murgh va naan*. It must have been a great meal as the town's name is a corruption of it. Margilan today has seen a gradual liberalising economically and politically. Under President Mirziyoyev, while Uzbekistan isn't exactly democratic, it is experiencing its own era of *glasnost* and *perestroika*. Corruption is still endemic, but now there is more freedom, particularly for younger people, to dress the way they want to, and it's *moda* to dress Muslim.

Around Margilan, most women wear grey or dusty-rose-coloured hijabs. There are even a few in niqab, showing only their eyes. Young men wear knitted prayer caps and ostentatiously straggly Islamic beards. It's Ramadan, and there's a furtive air in lunchtime restaurants as those who aren't fasting seat themselves away from the main windows lest they get spotted and judged by a passing acquaintance.

Despite the huge changes wrought during the Soviet era, there seems to be a seamless reversion back towards pre-Soviet life, not only in terms of clothing, but also with business. The Margilan Silk Factory, for example, is an enormous concrete building with a large Soviet mosaic over the front entrance depicting a woman weaving atlas silk, surrounded by abstract atlas silk motifs.

The factory closed shortly after the collapse of the Soviet Union, as orders for garish Soviet atlas silk designs dried up. Former factory workers, or those who had money or connections, started visiting the closed factory and purchasing or purloining looms. Soon domestic small-scale workshops had sprung up all over the city – just as had existed before they were banned in the late 1920s, when everyone was collectivised and forced into factories and farms. Now, walking down the street, you hear the muffled clatters of silk being woven behind courtyard doors. I track down several, deafened by the noise made by just seven factory looms once inside, and, not for the first time, unhappy about the lack of any ear protection for the women working there.

Some are weaving cotton and a few are weaving silk or *adras*. *Adras* is a blend of cotton and silk, with silk warps and a thicker cotton weft which remains invisible, due to the warp-facing style of weaving. The result is a material with the same luminescence of silk but with a bit more heft to it. *Adras* is often finished with a pleasing moiré effect that gives the shimmering fabric a lucid oil-on-water feel about it. It's a fabric mainly woven in Uzbekistan and has become extremely fashionable in posh upholstery shops in Chelsea.

The lightest and gauziest of silks are known in Europe as organza, which is a corruption of Urgench in Khorezm, where the silk was first woven. Even silk this fine is not made from one silk filament, but from a minimum of four filaments spun together. The lightness of organza scarves is often demonstrated by fitting them through a wedding-ring, such is their ability to shrink and then to open up, airily. Silk has the ability to be so light and take up so little space that during the Second World War it was used for parachutes, thanks to a tensile strength greater than steel, and also for secret maps, which could be stitched into the inner linings of jackets and clothing to avoid detection. If tautened, silk vibrates, making it a popular choice for Central Asian stringed instruments. While living in Khiva, I had lessons from a blind girl who taught me to play the dutar, an elegant two-stringed instrument that made silk sing.

Silk doesn't rot, which means that, once the pupae are killed, the cocoons can be stored in a dry place indefinitely. This property has also made silk the surgeon's choice for sutures. Silk also stretches, allowing silk stockings to cling rather than sag and tent guy-ropes to stretch in the wind and not snap. It's hardly surprising that silk is generally more expensive than other fabrics.

In one of the new domestic workshops, I admire the fine organza, undyed, as it emerges from the machine looms, and then retreat outside to the comparative quiet of the courtyard where pigeons are nesting in a quince tree. What I'm actually on the hunt for are workshops producing handwoven silk, with the distinctive warp-resist dye technique that is now a trademark for Central Asian weaving. The style is also found in Indonesia, where it is referred to as ikat, but here it goes by the name once given to silks that had been dyed seven times and were considered fit only for a king, or in this case, a khan; khan atlas.

I first saw the complex preparation for atlas weaving in the 1990s and remember watching, transfixed, as silk from twenty or so bobbins was tugged through a wire mesh and onto a huge warping wheel, two metres in diameter. This contraption enabled warps of 200 metres to be numbered off in groups without getting tangled. An old, bearded man in a black skullcap turned the wheel with one hand and with the other held a bowl of water to his lips, filling his mouth periodically and spewing a fine spray, whale-like, over the threads to help prevent tangles.

Near Margilan's main daily bazaar, there's a shop selling atlas silk. I go inside to make enquiries. The owner, Anwar, is pleased to have an Uzbek-speaking foreigner visit who is so interested in their craft. He leads me across the road and down a side street to an unprepossessing gate. We enter and he parts our way through bolts of electric-pink atlas cloth hanging on a line in long spools, dripping gently. Here is a small dyeing workshop which specialises in atlas. We pass vats as he leads me to a room where two artists are at work.

The 400-metre warp threads (the vertical part of a bolt of cloth) are measured and grouped into clusters of twenty by the warping wheel. These are tied into bunches and then looped and stretched on a low metal frame two metres in length. Two metres or so of the design will be drawn onto these warps which will repeat for the whole 400 metres of finished cloth. I enter the room where this design process takes place. Resting on a frame of taut silk warps are a mobile phone, a bowl full of charcoal mixed with water, a stick, and several metal rulers. Kneeling over the frame, checking a completed design on his phone every now and then, is 24-year-old Islom. He dips the stick into the liquid charcoal, and then measures out where to make his mark. The effect looks a little like the

dotted lines drawn beneath an eye or cheekbone by cosmetic sur-
geons. The overall design looks strangely squashed, which is very
different from all the atlas designs I've seen. I comment on this and
Islom smiles.

'This shape here that looks almost like an eye, will end up being
a long oval. That's part of the challenge for designers; we have to
imagine how what is currently squashed in one direction will end
up being elongated and stretched during the weaving process.'

I don't fully understand, but it's mesmerising to watch. Islom's
assistant brushes a dab of colour onto each section of each clump,
so that when the warps are taken for wrapping and dyeing, it will be
clear which parts should be left exposed to the dye-bath. Islom tells
me that he's been a designer for eight years. Sometimes he creates new
designs but most of the time he's copying older designs that he keeps
on his phone. His father and grandfather were both weavers, and his
grandfather worked in the only handloom factory permitted during
the Soviet times, now a thriving tourist destination called Yodkorlik.

Anwar leads me back outside to a bath where rosary-strings
of tightly bound silk with bulging open parts in saffron yellow are
in a rinse bath, lurking beneath the surface like brightly coloured
carp. Although I've seen the process before and know the theory
of it, I'm still struggling to understand how the whole thing will
fit together, until two of the boys remove teal-coloured warps
from another bath and begin to stretch and reassemble them onto
a metal frame. A beautiful pattern emerges from the chaos. The
unbound parts are teal but the bound parts remain white.

I'm distracted by a scratchy ripping sound from one of the
rooms. Here, Soviet machinery designed for twisting cotton to
make string has been adapted so that both ends of a two-metre
stretch of silk warps spin at the same time. A young man holds a
reel of Sellotape that screeches as it winds rapidly onto the marked
areas, binding it and making it dye-resistant. At his feet lie hundreds of discarded reels and clumps of crinkling tape that has been
cut away from the warps and discarded.

These warps have already been dyed and dried once, in a cherry
red colour. The tape from the undyed white parts has been removed,

and now most of the cherry red sections are getting the Sellotape treatment. Once each clump of warps has been Sellotaped, the warps will be submerged in a blue dye bath. After drying, the tape will be removed and the warps assembled in the correct order. A beautiful pattern of red and blue, bleeding into purple where they overlap, is what will emerge. It's ridiculously time-consuming and fiddly.

I chat to the two teenage boys who are wrapping the warps with tape. They tell me that they can complete two colours of atlas warps a day. If a more complex design requires, say, six different dyes, then it would take three days to complete the process. Do they do the dyeing? They shake their heads vigorously; dyers, warp wrappers and designers all keep to their own area of expertise.

'What happens to the warp threads once they're ready? Where are your weavers?' I ask Anwar, looking around.

'This workshop is just for men,' Anwar replies. 'We do all the warp designing and dyeing here. Then, the silk warps are taken out to the villages where women weave the cloth at home, bring it back to us and then we sell it in our shop. We have orders from abroad, too – mainly Turkey and Arabistan.'

This latter country is a somewhat vague appellation that generally refers to the Gulf.

I visit the Yodkorlik factory to see women hand-weaving atlas on their looms. This is generally a fairly simple affair, as the trickiest part was the dyeing of the warps. Now, a simple weft thread passes through the heddles on a shuttle and most women operate just two foot-pedals. The effect is beguiling with vertiginous designs that bleed their way down the length of silk, seeping into one another with a blurring of lines between them. Atlas used to be called *abr* silk, meaning cloud, and I can see why.

A few women work on more complex patterns which require six foot-pedals. They're producing satin, where instead of the over-under-over-under of plain weave, the cotton weft will go five over, one under, and so on, creating a looser weave with the silky side mainly showing.

My favourite story about the origins of atlas has a young male weaver who falls in love with a rich merchant's daughter.

When he proposes, she sniffs at him in disdain but lets him know that if he can dazzle her with a completely new fabric then she might give his proposal consideration. The weaver eagerly works on bolt after bolt of silk, but she shows nothing but disinterest for his creations. Finally, having spent a whole night weaving, and working so hard that he's made his fingers bleed, he visits her and presents her with the blood-stained silk. She is not impressed. Dejected, the weaver wanders outside and bends down to wash his bleeding fingers in the roadside water channel. The fast-flowing waters reflect the yellow from the sun, the blue from the sky, the green from the trees overhead, and mingle with the blood from his fingers.

Inspired by this vision, the weaver forgets all thought of sleep and returns to his workshop to recreate the flowing, vertiginous patterns he'd seen in the waters. The result is atlas silk and, of course, the merchant's daughter is suitably impressed and they fall happily, if shallowly, in love.

Given how labour-intensive it is to grow silkworms, and then the complicated stages needed to create atlas, it isn't surprising that khan atlas was only worn by the top echelon of society. The Tajik term for silk cloth was *podshoi,* meaning the Shah's clothing, because only royalty could afford to wear silk. However, by the latter half of the 19th century, trade, particularly in cotton, was leading to an emerging middle class with aspirational taste. So, silk, *adras* and cotton, and the various simplicities or complexities of their weave, stratified society and displayed anything from cheerful functionality to ostentatious displays of wealth.

Nowhere was this truer than in Bukhara, where men preened like peacocks, their generous beards and impressive turbans at odds with robes in bright pinks and greens, often covered in florals. For Central Asian men there was nothing 'girly' about wearing flowers.

Stephen Graham travelled through Bukhara at the turn of the 20th century and observed very few men or boys who didn't sport a rose, carnation or dahlia perched behind their ear. By then, Russian chintz had made its way to Central Asia and large pink roses on red or electric-lime backgrounds were a favourite for men's robes.

As for the atlas silk motifs, in Bukhara, the *boteh* was popular, referred to by some as the almond, but also reminiscent of the chilli, considered to protect against the evil eye. So was the pomegranate-and-comb design, the hand of Fatima, ram's horns, tulips, scorpions, flames, astral planets, pears and peacock feathers. Technically none of the men were supposed to be wearing these silk robes, as the Prophet told his followers that infidels would have silk in this life, but the faithful would have it in the hereafter. A selective interpretation of this injunction against men wearing silk argued that it applied only to silk against the skin. So, silk robes were given inner linings of cotton to avoid divine displeasure but still look fabulous.

Frenchman Henri Moser travelled through Bukhara in the 1880s and described the fabric hierarchy of the court. While the cut or shape of men's robes remained unchanged, lowly servants and commoners wore robes of simple striped cotton. Those of a slightly higher status wore *adras*. Next came pure silk atlas robes, and for the truly rich, there was silk velvet atlas, or imported silk brocades from China or India. Top of the pile were wearers of silk velvet atlas robes embroidered with gold thread and finished with the addition of a Kashmiri shawl.

Moser travelled with a French diplomatic convoy and received ten exquisite robes as gifts from the Emir of Bukhara. By the end of his stay in Bukhara, which was only a matter of weeks, he had amassed a collection of 140 robes, given by various officials. Most of these were re-sold to merchants, who were used to the recycling of gifts, and in some cases, having left a small mark on the inner linings of robes, he received the same one back again from a different official. At that time, even the Russians, Germans or other European minorities who lived in Bukhara wore silk robes rather than European clothing.

Danish explorer Ole Olufsen visited Bukhara in the late 19th century and also amassed a collection of robes, most of which he, too, recycled as gifts to local officials. The number of robes worn by a dignitary at any one time also denoted their social status. On one occasion, Olufsen called upon the *divanbegi*, or prime minister, catching him in a state of undress, wearing only two robes. The flustered *divanbegi* swiftly ordered a servant to bring in more and was soon a veritable mountain of rustling silk – the rustle being just as important as the look of it. Typically, the most impressive robes were larger in girth, partly because the girths tended to get larger, the more important the official, but also because, when several robes were worn at once, the most impressive one needed to be large enough to fit over the rest.

The Bukharan Emir would gift an entire new set of clothing to each member of his court every spring equinox, and valued servants of anyone in Bukhara were more likely to receive a robe than a raise for their efforts. Despite how fabulous these robes were, and how complex the weaves, Central Asians never quite mastered the concept of pockets. Indeed, there were no hooks, buttons or eyelets, but rather everything was held up and held together by a belt around the robe. For the wealthy, these belts would be plated with silver and studded with turquoise and coral or even precious stones. Different styles also denoted status, and for the Jews of Bukhara, the belt, or lack thereof, was an emblem of their second-class status.

At the turn of the 20th century there were more Jews living in Bukhara than in Jerusalem. Many had done well for themselves and worked as merchants, as well as monopolising the cold dyeing of silks in indigo blues and violets. Warm dyeing in reds and yellows was largely the preserve of local Tajiks. Jews were people of the book, along with Christians, so were not considered as lowly as idolatrous infidels. However, as non-Muslims they had to pay an extra tax and were permitted to ride only a female ass.

As for clothing, Jews weren't allowed to wear a turban, lest a passer-by mistake them for a Muslim and wish peace upon them. Instead, they contented themselves with a conical fur-trimmed hat, and instead of a belt were made to wear a rope around their waist as a reminder that they could be hanged at any point should they ever forget their station. 'The rope has in the course of time become thinner and thinner, and now they employ a thin twisted string in order to render the stamp of pariahs as little visible as possible,' Olufsen observed.* For Muslim Bukharans, only mullahs were supposed to wear white turbans, with others expected to wear white with an edging of red or blue. These were usually cotton and were often manufactured in England. Only those who had been to Mecca were permitted to wear a turban in green.

Summer and winter robes varied only in that winter robes were padded with cotton or occasionally camel wool. Within Bukhara itself there were guilds for apprenticing new weavers, and they even had their own saint. Today, in Turkmenistan, many carpet and silk weavers still intone a prayer to Bibi Risand, seeking her help and blessing, before embarking on a new piece.

The Khan of Khiva also distributed robes as rewards for service. Arminius Vambery, a Hungarian orientalist who disguised himself as a dervish, witnessed the Khan's treasurer dividing robes into separate piles. They were all in 'glaring colours' with gold-embroidered floral motifs, and were divided into four piles, the first referred to as four-heads, the second as twelve-heads, then twenty-heads and, finally, forty-heads. 'The nomenclature struck me as very odd, all the more so as there was not the slightest trace of a head to be seen on these garments.'† On enquiry, the treasurer cryptically told Vambery to come to the main square the following morning. There, a hundred dusty soldiers on horseback arrived, their saddlebags bulging, with captives tied behind their horses. Once the captives had been handed over, each soldier tipped out their sack, and the number of decapitated Turkmen rebel heads that tumbled out determined how fancy their robe would be.

* Olufsen, O., *The Emir of Bokhara and his country* (1911), p. 298

† Vambery, A., *Arminius Vambery – his life and adventures* (1884), p. 228

While robes and jewellery stratified society and displayed wealth, so did the universal means of transport: the horse. This was a man's most prized possession and Turkmen men made no secret of loving their horses more than their wives. For sedentary men whose women were covered, if they wanted to display bling, then the horse generally received preferential treatment, particularly as it was unheard of for a man of any standing to walk when he could ride. The result was equine jewellery worn around the harness, with silver tassels making a soft 'shing' sound as the horse trotted, tipped with coral and turquoise. Carnelians and silver might also stud the bridles. And a magnificent horse belonging to an owner of wealth would be covered in beautiful silk-embroidered caparisons, fringed with amuletic tassels offering the rider protection on his journey.

Knowing that atlas silk velvet is even more costly and complicated to weave than ordinary atlas silk, I set out to find someone in Margilan who can show me how it is made. After asking around, I meet someone in the bazaar whose neighbour is a velvet weaver, and we're soon crammed into a minibus heading to the edge of town. She knocks on a courtyard door and introduces me to Shirali. He's in his twenties and his courtyard is spacious enough to accommodate a vegetable patch, vines and a small orchard of fruit trees. One of the older rooms around the garden, with a mud-packed floor, houses Shirali's loom. The wooden loom itself doesn't look any different from other handlooms except for one important feature. Instead of one set of warp threads – weighted at the end to provide tension, and then feeding into the heddle – there were two sets. The upper set, I learnt, is a floating warp, and not integral to the structure of the cloth. It is what will become the pile of the velvet.

Shirali sits down at the loom and tugs on a pulley system that shoots a shuttle back and forth, alternating the warp threads with two foot-pedals. After doing this twice, he inserts a thin metal rod between the proper warps and the floating warps, and it nestles alongside the last weft thread. Then he weaves two more wefts and inserts another rod, repeating this pattern. I watch, full of questions but keeping quiet, waiting to see what will happen next.

Once he's used up the 50 or 60 rods he has at his disposal, which equates to around ten centimetres of fabric, he takes a sharp Stanley knife and scores along the length of each rod, removing it from the cloth. What is left is a luxuriant pile, produced by the remains of the floating warp. It uses the same principle as the pompoms we made at school. Now I understand why in 19th-century Bukhara, the only fabric more expensive than atlas silk velvet was imported brocade silk, or silk embroidered with gold.

The sumptuousness of these fabulous robes was captured in glorious colour by one of the pioneers of colour photography, Sergey Prokudin-Gorsky. His ingenious method of photographing in colour required three photographic plates to be taken of the same subject in quick succession. The first black-and-white image was shot on a red-tinted glass plate, the second on a blue one, and the third on a green. When the three plates were combined and aligned correctly, they created stunningly intense colour photographs. They weren't great for capturing movement – streams and rivers are a blur – but otherwise they so impressed Tsar Nikolai II that he commissioned Prokudin-Gorsky to travel throughout the vast Russian Empire, photographing it. Prokudin-Gorsky was even given permits to visit territories otherwise off-limits, and his own train-wagon was equipped with a darkroom.

His visits to Bukhara and Samarkand in the early 20th century give us glimpses into the colourful textile world at the time. He photographed the last Bukharan Emir, seated plump and proud as a peacock in a shimmering turquoise brocade robe with an enormous gold-plate belt and his upper chest littered with diamond-encrusted Bukhara stars. His *divanbegi*, or prime minister, was captured in a mint-green brocade robe complemented by a bright red silk sash, an ornate, jewel-encrusted sword and scabbard resting on his lap.

Bukharan noblemen wear robes of atlas silk but his photograph of the debtors' prison shows men crowded together in padded stripey cotton robes. Men on modest incomes still aspired to peacockery, and in another photo taken on the steps of one of the Registan's madrassahs, the majority of men and youths wear robes of Russian-printed cotton chintz, which favoured large repeating floral patterns. To me they look enrobed in old-fashioned wallpaper.

Central Asia is by no means the only place where silk has been used to stratify class and status. Where these codes have become enshrined in law, they are referred to as sumptuary laws. Ancient Romans banned all but princesses from wearing purple silk, as well as banning men from wearing it altogether, as we saw earlier. In China, commoners were forbidden from wearing silk satin or brocade. Farmers might wear plain-weave but merchants considered this too common. In Florence, sumptuary laws became a wealth tax of sorts, with the amount of gold coins paid determining how lavish the silken item might be. Medieval England allowed only knights of the realm and lords to wear silk satins or velvets. It was cotton, though, which caused the most European approbation, particularly in France, as we'll explore later.

The whole process from sowing cotton to harvesting it was full of exploitation in Russian-occupied Turkestan. However, there were winners, and a new emerging middle class of Turkestanis had disposable income and spent much of it on silk robes, leading to a renaissance of silk-weaving up until the First World War.

This was followed by the revolution and then the chaotic years of the early 1920s and the civil war waged all over the empire between Whites, loyal to the Tsarist Empire, and Reds who were a mix of socialists and communists, often teaming up in Turkestan with Muslims and nationalists calling for self-rule. These uncertain times of war and famine meant that there was little demand for silk robes, although some weavers, instead of weaving silk for money, were to weave silk money.

In 1920, Khorezm became an independent republic. It was short-lived, as the Bolsheviks eventually turned on their former allies, and with firepower from Russia, forced Khorezm to join the Soviet Union. During its brief existence, though, silk banknotes were woven and were legal tender. The money proved more durable than paper and, if it got dirty, you could simply launder your cash. After the collapse of the republic, these banknotes were repurposed and became popular, stitched together as wedding gifts, either as robes or quilts, wishing the new couple financial prosperity.

Then in 1928, the first five-year plan was rolled out throughout the Soviet Union, promising a hundred years of progress in just ten. Up until that point, small, family-owned and domestic businesses were permitted to operate independently. Now they were banned, as part of an attempt to break down pre-Soviet society and force everyone into collective farms or factories.

Centuries of artistic skill and talent was destroyed along with the complex guilds and training mechanisms that had been in place to pass down these skills. Weavers, dyers, metal-chasers, leather-workers, carpenters, jewellers and potters found themselves out of work and without the identity that had often shaped their sense of self and indeed had been their family identity for generations. 'The main difference between now and the old days,' recalled an elderly Bukharan, 'is that before the Soviets came, we *made* things. A man was a smith, or a jeweller, and his son would follow him. Or we sold things. After the Soviets came, everyone had to be a factory worker or a *kolkhozchi*. We had become peasants.'*

* Whitlock, M., *Beyond the Oxus* (2002), p. 65

Nor were the mainly Slavic Soviet rulers of Turkestan merely concerned with the economic aspects of society. They wanted to break down and remould everything. This desire for modernity made the Communist Party attractive to many within the *jadidi* movement of Muslim modernisers, who saw the oppression of the poor by the rich and women by men. Many of the first Turkestanis to join the party were *jadids,* who were easily recognisable in the streets, favouring European suits as symbols of modernity.

But what began as aspiration soon became coercive. European clothing became synonymous with progressive thinking and eventually there were even edicts informing Communist Party members of the correct attire for proper socialists. Robes and turbans became the preserve of the elderly, the rural, and those in opposition to Slavic rule. The one permitted item of traditional clothing for both men and women was the skullcap.

Before the 1930s everyone in Turkestan wore something on their head, which also marked out their region, religion, language or lifestyle. Nomadic Kyrgyz and Kazakh women wore high white beehive-shaped cotton turbans, while Turkmen women wore fabulously striking red and gold silk turbans with huge plated silver jewellery around them. Men from Khorezm and the Turkmen and Karakalpak tribes wore large, shaggy sheepskin hats in black or white, Tajik men in Bukhara and Samarkand wore skullcaps that disappeared beneath impressive cotton turbans, Jews wore conical fur-trimmed hats, and in Tashkent and the Fergana Valley men wore skullcaps, sometimes with a smaller turban wrapped around them.

Each region had its own style of skullcap, but during the first half of the 20th century, one skullcap design from Chust, in the Fergana Valley, came to dominate all the others and became a Slav-tolerated sign of Uzbek-ness and a national hat of sorts. It was black and square with white chillies embroidered on each of its sides. For girls, the white silk skullcap covered with cross-stitched roses popular in Tashkent became a national uniform. All good socialists were encouraged to wear European clothing, but the skullcap showed that you were an Uzbek-flavoured socialist.

English traveller Ethel Mannin was in Tashkent for the 18th anniversary of the October Revolution and watched the processions, including emancipated women in European dress, sporting velvet skullcaps. 'There are stacks of skullcaps of all colours ... some are very handsome in their gaudy fashion, with tassels and embroideries in gold or silver thread; others are very richly and cunningly embroidered in a multitude of coloured silks ... The embroidered skullcap is a compromise between the turbans of the Faithful and the head-dress of the godless West. It symbolises and typifies the conflict between Asiatic tradition and European modernism, religious, political, moral and social.'[*]

This road to modernisation, or rather Russification, was not a smooth one. Scottish traveller Ella Christie recalled in the 1920s: 'Such gay butterflies are the men, but the women are seldom or never seen out of doors, and if they are, one finds them smothered in dark-coloured or coat-like garments with elongated sleeves, the cuffs of which are fastened at the edge of the back of the coat.'[†]

She was describing the *paranja*, worn by nearly all urban women, and completely enveloping them, hiding their faces from view. And it was a war on the *paranja* – considered backward, religious and oppressive – that was to define much of the Soviet campaigning in urban Central Asia during the 1920s. Soon, the smell of burning silk was to fill the air.

....

[*] Mannin, E., *South to Samarkand* (1936), p. 286

[†] Christie, E., *Khiva to Golden Samarkand* (1925), p. 149

11. SILK IN FLAMES

Of all the treasures in my flat, my musical *sanduk* is probably my best bargain. It's a wooden chest with a flat lid covered in a fine lattice of decorative metal strips. I found it among broken samovars and other odds and ends in a tinker's workshop beside the disused railway tracks in Jalal-Abad. The tinker was surprised that I'd want something old and used, when shiny new wooden chests in garish colours were available just around the corner in the bazaar. He wanted the equivalent of £7 for it and ended up parting with it for £5. We both thought we'd got a good deal.

Before returning to live in Britain, I lined the *sanduk*'s outer sides and corners with cardboard, having stuffed my camel-down duvet inside, and at Osh airport I checked it in as hold baggage to the amusement of the airport staff. The chest got lost at Istanbul airport, and when it hadn't shown up on the carousel at Gatwick, I went to the lost-luggage office and tried in vain to explain to the bored administrator that my chest wasn't similar to any of the bag options I was expected to tick.

'It's not a bag at all. It's a chest. You know, like the things pirates fill with gold.'

She tapped a long, vividly red fingernail extension at the laminated options of lost luggage. 'You have to pick one.'

I opted for a bulky black suitcase which looked vaguely rectangular in shape, and was pleasantly surprised when the *sanduk* was delivered to my door the following afternoon.

To open the chest, there is a long, elegant bolt which slides out of three clasps. Once these are opened, the music starts. Calling it music is, perhaps, an overstatement. There is a lock, and as the key turns in it, a mechanism inside makes a jangling, vaguely melodic sound. This was part of its original appeal when I found it on the tracks, even though the key was missing. Why were chests musical? It was to help safeguard a woman's treasures from the most likely source of theft – a rival wife.

My chest was probably made in the early 20th century, when most wealthier households were polygamous. Having a second, third or fourth wife was a sign of status, particularly if they were kept at home in the women's quarters with nothing but gossip and embroidery to alleviate their boredom. A local woman in Samarkand in the 1890s summed up the feelings of many women when she stated how she prayed regularly for her husband to earn just enough but no more, for as soon as there was money to spare, his thoughts turned to purchasing another wife, and happiness would flee the home.

These additional wives were purchased as young as eight or nine, to husbands sometimes in their fifties or sixties. This meant that many first wives were more like mothers or even grandmothers to the terrified girls who had just been wrenched from the familiarity of home. Some wives found friendship with each other, but often there was rivalry and hatred between them. Mullahs and witches profited from this, as women regularly employed their services, purchasing amulets, love-potions or curses.

There were Koranic verses and prayers for protection, frogs to bury beneath the spot of a rival wife's sleeping mattress for curses, and potions to be slipped into a husband's tea with the whispered incantation, 'love me first'. For those unwilling to leave such matters to the spirit world, many would resort to poison, including arsenic, which could be inhaled during sleep to deadly effect. With no autopsies and bodies buried on the day of death, poisonings by family members were a fairly common occurrence.

So, life amidst such domestic strife meant that a locked chest was no guarantee of safety. Even if the first wife kept the key to her chest around her neck, during sleep it was always possible for a rival wife to silently slip it from the sleeper, but with the musical lock, it was impossible to open it quietly.

It seems appropriate, then, that I should keep some of my most precious Uzbek treasures in my own *sanduk*. These include a men's antique glazed cotton robe from Khiva which shimmers like silk. I also have a cloak made of silk warps and cotton weft, with thin black stripes running down it. It comes with elongated sleeves and a horsehair veil that fits over the front, shrouding the face and chest of the wearer. In the first half of the 20th century, it was both a symbol of women's oppression and of national resistance. Although there were regular public bonfires organised by the Soviet authorities to burn them, many women stubbornly continued to resist their removal. In Uzbek, this cloak is called a *paranja*.

When Russians first colonised Central Asia, they were often appalled at the treatment of women but did little to interfere with domestic affairs. Count Pahlen (commissioned by the Tsar at the turn of the 20th century to inspect the province of Turkestan) was less concerned by the *paranja* itself than with the damaging effects of child-marriage and the casual approach to divorce which could leave women penniless and homeless. He believed the primary need was for women to have education and employment opportunities.

Paul Nazaroff, a Tsarist Russian who eventually fled the Bolsheviks and was given sanctuary in an Uzbek home, witnessed domestic life first-hand. There were fights both between the husband and his wives, and between the wives themselves. These women were completely dependent on their husband financially; even the growing of silkworms required that their husband supply them with mulberry leaves. Beatings were common, and Nazaroff was also shocked at the ease with which divorce could take place. The mullah was called, the divorce declared, *plov* eaten, and then the wife and her young son were driven by wooden cart back to Tashkent whence they'd come. At least, Nazaroff reasoned, if a woman had somewhere to go, she could escape an abusive husband more easily than her Russian sisters.

In the Emir of Bukhara's harem, new additions often arrived because a man couldn't pay his debts and so was forced to part with a daughter. Girls were prized for their youth and virginity, but having been used once by the Emir, he rarely made further demands of them and passed them on to relatives or court officials. They would often change hands several times.

Arthur Koestler, a Hungarian visiting Bukhara in the 1930s, met Rakhat, a former member of the Emir's harem who was now a trade union official. Her father had died when she was twelve, and when no relative was willing to keep her, she was given to the Emir. He slept with her once and then later gifted her to his finance minister who was 75. She was seventeen. She bore him a son, but her life only really began when he died in 1922. Rakhat swiftly converted to socialism, unveiled herself, and found work in a factory, learning to read and write in her spare time. She married a peasant but he laughed at her for studying and attempting to better herself. 'So Rakhat Raikhova – one-time member of the Emir of Bukhara's harem, created by God as a slave of men, who could be bought and sold like chattel and was supposed to have no mind or will of her own – Rakhat went to the Registrar's office and obtained a divorce.' * Although ubiquitous at the turn of the 20th century, the *paranja* was actually a relatively recent phenomenon, becoming popular in the mid-19th century at the same time as Russian colonial expansion. It was partly a reaction to godless Slavs invading the land, but also a result of improved transport infrastructure allowing more men to make the pilgrimage to Mecca, where they saw covered Arab women and returned with religious zeal, determined that their wives would do likewise.

....

* Koestler, A., *The Invisible Writing* (1954), pp. 140–1

Wealthier kept women no longer walked the streets with the *mursak*, a simple white silk headscarf, but now enveloped themselves in their cloak-like *paranjas* and horsehair *chedras*. As with men's robes, some *paranjas* were made from silk velvet while others were simple cotton, also stratifying the wealth and status of the wearer. Some girls eagerly anticipated veiling as a sign of maturity, while others dreaded the day when they would no longer be allowed to play freely outside with other children.

So, during Tsarist rule, women were largely invisible in urban public life. In fact, for many women the *paranja* was what allowed them to escape the women's quarters of their homes and get out on the street to visit others. The only open-faced women seen on the streets were Russians and Tartars, or aged beggars or prostitutes. Women would rarely frequent the bazaar but were permitted to visit other women. For covered women, before donning their *paranja*, they would wear a brightly embroidered skullcap and possibly a headscarf. Over this, there would be placed a thick, black rectangle of woven horsehair with a band at the top end which could be fastened around the head to keep it in place. The veil would then hang over the face and chest. It was referred to as *chachvon* or *chedra*. In Khorezm they used the Persian *perdeh*, meaning veil or screen, and from where the Urdu word for female seclusion or purdah originates.

'The strangest thing about the *paranja* is its long tapering sleeves, which, too narrow for use, are thrown back over the shoulders and pinned together behind,'* stated Meakin. She was told that the elongated sleeves originated in women wearing their husband's robes over their heads as cloaks. As the sleeves constantly got in the way, they were elongated and fastened together at the wrist, becoming merely decorative. I was told that they were fastened behind the back as a symbol that the wearer was her husband's slave.

---

* Meakin, A., *In Russian Turkestan* (1903), p. 204

While men's silk robes were fabulously floral and colourful, *paranjas* were usually dull-coloured or in muted blues and purples, and any embroidery was usually black. However, unlike men's silk robes (which were dutifully lined with cotton chintz so that silk would not be against their skin after the Prophet's injunction against men wearing silk), the inner linings of better-quality *paranjas* were often a colourful riot of atlas silk, their beauty kept hidden until they unveiled in the presence of other women.

It would take more than a colourful silk lining to win over Ella Maillart, a Swiss explorer to Uzbekistan in the 1930s. 'Numbers of veiled women in the stiff unbroken lines of their *paranjas* look like silhouetted upright coffins, with some package or basket balanced on every head. It is nonsense to call them veils; trellis work is far more to the point, so dark and rigid is the horsehair which scarifies the tips of their noses, and which they pinch in their lips when they bend down to see what quality of rice is being offered them, for their sight is only able to filter through when the "chedra" is hanging straight down in front of them.'*

Before the revolution, the Muslim modernist reformers known as *jadids* had campaigned against the veil. They wanted to retain Islamic identity and practice, but to modernise it as was to happen under the rule of Mustafa Kemal in the newly created secular republic of Turkey. In Turkestan, a few brave *Jadidi* women mixed in male company, although they would still veil themselves outside.

Then came the Bolshevik Revolution. Initially, the Bolsheviks were occupied with combatting both the Russian regime loyal to the Tsarist Empire and the independence movements among the empire's diverse ethnic and religious groups. As they sought to

---

* Maillart, E., *Turkestan Solo* (1934), p. 171

control Russian Turkestan, local resistance movements sprang up, vilified in the Soviet press as nothing but bandits and referred to collectively as *Basmachi*.

More Bolsheviks were brought in from the wider Soviet Empire to help bolster the tiny number of actual communists now ruling over Turkestan. The majority of these were Slavs and they generally lived in the colonial cities that had been built by Imperial Russia. Even with this influx, the non-natives made up only 8.5 per cent of the population. The Bolshevik hold on power was far more tenuous than the propaganda of the time would ever admit.

The guiding principles and certainties of Marxism, dictating that an urban proletariat must rise up against their oppressors, did not seem to be working in the Central Asian context, despite redistribution of land and water rights. Instead, suspicion and opposition to Slavic rule remained firmly entrenched. Rather than being viewed as class liberators, Bolsheviks were perceived as just more colonial oppression under a different banner.

What the Bolsheviks desperately needed was for an indigenised movement of committed communists who would turn others to the cause. But there were few allies among the local population; hardly surprising given the atrocities and exploitation that took place under Tsarist rule. So, Bolsheviks were constantly looking for segments of the population they might win over, but tended to focus initially on class.

There had been initial, rather clumsy attempts to liberate veiled women in Tashkent. Local women who were already unveiled were commissioned to go house to house, dressed in leather jackets, preaching the gospel of emancipation. The problem was that these women were usually unveiled because they were prostitutes. As Nazaroff wrote, 'The Mohommedan women saw in this an insult to themselves, and all the emancipated ones had their throats cut.'* The next wave were equipped with revolvers, which may have

....

* Nazaroff, P., *Hunted Through Central Asia* (1932), p. 51

kept them alive, but simply entrenched the idea that an uncovered woman was one with no morals.

More successful was the establishment of Women's Departments in every major city, combining the Russian words for 'women' and 'department' into 'Zhenotdel'. American communist Joshua Kunitz met one of the first Slavic women to establish a Zhenotdel in Tajikistan. Like most Slavs in Turkestan, she spoke no Uzbek or Tajik and understood little of the local culture. She was, however, appalled by the condition of local women, and endeavoured to do something about it. Her bridge into the local communities was local Tartar women, who were Muslim, but were more Russified and often spoke Russian.

Initially the women's outreach targeted women from wealthier and more educated families, with little success. They soon learnt that it was the most destitute women, with nothing to lose, who were willing to discard their veils or break other cultural taboos in exchange for provision from the Zhenotdel. Beyond this segment of women, female cotton weavers, who were often widows supporting their families financially, started to join the new women's clubs set up by Zhenotdel. They were attracted by free literacy classes and Russian classes, primary health education, women-only shops that were usually well stocked, and the opportunity to socialise with other women.

By the early 1920s, the Zhenotdel was making steady progress with the establishment in Tashkent of all-female midwifery, pharmacy and nursing colleges. Abortions were available freely and considered simply a method of birth control. Runaway child brides were taken in and given places in boarding schools. The Zhenotdel leaders urged the Communist Party to take the oppression of local women seriously, but the party was preoccupied with attempts to win over the working classes. Ethnic, linguistic and religious identities were far more resistant to Slavic communist attempts to create brotherhood across class lines than had been anticipated, and the Bolsheviks were running out of options. So, they began to take the Zhenotdel's proposals seriously.

What if gender became a proxy for class? The emancipation of women could potentially win over at least half the local population who could then convert their husbands and sons to the cause. There were few Uzbek female party members to point out any potential pitfalls that might lie ahead. Soon, it was decided to make the emancipation of women a socialist priority, with a particular emphasis on unveiling.

So, in 1927 on 8 March, International Women's Day, the Communist Party launched its new campaign. They called it the *hujum,* translated as 'attack' or 'assault'. Its brief was to raise the age of marriage for both boys and girls, with the minimum age for girls being sixteen. It would make polygamy illegal, along with the *qalim,* or bride-price, which had incentivised the selling of particularly young daughters. Divorce laws would also change. Divorced women would now have the right to claim financial provision from their ex-husbands for the upkeep of their children. Above all, and as the most visible marker of its success, the *hujum* would free women from the *paranja* and allow them to walk boldly and bare-faced into a bright new Soviet future.

The original timescale for the *hujum* was a blindly optimistic six months, to end just in time for the ten-year anniversary celebrations of the October Revolution. The plan was that the wives and daughters of Uzbek communist party members would unveil first, inspiring the wives of more socialist-leaning factory workers, union members, schoolteachers and the like to follow suit. There seemed to be little awareness that social engineering on such a scale and to such an invasive degree had never been carried out by a colonial power before. The Communist Party were totally unprepared for what happened next.

The introduction of the *hujum* at the International Women's Day celebrations began well enough. In numerous cities, crowds of women gathered and there were rousing speeches espousing women's liberation, culminating in the visually arresting spectacle of women throwing off their *paranjas* and horsehair veils, casting them into bonfires lit for the occasion. The air filled with the acrid crack and sizzle of burning horsehair and the curiously meaty smell of burning silk and – if official reports are to be believed – over 100,000 women renounced the veil.

However, this initial success was short-lived and provoked a furious backlash. For many Uzbeks, female face-baring was so closely associated with prostitution that when unveiled women returned to their neighbourhoods they were spat at, propositioned, or verbally insulted on the street, called whores, *sotilgan* (someone who's sold themselves out) and unbelievers. Husbands, fathers and brothers who considered themselves publicly shamed usually responded with physical violence and worse. Over the next two years hundreds of unveiled women were murdered, nearly always by their husbands, fathers or older brothers in an epidemic of revenge shame-killings.

Some women who unveiled that day remained uncovered. They were either wives of senior communist officials or those with *jadidi* sympathies. However, despite the speeches, the reality was that a Muslim unveiled woman was still considered of questionable character. Women who had run away from home or been divorced, or had been prostitutes, but now relied on provision and employment from the state, living in factory dorms, remained unveiled. These women, having completely broken away from their cultural background, often adopted European dress and cut their braids into fashionable Russian bobs. Newly unveiled women hardly wanted to be associated with any of these categories and it took very little public shaming – never mind the risk of domestic violence – for them to swiftly don their *paranja* once more.

Uzbek women now faced a treacherous and shifting cultural landscape, pinioned between the forces of Mohammed and Marx. To remain veiled might risk their own economic prospects or the careers of their husbands if they aspired to join the party or take an administrative position within government. To unveil guaranteed opprobrium on the street from neighbours and violence from male relatives. More pious women found that the war against the *paranja* actually limited their freedom because now they simply didn't leave the house at all but remained sequestered for months and even years on end.

A pragmatic solution adopted by many was to leave their neighbourhoods veiled and then unveil before entering a factory or communist meeting, where veils were forbidden, before re-veiling on return to their own neighbourhoods. Some women substituted a shawl or robe for a *paranja*, still concealing their faces and bodily form from men, but technically not wearing the *paranja*. None of these half-measures sat well with party activists or Zhenotdel.

Wives of communist party members who'd often assumed their husband's support swiftly discovered that, while they might publicly back the party's aims, when it came to their own family members, they were definitively anti-*hujum*. According to government reports, only 10 per cent of the wives of communist party members remained unveiled.

Then there were pious wives of communist party members who were forcibly unveiled in public by their enthusiastic husbands and would shriek or even faint at the trauma of being stripped in public. Those Uzbek and Tajik women working within Zhenotdel itself found interactions with local male communist party members challenging. Their unveiled status meant that assumptions were made about their own morals, and many were propositioned and sexually harassed, whatever the public party line might have been.

As the Communist Party noted the lack of success with the *hujum*, they cast around for scapegoats, but there were no easy answers. When a woman re-veiled, was she expressing doubt or even mistrust in the Soviet state, or was this the result of family pressure and coercion, or because of the treatment she received on the street? It was also hard for the central executive to monitor the progress of the *hujum*, because reports were often wildly inaccurate in attempts to impress. One report claimed that more women had unveiled the previous week than even lived in that particular city. Socialist-minded students and members of the Communist Party's youth wing, *Komsomol*, were recruited to patrol neighbourhoods and count the numbers of veiled or unveiled women. In the end, blame was inevitably laid at the feet of class enemies who, in this instance, were considered to be the mullahs and the merchants.

With mosques and markets on one side and the Zhenotdel and Communist Party on the other, the opposing sides were drawn up and ready for a culture war.

One weapon in the Zhenotdel's arsenal was medical science. The *paranja* was declared dirty and unhygienic, preventing skin from receiving sunlight and lungs from breathing in fresh air. According to one article, it caused flabbiness, premature ageing and muscular weakness. Women who remained in seclusion, they stated, had poorer circulation due to lack of exercise, resulting in a build-up of toxins which they then passed on to their children through their poisoned breast milk.

Another weapon was the arts. Writers such as Hamza Niyazi produced songs and plays with themes of social injustice and female emancipation. He was eventually stoned to death by a religious mob. Tamara Khanum was the first local woman to dance unveiled in public and joined the Tashkent Russian Opera and Ballet troupe in 1921. Nurhon Yulduz Hojaeva followed suit a short time later, having run away from her home in Margilan. On a return visit to her family home, she was stabbed to death by her brother in a shame killing ordered by their father. Often women were tortured before being murdered, or their bodies were mutilated afterwards. The Communist Party were unsure whether to publicise these deaths in order to create heroic new martyrs, or hush them up lest they scare off women from unveiling altogether. Show trials and executions of male family members of murdered women soon became the norm.

Art was employed for *hujum* purposes. Typical paintings – usually by Slavic artists – often portray a quietly defiant teenage girl clutching a textbook or walking to school, ignoring the glare from her father or gossip from veiled women. Women's newspapers written in Uzbek, such as *Yangi Yol*, or New Path, included comic strips in which opponents to the *hujum* were always brought to justice. Propaganda posters pictured Slavic women calling on their Uzbek sisters to unveil, pointing out the employment opportunities for the female workforce. I have a reproduction of one on my wall, which calls on women to unveil and start driving tractors. Tractors featured heavily in propaganda posters of the time, as Central Asia received the first tractors produced in Belorussia long before they were available to rural Slavic communities. They were seen as powerful Soviet symbols of progress, and Central Asia was prioritised in an attempt to impress the local population and win them over to socialism, even if the first ones simply sat unused because no one had thought to also ship out diesel.

Inducements helped persuade women to unveil, such as possible employment in women-only factories, or free literacy classes. There were even a few Zhenotdel workers who simply resorted to bribery, offering money or other gifts to women who would renounce the *paranja*. Where inducements failed, there was the force of the law.

Hefty fines were given to those who broke the new rules governing the age of marriage and bride-prices. They also raised new social questions. If a man had several wives, who should stay and who should go? Similarly, how was one to determine if a girl given in marriage was sixteen or older when there were no birth certificates and forged ones were readily available on a burgeoning black market? So many young girls lied when questioned by Zhenotdel that eventually only an invasive medical examination by a Slavic doctor was considered 'proof'.

Finally, town-planning was used to reshape Uzbek domestic life. The winding alleyways of mudbrick courtyard houses, devoid of outward-facing windows, were gradually demolished and replaced with wide, paved streets and later with apartment blocks. In 1933, Arthur Koestler visited Bukhara and was woken not by the muezzin call to prayer but a loudspeaker rigged up in the central square announcing, 'Get up, get up, empty your bowels, do your exercises, do your exercises, ten minutes of physical culture, eat your breakfast, eat your breakfast and now it's time to go to work.' He mourned the demise of the covered souks which were crumbling into ruins, as were those madrassahs that hadn't already been converted into schools or offices. The chairman of the town-planning committee told him that within four years, Bukhara would be a European city.

It's still possible today to take a turn down a timeless alley in the Jewish quarter of Bukhara and emerge squinting in the blinding sunlight of an enormous concrete square, replete with disused fountains, manicured flowerbeds, brutalist concrete Soviet hotels, a sports stadium, and the former KGB headquarters.

Resisters of the *hujum* campaign were also armed. Their most potent weapon was Islam. Despite Bolshevik campaigns against religion, mullahs still held great status and influence within society. The Quran was quoted, with specific edicts for women to be shielded from the gaze of the male stranger, and there were regular Friday sermons railing against the *hujum* and its desecration of piety and tradition. The *hujum* was framed in apocalyptic terms as a great testing of the faithful by God, with damnation assured for those women who forgot their place and their morals. Natural disasters were immediately accredited to divine judgement and men were regularly warned to get their households in order.

Harassing unveiled women in the streets became a socially acceptable, even pious, form of resistance. Some men exposed themselves to these women. Rape was weaponised, tolerated and even approved to help teach women a lesson. Those who murdered their female relatives were lionised as heroes and remembered as martyrs to Islam after their arrests, convictions and executions.

Although the Soviet state had mass media and newspapers running stories denigrating the *paranja* on a regular basis, literacy levels were still low and resisters had a far more formidable and effective weapon: the rumour. Hammams, teahouses and bazaars were perfect places to disseminate misinformation. Some rumours were true, such as the likelihood that veiled women attending Zhenotdel clubs for something as innocent as hygiene classes were also being encouraged to unveil. Most rumours were wilder: communists plan to unveil our women so they can choose the prettiest ones and share them in common, just like they redistribute our land. The *paranja* is only the start; soon the party will require all women to undress completely and parade around the streets naked.

Petitions were handed in to local offices demanding a reinstating of the veil. Anti-*hujum* songs and taunts became popular, often using humour as a mark of resistance. Veiled women marched against the *hujum,* as noted with concern in secret police reports, for opposition to the *hujum* was beginning to look rather like the will of the people, which was supposedly what the Communist Party represented. One march of 200 particularly spirited women in Andijon resulted in the threatening of police officers with knives, as well as the beating of unveiled women found on the streets.

Ironically, perhaps the most effective weapon of resistance to the *hujum* was the *paranja* itself. The Communist Party had made it the embodiment of all that was wrong with traditional, religious society and the oppression of women, constantly associating it with all things traditional and Uzbek. At the same time, there was an emerging sense of what Uzbek-ness meant, particularly in opposition and resistance to Slavic cultural imperialism. The *paranja,* then, became a symbol of national pride and resistance to Russification.

Few women wanted to be Europeanised, and most were very aware of the intrusion of the state into their traditional cultural norms. Before the *hujum* began, few rural women working in the fields would veil themselves. Now, though, as the *paranja* became a symbol of Uzbek identity, they, too, began to wear them in rapidly increasing numbers. Also, for many women, the *paranja* actually represented freedom of movement, as it granted them the freedom of anonymity, avoiding neighbourhood gossips and sexual predators alike.

Had the Communist Party allowed the call for unveiling to rise naturally from the local population, rather than be imposed by European outsiders, this might not have been the case. However, they had largely viewed the *jadidi* movement as competitors rather than allies, which had alienated the people most likely to support their cause, and resulted in a rushed, ill-judged and hard-line approach to the *hujum,* lest the *jadids* got there before them. This ultimately backfired, as soon even more women were veiling than had been at the start of the campaign.

By the 1930s, hundreds of women had been raped or murdered for unveiling, and the *paranja* was ubiquitous. Lenin's widow, Nadezhda Krupskaya, announced at a women's conference: 'We should like, of course, to send the *paranaja* and *chachvon* to hell, but we cannot always get everything we want by issuing decrees.'* This unwillingness to ban veiling by law came as a bitter blow for women activists, but as soon as unveiling was enshrined by law, it would undermine any sense of actual liberation and the prisons would be unable to cope with the number of women who would still refuse to unveil.

The *hujum* only worked where a slow and thought-out approach was taken. Khoziar Markulanova, herself a local, unveiled woman, explained to Joshua Kunitz that the first woman to unveil in a community set the tone. If she was of good standing, then others were far more likely to follow. They generally counselled women against unveiling too soon, ensuring that they were resolute in their beliefs and prepared to be a pioneer and to handle the backlash that would inevitably follow. They also learnt to incentivise women. 'By opening silk and textile factories, by opening cotton-ginneries,

* Northrop, D., *Veiled Empire* (2003), p. 284

by paying more than a woman can possibly earn in her primitive home-crafts ... we lure women out of seclusion, gradually but irretrievably."

Women who had embraced emancipation were discovering a new concept now open to them: a career. Gustav Krist met a woman who a decade previously had been the illiterate second wife of a rice merchant. She was one of the first to unveil in her village and had shown such resourcefulness and initiative that she had risen up the ranks and was now the chairman of her Soviet village, the equivalent of mayor.

Similarly, Langston Hughes visited a silk factory in 1930s Samarkand named 'Deliverance of Women', which provided housing for the 1,200-strong all-female workforce, a cafeteria, childcare and literacy classes. There were three seven-hour shifts a day, and no one was veiled. The Bolshevik Revolution is often referred to as the Russian Revolution, but far more dramatic social changes took place in Central Asian society than in Russia itself.

Women eventually outnumbered men in collective farms, although many would still wear the *paranja* whenever possible. However, by the time Fitzroy Maclean visited Tashkent in the late 1950s, veiled women had become a rarity. Several factors led to the veil's eventual demise. The first, ironically, was the result of the *hujum* shifting away from unveiling to focus on educating schoolgirls, raising a new generation outside the home and with work opportunities the previous generation couldn't have imagined. Eventually, Uzbek women knew about *paranjas* only from museum exhibits and history books.

The Second World War also played a crucial role. Slavs and Central Asians experienced extraordinary suffering brought about by a common enemy, and this proved a greater leveller and unifier than most communist policies ever had. At least 26 million Soviet citizens perished in the war, and despite Uzbekistan being nowhere

---

* Kunitz, J., *Dawn Over Samarkand* (1935), p. 300

near the front, large numbers of men were called up, leaving job vacancies that were then filled by women.

Stalin, paranoid about minority groups and their supposedly separatist tendencies, had Koreans, Chechens, Poles and Tartars deported en masse to Tashkent, and from there to other parts of Uzbekistan, creating a less polarised and more cosmopolitan environment. Many Russian orphans were also sent to Tashkent, and a number of Uzbek families adopted or fostered them. All this helped to create a new sense of common Soviet identity and heal some of the previous divisions.

Women created new forms of head-covering as compromises between the *paranja* and the skullcap. In Southern Uzbekistan, *jeleks* became popular. These looked a little like mini-*paranjas* with tapering sleeves sewn together at the back, but were brightly coloured, decorated with shiny buttons and beads, and worn as headscarves, coming just halfway down the back, and left unhemmed in the belief that this would help prevent infertility. They were never worn with a face veil. Similarly, Turkmen women continued to wear their *chirpy*, which were similar in style to the *paranja*, but had never received the same Soviet disapproval because there was no face-covering. They were also far more beautiful, made of silk and decorated with a blizzard of fine silk embroidery. A Turkmen woman would only wear three in her lifetime: the first in darker colours as a young woman, then a yellow one in middle age, and in old age a *chirpy* in white.

Despite regular debates on the matter, the Soviet Union never actually banned the *paranja* and horsehair veil. In fact, face-veils or *niqab* were only banned in Uzbekistan after the collapse of the Soviet Union during the Karimov reign. The banning was introduced a year before I moved to Uzbekistan, and police coercion was not restricted to women's clothing. Soon any young man with a beard could be called in for questioning by the secret police, and only gypsy-style headscarves were permitted for women. Now, there is relative freedom for men and women to dress however they want, but this then brings with it a social coercion as Islam re-exerts its influence, every bit as effective, which polices what is acceptable clothing and what isn't.

The governments of independent Kyrgyzstan and Kazakhstan had not sought to legislate on religious clothing, which meant that the increasingly pious Uzbek minority in Southern Kyrgyzstan, influenced by Saudi-funded Wahabi missionaries, changed what they once wore.

'I used to wear a headscarf and I thought that was enough,' sighed Oisha, my Uzbek host mother, in our courtyard in Jalal-Abad. 'But now, you also have to wear the Islamic headscarf as well when you go outside.'

'Who says you *have* to?' I asked.

She shrugged. 'If you don't want gossip, then you have to.'

On New Year's Eve, we celebrated quietly indoors, stepping out into the snowy courtyard only at midnight to watch the fireworks. While the Kyrgyz still considered this Soviet holiday a firm favourite, Uzbeks were now told it was un-Islamic. 'In the Soviet times we'd all be outside, lighting bonfires,' Oisha smiled sadly. 'There were Uzbeks, Kyrgyz, Russians, Tartars, Chechens, Kurds, Germans, we were really international, and everyone made their traditional food and laid it out for their neighbours to sample. Now we can't even put up a new-year tree and tinsel without some self-appointed cleric turning up to tell us off. I made sure that the neighbours were watching when I threw out our old plastic one.'

After I'd left Kyrgyzstan, Islamic piety gained popularity among urban Kyrgyz as well. In 2016, I spent the summer back in Kyrgyzstan and noted the growing number of young Kyrgyz women wearing Arab-style hijabs. There were also huge government posters displayed in prominent positions, speaking out against this practice. They depicted a series of three pictures. In the first were a group of Kyrgyz women in traditional national costume, wearing white beehive turbans and lots of silver jewellery. The second and third photos were black-and-white with faceless women shrouded in black niqab. A caption beneath them read, 'Oh my people, where are you going?'

A Canadian friend living in Osh, which was generally more religious, told me what had happened to one of these posters displayed there. During the night someone had replaced the two black-and-white images – requiring a lot of planning and preparation. The colour image of Kyrgyz women in their national costume remained intact, but now the second picture showed Soviet Kyrgyz women in short skirts, and the third was of Kyrgyz girls in thongs and high heels pole-dancing. The slogan beneath still read, 'Oh my people, where are you going?'

The battle continues unabated between liberal and conservative, Islamic and secular. Women and what they wear remain at the centre of this storm.

And so, we reach the end of another road. While the heritage of handwoven silk was destroyed along with most artisanal skills during the turbulent years of the *hujum* and collectivisation, the Silk Road is seeing a revival today. Tourism has created a demand for traditional handicrafts, and countries such as Uzbekistan have increased their sericulture production and are reviving and rediscovering weaving and dyeing skills, using them to bolster a sense of national identity and Uzbek-ness. Once more, the bazaars shimmer with bolts of glittering silks.

But it is not the Silk Road that has most influenced Central Asia. Today, the borders of nation states created by Soviet Slavs, the ongoing misery of a dead sea, and the international censure and boycotting of one Central Asian product are all connected to our final road. It is named after the plant that has been responsible for more exploitation, environmental catastrophe and human suffering than any other legal plant.

It is the Cotton Road.

PART THREE

The Cotton Road

embroider
/ɪmˈbrɔɪdə,ɛmˈbrɔɪdə/

verb

1. decorate (cloth) by sewing patterns on it with thread.

2. add fictitious or exaggerated details to (an account) to make it more interesting.

12. A PLANT THAT KILLED A SEA

It's the summer of 1999 and I gaze out of the window of our little red van as we judder and bounce along a potholed road an hour or so north of Nukus, the capital of Karakalpakstan – land of the black hats. It's a semi-autonomous region within Uzbekistan – whatever that means. Many Karakalpaks would prefer independence or amalgamation with neighbouring Kazakhs, who are culturally and linguistically much closer and who also have nomadic roots. I may be sweating, but the landscape seems caught in the depths of winter. There's a crust of what looks like hoarfrost over the dull, featureless sand, but it isn't cold.

This is saltpetre, a mineral salt from the earth that leaches to the surface. Ninety per cent of the soil in Karakalpakstan is now affected by this salinity, which makes for poor harvests. In Khiva, the saltpetre isn't as bad but still wreaks havoc on buildings, creating white blooms that bubble and blister the walls of newly painted concrete buildings. I've never seen the saltpetre as thick as in this region of northern Karakalpakstan, and it's a wonder that the pink tamarisk bushes and other desert scrub manage to survive.

Most wildlife hasn't, for this is a place of environmental devastation on a truly epic scale. The cost to human health is estimated as even greater than that other well-known Soviet environmental disaster: the explosion of the Chernobyl nuclear power plant near Pripyat. Had I visited the wasteland outside the van window as a young child, this road would have passed by huge expanses of wetland, created by the Amu River as it formed a wide delta before emptying into the Aral Sea, with reeds tall enough to hide a man on camelback, full of rich and diverse birdlife and a thriving musk-rat fur trade. The clouds of mosquitos that also flourished made sheep-rearing difficult, so only hardy goats and cows survived. But for them and their herders, there were much larger threats than mosquitos.

In this 'reed kingdom', as the Russians referred to it, the Aral tiger was once prolific, hunting boar and even people; there were over 200 attacks between 1886 and 1891 alone, with many Karakalpak fishermen ending up as dinner, as well as the occasional Russian commander from the nearby fort.

The last Aral tiger stands stuffed and glassy-eyed in the national museum in Nukus, having been shot in the 1970s. The museum, which is arguably the best-kept secret of the global art world, is one reason for making this trip up through the desert from our home in Khiva. The guidebook we're writing mainly focuses on Khiva itself, but we're keen to include surrounding sights of interest. Nukus is not that far away, although bad roads make it feel further. The roads worsen beyond Nukus as we head for our destination, a small town that has become increasingly popular for disaster tourists.

It's too small to justify the derelict airport, but that's a legacy from the days when this was a resort town frequented by Soviet officials who flew in for their seaside holidays. It was also a bustling fishing port, employing 30,000 people in its fishing fleets and canning factory. Not anymore. A year after our visit, a journalist from the *Sunday Times* will dub it 'The worst place on earth'. We're heading for Moynaq.

Catriona, my Scottish co-writer, is driving the van. Our English friend, Daniel, who lives in Tashkent, has come along for the ride. We've also invited Ira, a student from Nukus, to help us with translation. Karakalpak is just different enough from Uzbek that we might need her help, and many locals prefer to speak Russian over Uzbek. This is the first time Daniel and Ira meet, but even a trip to an ecological disaster zone can't dampen their attraction, and they'll go on to marry and have a family.

The fifth member of our group is already in Moynaq, which is where he was born and raised. Oktyabr now lives in Nukus but is visiting his brother back home and has agreed to show us around. We pass herds of grazing camels and eventually come to a triangular concrete road sign with 'Moynaq' written in large Cyrillic letters. Beneath it, without any trace of irony, are painted blue waves with a fish leaping out of the water. How things have changed.

We finally arrive at a cluster of houses with dusty corrugated asbestos roofs and fenced-off dirt yards. A few anaemic trees grow but provide little shade. There is a washed-out, colourless, dustbowl feel to the town. The layout of the buildings seems weirdly cramped, but that's because this used to be a peninsula jutting out into the Aral Sea. The houses stop abruptly at what had been the shore but is now just a continuation of the desert.

We ask for directions. An old woman with crinkly eyes wearing a white headscarf nods wearily and points us in the direction of the boat graveyard. It's where all foreigners go, and Oktyabr jokes unsmilingly later that if every visiting disaster tourist, environmental scientist, diplomat or journalist brought a bucket of water with them, the Aral Sea would soon be replenished.

We see the rusting hulks below us in what was once a harbour but is now just sand dunes and hummocks of seagrass. Beached and rusting, paint flaking, are a fleet of obsolete fishing vessels. And as for the sea? Well, it's gone.

A few cows and a camel ruminate in the shade of one of the boats, chewing meditatively. There are deep dry channels that were dug back when the sea first started to disappear in a desperate attempt to keep the fishing industry alive. Back then, although the remaining sea was getting steadily saltier as it shrank, there were still some fish to be had.

This may not seem an obvious place to begin a journey along the Cotton Road. The terminus at one end of this road is in the lush wetlands of Bengal, and at the other, the textile factories of Moscow or Lancashire. But this is perhaps the place most impacted and damaged by cotton. The current borders of 'the -stans' and the heavy imprint of over a century of Slavic colonisation, first with

Imperial Russia and then the Soviet Union, are in large part due to the ability of one plant to thrive during the long hot summers. However, cotton, a member of the marsh-loving mallow family, is a thirsty crop, requiring ten times as much water as wheat. Central Asia may have the sun and heat for this crop to be grown widely, but it doesn't have enough water.

And the results have been devastating.

The Aral Sea was once the fourth-largest inland sea in the world, roughly the size of Sri Lanka or Georgia, and yet within just a few decades, it has all but disappeared. Water from the two great rivers that fed it (known by the Ancient Greeks as the Oxus and Jaxartes) was syphoned off to reclaim desert lands for cotton-growing. According to one World Bank report, around 60 per cent of this water didn't even reach the fields, due to unlined and poorly maintained irrigation canals.

We trudge over to the rusting hulks, hot to the touch in the midday sun. I clamber onto a boat that lists almost on its side. It's disorientating to lurch through rusting metal bulkheads at unfamiliar angles. I stand on the bridge in the place where the wheel would have been. The dials and other machinery have rusted away, and the place was long ago picked clean of trophies and souvenirs. Then the schoolboys arrive. They look around ten or eleven, but are probably older. The ecological devastation as a result of the dying sea has severely stunted growth, particularly among boys. They're in high spirits and clearly treat the graveyard as their personal playground. Keen to impress me, one of them clambers up to the prow and stands with his arms wide. 'Look at me!' he shouts in Karakalpak, 'I'm Jack! I'm the king of the world.'

He's mimicking a famous scene from *Titanic* which has recently been a rare Hollywood hit in Central Asia. 'You're not Jack,' jeers his mate. 'You're Rosa!'

They want me to take their photo, so we all pose on the rusting bow. When I jump down onto the sand dunes, my feet crunch. I hunt and find small shells just as you would along any seashore. I collect a few and pocket them, knowing that I'll value them more than anything else I've ever beachcombed.

The Moynaq fishing fleets and others in Aralsk, a former Aral Sea port in Kazakhstan, provided the whole of the Soviet Union with up to 10 per cent of its fish. During Stalin's famine, fishing helped save the lives of many Kazakhs who would otherwise have starved to death. If you visit Aralsk today, it still has a jetty which juts out from the port but it ends abruptly in scrubby desert surrounded by similarly beached and rusting fishing fleets.

'You get a good view from here,' Catriona calls out. She and Ira have managed to climb up on the tallest of the boats and stand at its prow. I give Daniel a leg up and we join them. In one direction, houses curve following the line of the former shore, but in the other, as far as the eye can see and much further, is Aralkum, the new Aral Desert.

It was obvious to anyone with a basic understanding of water evaporation that when the Imperial Russians, and then later the Soviets, began diverting huge quantities of water from the Amu and Syr Rivers to irrigate reclaimed desert for cotton and wheat, there would be consequences. However, when Imperial Russian scientists, water-engineers and agronomists were summoned to advise the newly formed Soviet government on increasing cotton yields in the 1920s, those who expressed concerns about the unintended consequences of reclaiming the desert were promptly imprisoned or sent to gulags.

At first, the sea level did not drop noticeably. But by the 1950s, cotton production had ramped up and the Karakum Canal opened. This diverted huge quantities of water for the burgeoning Turkmen capital of Ashgabat and other desert-bound cities and cotton fields.

That was when people really noticed the sinking sea levels. At first, there were few adverse effects. Moynaq was still canning around 26,000 tonnes of fish annually, but by the 1960s, there were discussions about the Aral Sea issue and what was to be done about it. In the end, the economic benefits of cotton were considered too great for anything more than talk. The sea then shrank rapidly, and much quicker than anyone had predicted. The channels dug to get the fishing fleet to the retreating sea were futile, as the remaining water was soon too saline to support fish. In a breath-taking example of how a command economy can work, fish were then transported all the way from the Pacific Ocean to be canned in Moynaq.

The retreating sea left behind in its wake a toxic chemical cocktail of sea salt and dust, blended with the residue from pesticides, herbicides, cotton defoliants and huge quantities of DDT that had been sprayed for decades all over Uzbekistan and had washed into rivers, ending up eventually in the Aral Sea. Cotton is particularly vulnerable to blights and pests, and given how much of a monoculture it had become in Central Asia, everything depended on a good harvest. There was no stinting on the amount of DDT used, even after it had been banned in the rest of the Soviet Union due to its adverse effect on human and animal health. In just one decade, Uzbekistan was doused with 60,000 tonnes of DDT, which also wiped out the malarial mosquito.

Even today, around a quarter of the world's pesticides are used on cotton, and in India cotton takes up only 5 per cent of agricultural land but accounts for half of the pesticides used. Cotton is known as a frontier crop because of how badly it depletes the soil, so whenever it is grown in the same place continually, it inevitably requires additional fertilisers to maintain the same yields.

The toxic Aralkum dust gets whipped up into the air and breathed in, causing respiratory diseases, contaminating drinking sources and travelling throughout our atmosphere. Deposits have been found in countries on the other side of the world, as well as on glaciers, where it exacerbates their melting. Persistent organic pollutants, such as DDT, once ingested by animals, cannot be excreted using the usual kidney/liver function and get passed up the food chain, showing up in human blood and breast milk. Today, around 5 per cent of Karakalpak children are born with abnormalities, and their DNA mutation rate is 3.5 times higher than in most other countries.

I find out more when we locate the address of Oktyabr's brother and meet him there. Oktyabr, with his wonderfully communist name, has the slanted eyes of a nomad, crinkled for the most part by a wide smile. He is lean, good-looking and in his early forties. He tells us how people in his town are 27 times more likely to get throat cancer than the global average. Lung cancer is also rife, with tuberculosis an issue all over Karakalpakstan, along with severe anaemia. Lots of people have eye problems from the dust. Infant and child mortality rates are both alarmingly high, and the number of birth defects is rising. The sea used to regulate weather temperature, but now summers are hotter and winters are colder and longer.

'It wasn't always like this,' Oktyabr assures us. 'If you could have seen this town as I knew it when I was a child ...' He looks up, resolute. 'Come, I want to show you something.'

We pile into the little red van and drive out of the town and up to a ridge where a dusty Second World War memorial stands. There's one in every Soviet town. Every bride and groom will go there to lay flowers on their wedding day. Oktyabr ignores the monument and beckons us to stand with him. We perch on the edge of a cliff, and ahead of us is the desert.

'People say we have to learn to live with the situation,' Oktyabr says. 'The Uzbek government wants to just relocate us and take us far from our land and the place of our ancestors. But look down there.' He points at rocks below us. 'When I was a boy, I swam down there with my school friends. It's where we spent our summers. The waves would crash against these rocks.' His eyes blaze with fury and heartbreak as he holds our gaze. I don't look away. That would be too easy.

For this chapter, I called up my old friend Desiree to chat about the two years she lived in Moynaq – one of the few foreigners to have done so. Having spent a decade working for Nike in Shanghai, Desiree, a committed Christian, wanted to give back and use her acquired business acumen to help others. She initially worked for an NGO in Nukus, but then moved up to Moynaq with an Uzbek colleague to run a Tearfund-sponsored micro-finance scheme. She never had any health issues herself as a result of her time there, but saw the day-to-day struggle of many.

'All the women we worked with were really anaemic, but that wasn't just in Moynaq, it was in most of the country. They drink a lot of black tea with their meals and that inhibits your body from absorbing iron from your food. They also weren't able to afford much meat, and what meat there was tended to be eaten by the men. Many women had really brittle fingernails that snapped easily. I paid for blood transfusions for one or two women who kept blacking out. It wasn't a solution, just a stop-gap measure, but I had to do something. They also had far more urinary and kidney infections than normal due to the high salinity of our drinking water.

'Wounds got really badly infected in a way I'd never seen before. A simple cut could lead to a strep infection and even amputation. The whole town still got sprayed by crop-dusting planes with some kind of chemicals, apparently to get rid of fleas, which were a problem. We spent most of our time working as there wasn't a lot else to do. We used to hike into the Aral Desert, across the old seabed, feeling like Moses walking through the Red Sea, and we took visitors to the ship graveyards. One of the boats got painted by a film crew who wanted to shoot a music video there but thought it looked too old, which was weird.'

Desiree talked to the middle-aged townspeople who had witnessed the sea vanish. 'They said that it happened gradually, but then very suddenly, and within the space of just a few days, the water level dropped by several metres. That seemed really strange and like something else was going on, and not just water evaporation.'

I asked Oktyabr about this, and his theory is that the Soviet nuclear weapons testing that took place in the desert between the Aral Sea and the Caspian opened up fissures in the earth. The Caspian Sea is 68 metres lower than the Aral, and there are reports that its level increased at the same time as the sudden drop in Aral water levels, suggesting that water found its way through the fissures and drained from one sea into the other.

I asked Desiree what the biggest challenges had been, living in a place like Moynaq. 'Even more than the isolation was the suspicion towards me. I mean, I was used to people's curiosity about me being an American and having to justify why I was unmarried in my thirties – that already happened to me in Nukus. What I hadn't expected was to have the KGB show up regularly and unannounced, hoping to catch me in the act of espionage or terrorism, or something. The only internet connection in the whole town was dial-up from the post office, so I used to turn up there with my laptop and plug in. The locals would hear all the weird sounds dial-up makes, and think it was some kind of witchcraft. One time the main KGB guy showed up, narrowed his eyes and told me that he knew exactly what I was doing, and that I was connecting to this thing called the internet. I mean, yeah? He seemed surprised when I didn't deny it, or see anything wrong with that.

'Then they showed up at our office and spotted the map on our wall. We'd got hold of an old Soviet map of Moynaq so we could mark out the locations of the different businesses and enterprises we were helping to finance through our project. They took one look at this map and wanted to confiscate it. When I asked why, that same KGB guy jabbed his finger at the airport, which was still showing on the map, and thought I was giving away military secrets. I mean the airport was just a disused wasteland, like the canning factory. He seemed to think this was proof that I was a spy, and that I was going to bomb this derelict airport that was no use to anyone. It was insane!'

Desiree once met an American army official who was part of a biological hazard clean-up operation. It was then that she learnt of the Aral Sea's other dirty secret, which helped explain some of the paranoia she'd experienced towards her. It might seem that this destructive tale of a plant that killed a sea, leaving poisoned land behind, couldn't get any worse – but it's about to.

The word Aral means 'island', and the island of Kantubek in the middle of the sea drew interest from Red Army generals as early as the 1920s. Its remote location and sparse surrounding population made it the perfect place for a biological weapons research facility. If something went wrong – as it would – at least it was far away from Moscow.

Over the years, a bio-weapons facility, known as Aralsk 7, was built, complete with outdoor pens for animal test subjects and indoor cages rumoured to sometimes contain humans. Around the facility grew the town of Kantubek, comprising houses and apartment blocks for around 1,500 inhabitants, schools, shops, a sports stadium, an airfield and a park. The Russians referred to the island as Vozrozhdeniya, meaning 'rebirth', although it never appeared on Soviet maps. Gamers might be familiar with it as one of the locations for *Call of Duty: Black Ops*.

Diseases were modified and enhanced to make them more virulent and resistant to medication. These included weaponised anthrax, with spores made smaller so they couldn't be so easily caught and filtered by nasal hairs. They also fused these anthrax spores with genes from *Bacillus cereus*, which rots human tissue. If breathed in and lodged in the lungs, the spores would multiply, leading to a slow and horrible end. They also weaponised small-pox, along with botulinum, tularaemia and equine encephalitis. The first tests were carried out in the 1930s, but it wasn't until the 1950s that the town was built.

Inevitably, there were accidents. In 1971 there was an explosion of weaponised smallpox, releasing a murky yellow cloud that rolled out over the sea. A scientific research vessel crossed its path and one of the scientists on deck got infected, despite being vaccinated. When she got back to the port town of Aralsk she unwittingly infected nine others. While she survived, three didn't. One of the fatalities was her younger brother. Then there were fishermen found dead on bobbing boats with no signs of bodily trauma. In 1976, huge shoals of fish died suddenly for no apparent reason and were discovered floating belly-up. Entire flocks of sheep lost their wool, and in 1988, half a million saiga antelope – a third of the world's population – dropped dead within an hour.

The island's soil was contaminated due to open-air testing in some parts, and so the Soviets decided to make it a dumping ground for all their stockpiles of weaponised anthrax. By then, the Cold War was on the wane, and there had been an accident at a bio-weapons facility in Perm, Russia, that had caused the deaths of over 100 people. The anthrax spores were mixed with bleach to kill them, and hundreds of tonnes of anthrax-and-bleach slurry were taken to the island, dumped into pits and covered. However, spores can remain inactive but alive for hundreds of years and are resistant to extremes of heat and cold, and even to disinfectants. Also, spores often clump together, so while some might have been killed by contact with bleach, others could still be alive.

All this time, the island's landmass was growing steadily in size as the waters receded, until it joined up with the mainland of Karakalpakstan. Now, animals could wander unwittingly over to the island. When I lived in Khiva, I heard rumours of camels discovered in the desert haemorrhaging or foaming at the mouth. The whole town of Kantubek and its biological weapons facility was finally closed down in 1992 in the wake of the Soviet Union's collapse. However, the hastily disposed slurry of bleached anthrax was considered enough of a potential bio-terrorism risk that after the World Trade Center attacks in New York in 2001, and subsequent letters filled with anthrax spores, the US intelligence community began researching the global whereabouts of anthrax stockpiles.

A Soviet scientist who had defected revealed the existence of the island. The Americans worked with the Uzbek government on a six-month operation that employed hundreds of local people, digging up the anthrax remains and disposing of it properly.

One of the American military personnel at the time met Desiree in Moynaq.

I interviewed Nick Middleton, an Oxford professor, explorer and travel writer, who managed to visit the island by boat in 2005. At the time, there was still a body of water between the port town of Aralsk and the island itself. Nick went with Kazakh smugglers whose reasons for visiting the island weren't entirely clear, but ostensibly involved scavenging for scrap metal. Also accompanying him was Dave Butler from the British military, who was an expert in biological weaponry. He insisted that they wear gas masks and hazmat suits despite the sizzling summer temperatures.

They were shocked to discover just how much of the weapons-testing facility was still intact. It looked as if there had been a very hasty departure as they walked gingerly among the detritus of rusting cages, broken glass vials and petri dishes that had once contained all manner of horrors. They didn't stay long, and stripped and scrubbed outside after their return to Aralsk, doing everything they could to ensure that not a single stray anthrax spore had hitched a ride. I asked Nick what – all these years later – he remembered most.

'Just the spookiness of it,' he stated. 'The complete absence of birdsong or of any animal noises, and the fact that it hadn't been cleaned up properly; just abandoned. My natural instinct was to touch things that I found fascinating but, of course, we couldn't touch anything, not even with gloves on. You can't see, taste or feel anthrax spores but we knew they could still be floating around. There was a sense that one wrong step and things could turn really ugly, maybe even fatal.'

I asked him what he thought the future was for the Aral Sea region. He shrugged. 'Well, the Kazakhs have dammed the top part and that's refilling, but the rest is just going to be desert. The human demand for irrigation water to keep the cotton growing is just too great. The Uzbek government's main strategy seems to be relocating Karakalpaks to other parts of the country, but that might also be a strategy to reduce separatist components. Apparently, the World Bank is funding programmes to plant saxaul saplings on the seabed, which might help anchor the soil.'

The World Bank also funded the eight-mile-long dam, known as the Kok-Aral, or Blue Island Dam. Now, instead of receding, the water level in the Little Aral is gradually rising again, fed by the Syr River. The salinity has reduced and fish have been reintroduced to the waters. The hope is that one day, the wooden jetty in Aralsk might end at the sea again. For Moynaq, though, the sea is gone forever.

The global textile industry is the second most polluting industry after the fossil fuel industry and consumes vast quantities of water. To manufacture just one pair of jeans requires 11,000 litres of water. The ecological fallout from all this isn't always as stark as the fate of Moynaq, but is still causing all manner of environmental devastation, particularly as clothing prices in Western countries remain low and clothing has become almost disposable.

Before we leave Moynaq, Oktyabr takes us to visit a women's cooperative, known as 'Golden Heritage of the Aral', recently established to provide local women with an income and to revive the extraordinary embroidery for which Karakalpakstan was once famous. Women sit on cotton-filled mattresses, pieces of cotton cloth or synthetic velvet in their hands, reviving the complex embroidery that makes Karakalpak wedding outfits by far the most impressive in Central Asia.

I still have a wallet made in Moynaq which I purchased from the women's cooperative. You have to look closely to fully appreciate the intricacy of the needlework, and I treasure it. The women grinned and cracked jokes as we chatted with them. I wasn't sure if it was redemptive or ironic that these women were making something beautiful out of cotton, after all the ways in which cotton had so negatively impacted them and their town.

Traditionally, the bridal clothing known as *besh kiyim* was tailored and embroidered by the bride herself. The aim was not only to look fabulous, but also to justify a high bride-price by demonstrating worth through proficiency with the needle. All girls were expected to have 'pierced fingers' before marriage, having practised their needlework extensively throughout childhood. Girls would start learning from the age of six or seven, gathering in yurts under the tutelage of older women.

The most ornate part of this outfit was the red *kimeshek*, a square of red Russian broadcloth with one corner removed. A diagonal band of additional cloth went along the underside of this open corner, creating an aperture through which the bride would fit her head. The broadcloth, framed with incredibly intricate embroidery, would hang down behind her like a shawl, while a triangular mantle was worn over her front, densely covered in a blizzard of tiny embroidered stitches. These were a blend of chain stitch and – more unusually for Central Asia – minuscule cross-stitch. Motifs included the ubiquitous ram's horn, along with goose neck, crow's claw, scorpion tail, fenced flower, ant-waist, snowflake, camel's foot, apricot flower, and a circle with wedges of alternating colour creating a cross motif and dubbed, delightfully, 'queen's spit'. Under this mantle, a bride would wear a long waistcoat, tunic and baggy trousers.

There was also a magical aspect to this embroidery. *Kimesheks* were so dense with talismanic motifs that they were considered virtually medicinal, so that when a child or elderly relative was sick, a *kimeshek* would be draped over them like a magical blanket. Pieces of *kimeshek* were sometimes cut off and burnt to create smoke inhaled by the sick to supposedly cure them. When an old woman died, her *kimeshek* would be hung on a pole above her yurt for seven days and then given to family members. If the woman had lived particularly long or had been unusually fertile, her *kimeshek* would be cut up and the pieces highly sought after, considered to bring luck and blessings when patched onto a younger woman's garments.

In fact, there is a whole world of spiritual belief and superstition that maps itself in the clothing and soft furnishings of Central Asian homes, whether made of brick or wool. Crowning this belief system is fear of that most malevolent of entities: the evil eye.

13. MAGICAL PROTECTION

The ram tethered outside my ground-floor bedroom doesn't bleat or baa, it bellows; short, loud bursts that begin at dawn. Sometimes the interval between bellowing is long enough for me to try and get back to sleep, but then it starts up again. The previous three mornings have been like this, but – I remind myself sleepily – this will be the last time, because the wedding is today, and soon the ram will play its unwilling part in the catering arrangements. I grab my towel and washbag and head outside. It's summer and it already feels hot in the sun, although still cool in the shade. Behind the poplars and fruit trees around me loom the Badakhshan mountain ranges. Khorog is a valley between them. At the bottom of the garden is the pit-latrine and next to it is a small bathhouse – one of the reasons I chose this particular host family.

I've only been living in Khorog for a few months, but have already grown attached to my generously sized bedroom. The fact that my windowpanes are held in place with small bent nails, with gaps between the window frames, doesn't really bother me. It will later, when winter comes and I resort to stuffing raw cotton into every gap and crevice to keep out the icy cold. Then, I'll also learn that our neighbourhood is on the dark side of the valley. We live in the shadow of a mountain which the sun never crests in winter, leaving us in permanent shadow and ice for several months. I'll gaze up longingly at the houses perched on the south-facing valley in the unfortunately named village of Horfuk that get bathed in winter sunshine. By then, my breath will fog in my bedroom and I'll mention this politely to my host family. Grish, my host dad, will nail plastic sheeting over my windows in an optimistic attempt at double-glazing. I'll return from work one evening to find a large brick on the floor beside my mattress, with a maze of indentations on its top side. Fixed into these indentations will be a coil of wire snaking up to the socket with two live wires jammed into it. The coil will glow and keep off the worst of the chill. Each morning I'll start the day with a quick prayer of thanks that I wasn't incinerated the night before. Eventually, though, the allure of a south-facing home will prove irresistible, and I'll move.

That's all to come. For now, it's the beginning of summer, and the mood in our house is one of excitement, because today, my host brother is getting married. Breakfast is *shir choi,* a staple for most people at breakfast and lunch, consisting of bread dipped into salty, milky tea with a dollop of ghee swimming on top. When made with real milk in the villages, and with the addition of walnuts, it's passable as long as you think of it more as a soup than tea. Up in the High Pamirs, it's made with yak milk and actually tastes pretty good. In Khorog, though, milk is in short supply, so powdered coffee creamer is substituted, or a Korean brand called 'soul of milk' which lists milk as its seventh ingredient. I've lost a lot of weight.

As I eat, relatives arrive and start chopping vegetables. An uncle sharpens his knife and soon we hear the ram bellow for the last time. After breakfast, I go outside and insist on helping chop carrots on the porch for the greasy *plov* that is to come, even though some of the relatives are unhappy about a male foreign guest demeaning himself in this way.

'Where's Raoul?' I ask one of them. Raoul is the groom. One of the aunties nods to the bathhouse. One of his two groomsmen emerge from the bathhouse, smartly dressed and wearing a red circular skullcap that flashes where the sequins catch the light. He calls over and several aunties pick up their tambours – large flat hand-held drums – and begin to mark out a rhythm. We abandon the carrots and head towards the bathhouse. I'm not sure why. The relatives begin to dance and clap and chant, 'The king is coming.' Next to emerge from the bathhouse is the second groomsman, also freshly shaved and bathed, and dressed the same. However, when Raoul makes his entrance, although washed, he's still in T-shirt, joggers and sliders. They lift him on their shoulders and parade the king around the garden as we follow, clapping and singing, before heading for the house and whatever will come next.

I have limited uses, but am the self-appointed photographer. Far more important is the videographer, to whom everyone defers, and who is always in the thick of the action. The resulting eight-hour wedding video is almost as important as the wedding itself, and will be rewatched in its entirety several times in the subsequent weeks. Raoul is sat on a chair as a basin of hot water is brought in. To the accompaniment of clapping and singing, his two grooms-men lather his face and then shave him. He has already shaved his armpits and pubic hair, as I'll discover shortly, and once his face is shaved and sprayed liberally with thick-smelling aftershave, he stands.

For the next part of the ceremony, a third man is needed. I'm roped in and given the corner of a large cotton sheet. One of the groomsmen holds the other corner and gestures to me that we should lift the sheet to make a screen. Raoul then strips behind it, to catcalls and cackles from middle-aged aunties and calls for us to drop the sheet. Soon he wears nothing but a leather band strapped around his right upper arm. This is his amulet, and inside, sealed in a bulge of wax and leather, is the actual talisman, paper with written spells or holy writings to grant him virility, good fortune and protec-tion from harm, each transcribed by the local *khalifa* or Ismaili holy man. He grins at me, sensing my surprise. After all, I thought the only person who'd be seeing him today in nothing but his amulet was his new wife.

The other groomsman collects the offerings. First is a new pair of boxer shorts, still in plastic packaging. These are passed over the sheet to Raoul who puts them on. Next comes a brand-new white cotton shirt with a silk tie, trousers, a belt, new black shoes and, finally, a black jacket. Once fully dressed, he's presented with a red

Pamiri hat, and we can now drop the screen to reveal the emperor in his new clothes, who is then applauded. This tradition has its roots in the custom of emirs and khans to gift *sar-o-par* (head-to-foot) sets of clothes to members of their court for celebration days, but there's more to the importance of new clothing, as I'll learn later.

I now discover that our song 'the king is coming' has a second verse, 'the king is going'. We sing this as Raoul is accompanied by his groomsmen, younger friends and relatives to a car waiting outside. It has plastic red-and-yellow flowers on the bonnet that spell out the word 'love' in English. The car drives slowly and we accompany it on foot. The bride's house isn't far, and I chat with my friend Farid, who is Raoul's relative and speaks English. He tells me how the couple met at university.

We arrive at the bride's house, which is built in the traditional Pamiri style, with a pillared hallway leading into one large, multi-purpose room framed with pillared platforms at various heights. On one platform are piles of new mattresses and carpets beside new chests, and everything else that the bride will take with her to her new house. Tucked away near this is another bundle of what appears to be brightly coloured laundry. It moves. This is the bride. She wears seven veils and can see nothing through them. She must be guided back to Raoul's house by her girlfriends after the groom's guests have been fed with bread soaked in milk and butter.

Here, the wedding rites will be performed by the *khalifa*. First, though, an older couple who know the bride well step forward. They have been given the honour of unveiling her, and this ritual will bond them to her for life as surrogate parents, a little like the concept of godparents. The veils themselves are bright magenta and red cotton chintzes, often shot through with gold. By the time the last veil is lifted, the bride is sweaty but happy, gulping fresh air. She is given a new gauzy red veil by the older couple, which sparkles with gold sequins and is draped over her red Pamiri hat that matches her husband's. She wears a long tunic of red velvet and sparkling sequins, with baggy trousers protruding from them. She has strong, shapely eyebrows, a straight nose, full lips and a slim build. Raoul has done very well for himself.

Once the *khalifa* has completed the ceremony and Raoul has kissed his hand (the only public kissing that will take place) we'll head to the wedding hall for a reception where I will perform songs on guitar and vocals. There are three songs in English that are known by most people – excluding 'Happy Birthday'. Most popular is The Beatles' 'Yesterday', but even if they don't understand the lyrics, it is definitely not wedding-appropriate. So, I will be singing 'My Heart Will Go On', known simply as 'The *Titanic* song', followed with 'Hero' by Enrique Iglesias. Pamiris, I have learnt, love a cheesy power ballad.

It's only later, as I start to research the magical role of textiles, that I understand some of these wedding practices. Unlike Western weddings, where the emphasis is on the bride and her special day, in the Pamirs it's all about the groom having his one day of being king. This might be patriarchal, but it could also be protective, for it is believed that a woman is at her most vulnerable on her wedding day, when the jealous stares of others might afflict her with the evil eye.

Belief in the evil eye is why the Pamiri hats worn by both bride and groom feature a complicated pattern of woven strips around the rim. Embroidery, braiding or yarn manipulation to create patterned piping, hemming or edging is thought to confuse the evil eye with its busyness and refraction, and help keep it away. Similarly, the sequins that sparkle on the hats and bridal veil will dazzle the evil eye, blinding it or fascinating it with its own reflection. Raoul's entirely new outfit and the ritual way in which this was bequeathed was also important, because clothing previously worn can transfer either good fortune or bad luck from the previous wearer. This is even true of a patch sewn on from another garment. The fear of not knowing the fate of the previous owner means that second-hand clothing shops are all but unknown in Central Asia.

Bridal veils are common in a variety of cultures and often are more about magical protection than modesty. Even the translucent veils of Western weddings are usually patterned with lace or studded with seed pearls or sequins, with origins in protection from the envious stares of other women – particularly unmarried or barren ones. In Khiva, brides were so weighed down and blinded by heavy blanket-like veils that they would bend over, holding on to the waist of an older female relative to be led blindly into the presence of their new in-laws, reminiscent of the back half of a pantomime horse.

Another legacy of magical protection still employed in Western weddings is the use of decoys, whom we refer to as bridesmaids. Given how vulnerable a bride is, having several other young women dressed the same as her confuses the evil eye and makes the bride less of a target. And as for the recent popularity in Britain of women wearing fascinators on their heads at weddings? Little do they know the connection between their headwear, the evil eye, and an erect penis. But we'll return to that shortly.

Belief in the evil eye is perhaps the widest-spread superstition in the world and has been around for millennia. Around 40 per cent of the world today hold some level of belief in it. While there are variations, the basic concept is of a roaming malicious spirit that attacks people, particularly women and children, causing sickness or misfortune, and is provoked either by the jealous stares of others, or by the hubris caused by a person's beauty, prowess or lack of modesty.

No one knows when or where the concept first came about, although it appears in Chalcidian drinking vessels from the 6th century BC and in ancient Egyptian hieroglyphics. Blue glass beads, worn to fool the evil eye into thinking the wearer already belongs to it, have been found dating back to 1500 BC. Similar beads are sold in every bazaar in Central Asia, and in Ankara, where I was born, I was considered particularly vulnerable to the evil eye as I was a blond, blue-eyed, chubby, first-born son.

My mum was regularly presented with strings of evil-eye beads for me to wear around my wrist by anxious neighbours or local friends. These were graciously accepted and then disposed of. Loud insults were considered inverse compliments, as a means of magical protection. 'He has the face of a pig,' one woman would say loudly to the room. 'No, like the backside of a pig,' another would chime, all in an attempt to protect me.

The same principle applies to the large blue glass *nazar,* or eye, pendants, which often hang in Turkish or Greek homes and restaurants. It's also why many older religious and municipal buildings in Europe sport gargoyles and grotesques. While gargoyles also act as waterspouts, in both cases their primary function is to look demonic so that any passing evil spirits consider the property already occupied and move on.

In the nativity story, Mary visits her cousin Elizabeth, who has become miraculously pregnant in her old age. As a result, Elizabeth goes into confinement. This concept of hiding away pregnant women or new mothers is to protect them from jealous glances. Uzbek and Tajik mothers return to their own maternal home after giving birth, where they're looked after and kept in confinement for 40 days. My sisters visited me in Uzbekistan and went to the women's hammam or bathhouse in Bukhara. There they witnessed a mother emerging from her confinement with a sagging paunch, having been confined to the house for the required 40 days. She lay down on the hot stone slabs while two other women rested the soles of their feet on either side of her middle and then began to push, squeezing it back into shape.

Newborn babies are considered very vulnerable to the evil eye and receive their own confinement, spending their first six months swaddled and then strapped into wooden cradles, called *beshiks,* which are covered with sparkling cloth. A knife is slid under the mattress and a triangular amulet along with a dried chilli are hung from the cradle to offer additional protection. Toddlers will wear either an elastic band of black-and-white evil-eye beads around a wrist, or have one bead and a chilli amulet pinned to their clothing.

Lady Macartney, wife of the first British ambassador to Kashgar at the turn of the 20th century, got into trouble for complimenting babies, which might make Allah want to take them back, and was told that if a child died young, the next born would be given an ugly name, such as 'stone' or 'broom', to make the evil eye uninterested. Fathers of newborns were very particular about whom they allowed to visit the house or touch the baby first.

Mosaics from Roman archaeological sites, such as Leptis Magna in modern-day Libya, depict a large ejaculating phallus blinding a disembodied eye. This may help explain how erect phalluses became such popular talismans against the evil eye among Romans of both sexes. They were known as *fascinus*, meaning 'to cast a spell', which is the root word behind the English term 'fascinate' and the fascinators worn at English weddings. Phalluses were often winged and sometimes had legs and usually a smaller phallus of their own. Pompeii was full of them, particularly as windchimes. Phallus pendants were popular with Roman soldiers, and a number have been unearthed in Britain.

For Romans, an alternative to wearing phallus talismans was to simply make the sign of a phallus. This was a closed fist with the thumb protruding between the index and middle finger. Metal fists making this sign can still be found as doorknockers in some older Mediterranean houses.

The evil eye, along with a fear of jinn, is everywhere in Central Asia, even in the air you breathe as you walk around a bazaar. Roma girls or destitute older people, too proud to beg, wander the stalls wafting pans of smoking herbs called *isfan*. The smoke supposedly wards off the jinn, and you're expected to tip them for their service. A pan of *isfan* was burnt in our home before Raoul left to claim his bride, in an attempt to keep everyone safe. The belief was so entrenched in Russian Turkestan that the Soviets were unable to outlaw the practice; instead, they pragmatically declared that the smoke actually killed microbes. Now, women in facemasks and lab coats can be seen in schools or hospitals wafting smoking pans if there is an outbreak of flu.

Belief in the evil eye makes the usage of compliments dangerous territory. A compliment might provoke the evil eye unless followed with 'may the eye not strike', or by miming spitting on the heart. For the casting of the evil eye is not always intentional, and unmarried or childless women are considered particularly dangerous, either when complimenting a child or spending too much time with it. This, of course, simply compounds the stigma and social isolation these women already feel.

'Listen, Aslan, you can dismiss the eye, but it's no joke,' explained my friend Zafar in Khiva. 'I grew up in Soviet times and went to Russian school and learnt all about Lenin and atheism and all that, but I'm telling you, the evil eye is real. Look at my wife, Minerva, she was the sickly one as a child. Her twin sister was healthy and strong. Then, their mother was at a circumcision or wedding and a woman with hard eyes came over to Minerva's sister and played with her and told her how beautiful she was. That night, the child sickened and even though they took her to hospital they knew the eye had got her and that she would die, which she did.'

I heard something similar from an American couple who had lived in Cairo. Their five-year-old son played with a boy of the same age in the flat next door and the two were inseparable. The wife was a little on the gushy side, always complimenting everything. When their neighbour's boy sickened and died, a mutual Egyptian friend came and warned them to pack and get out because their neighbours would blame her for putting the eye on their son and would seek vengeance.

Hung outside most houses in Khiva are dusty strings of dried chillies. For reasons unknown, the evil eye doesn't like spicy things, and also chillies have dagger-like points which can pierce it. Even the mere symbol of a chilli, such as those embroidered into the ubiquitous black skullcaps worn by men in Uzbekistan, provides protection. Erna, the Swiss English teacher in Kokand, told me how all the Uighurs she knew slept wearing a headscarf or a skull-cap, in order to protect their minds from jinn that might send them nightmares. Amuletic motifs allowed for a good night's sleep.

Camel wool among the Turkmen is considered magical protection, and even a twist of it wrapped around a button on a woman's cardigan is enough. Decorative flourishes, such as pom-poms, tassels and bells, whether on clothing, hanging from yurts or horse bridles, also confuse and disarm the evil eye.

Sometimes a motif of the very danger the wearer wishes to avoid is embroidered onto clothing in sympathetic magic, the act of visualising the enemy to gain dominance over it. Motifs of scorpions, thorn bushes or biting ants on carpets or around the hems of baggy pants, for example. Cotton shifts made for Turkmen infants are often decorated with coils of braided cotton or wool with black markings that make for impressively life-like snakes, in the hope that real snakes will stay away.

Tajiks in Samarkand hold aloft an embroidered *suzanis* as a protective canopy over couples on their wedding day, similar to Jewish custom. The magical motifs often included are circular blue shapes that represent the eye itself, ram's horns, and the ubiquitous triangle, the *tumar*. Sexual potency has always been efficacious when it comes to the evil eye. While for Romans, male potency in the form of an erect phallus offered the best protection, or for Central Asian nomads the ram's horn motif, female sexual potency also offers magical protection and is symbolised by a triangle – the female sex – known as a *tumar*.

Maria Navalkina, a Russian living in an Uzbek town in the late 19th century, noted how if a wife thought her husband's affections were straying, she would go to the mullah who would give her a *tumar* containing a talisman, or bless an item of food, such as a dried apricot which must then be eaten unawares by the husband in order for the love magic to work. Conversely, if a wife wanted to kill her husband, she had only to secretly feed him donkey brains and he would soon go insane.[*]

In the Khiva carpet workshop, I initially had four wooden looms made, each sporting two enormous crossbars. However, these were no match for silk; after the first crossbeam had snapped, the weavers on the other looms hung triangular *tumars* to protect them. Still, each crossbeam inevitably succumbed, and we learnt that the uglier metal looms that we had commissioned from disused Soviet

---

[*] Navalkin, V. and Navalkina, M., *Muslim Women of the Fergana Valley* (2016), pp. 128–9

factory parts worked far better, even without amuletic protection. When I first arrived in Central Asia, *tumars* would dangle from the rear-view mirrors of most cars, often with strings of cloves, which are both spicy and piercing. These days, they've largely been replaced by shiny plastic disks depicting pilgrims circling the Kaaba in Mecca, or a verse from the Quran.

Perhaps one of the areas the *tumar* appears most, reflected and refracted, is in Central Asian patchwork. Popular with both sedentary and nomadic women, patchwork has traditionally been a means to create something beautiful from recycled scraps of material, but it also has magical benefits. The refraction within patchwork confuses the evil eye, so a band of patchwork squares rims the outside of most yurts. Inside houses of wool or mudbrick, intricate patchwork hangings drape over piles of bedding or are worked into pillows and other stackable bedwear. Older patchworks blend squares and triangles of Russian-printed cotton chintz with pieces of locally dyed *adras*, often repurposing a robe that had been torn or seen better days.

Patchwork also transfers blessing. So, a wandering dervish or holy man might tear a piece from his robe and bequeath it to his disciple or devotee. By stitching that patch to their own robe, they take something of the dervish's spiritual essence with them. The dervishes I saw in Northern Afghanistan, eyes hazed with opium, all wore ragged patchworked robes. In Tajikistan, if a mother has had a difficult birth or a number of previous miscarriages, she prepares a patchwork tunic for her infant and makes sure to include material gifted to her by women with particularly large families in the hope that their fertility and good fortune will be contagious.

You may be wondering what the difference is between a charm, an amulet or a talisman. A charm is for good luck, and a talisman for protection. Talismans are the spell itself. Sometimes this is etched into precious or semi-precious stones, or more commonly written on paper. It is the vessel which holds the talisman that is the amulet. Sometimes these talismans simply consist of writing in black ink, but more often – particularly if the clients are illiterate – they contain magic number grids which act as a kind of mystical

Sudoku, with all the numbers on each line adding to the same total, and visual symbols such as the Star of David.

Over time, the amulet holding the talisman has become talismanic in its own right, so that the form of the amulet – such as the triangular *tumar*, with three or four hanging tassels below it – has itself been imbued with spiritual power and is powerful enough to be included in the designs of *abr* silk robes or woven into Turkmen carpets.

The most wearable amulets are jewellery. Thin silver tubes, studded with turquoise and coral, contain rolled-up talismanic scrolls, while flat, silver square boxes, also bejewelled, have their talismans simply folded up. Turquoise – literally, the colour of the Turks – has often been associated with the evil eye in Central Asia, even though blue eyes are a rarity. As for coral, belief in its magical potency prevails in coastal parts of the Mediterranean today. Babies in Corsica are presented with amulets of coral shaped into tiny fists with the thumb protruding between the fingers. Central Asia – so far from any ocean – has always treated coral as precious, and perhaps its most impressive use is in the traditional wedding headdresses of the Karakalpaks. These helmet-like pieces have coral beads of varying sizes clustered along the forehead and around the temples of the bride, to great effect.

Another weapon in a woman's arsenal of magical protection is the cowrie shell. Like the *tumar*, it also draws on female sexual potency with its vulva-like opening and, like coral, is valued due to its scarcity. Decorating plain cotton or silk with cowries, silver coins, shiny buttons, or anything that reflects light, dazzles the eye. Mirror work, particularly in Pakistan and India, has been used to embroider cotton with pleasing results, and is popular on bedspreads which keep the sleeper safe throughout the night.

Sharp objects, such as pins and knives, can pierce the eye, and so are employed literally, such as the knife under the cradle-mattress, or figuratively, with knife motifs embroidered into *suzanis* or onto Turkmen *chirpy*, or woven as motifs into their carpets. Spiky tulips and bristling thorn bushes are also popular Turkmen motifs for the same reason. In Dushanbe, many Tajik homes have a clump of mountain bush-thorn nailed above the front door to pierce the eye should it attempt a home invasion.

While belief in the evil eye may have resulted in some beautiful jewellery and textiles, it also causes fear, judgement and gossip. It's easy, therefore, to dismiss the amulets as simple signs of backward and corrosive superstition. However, when I see examples of Turkmen and Uzbek toddlers' clothing, I choose a different interpretation. The same cotton shifts are worn by boys and girls, with a wide neck and a button at one shoulder to fasten it. Despite the lavish embroidery or patchwork, these shifts are always left unhemmed in the belief that to hem will cause the mother barrenness or prevent the child from growing. Owl feathers, cowrie shells, buttons, tassels, silver coins, silver jewellery, beads, snakes of camel wool and rams' horn motifs are all used, along with little pockets where talismans can be secreted. And triangles are everywhere, in patchwork, or simply embroidered. Ultimately, whether or not these decorations and embroideries are all just superstitious nonsense, they represent the fierce devotion of a mother towards her child in places where life is precarious and just one failed crop or dried-up well can spell disaster, and where infant mortality was once alarmingly high. Here are women with needles and threads in hand, doing all they know how, to try and keep their loved ones safe.

Although there are still examples of antique clothing from Central Asia festooned with amuletic motifs, there is one fabric, a cotton which was worth far more than silk, which no longer exists. It was a fabric of exquisite beauty, and to produce it took enormous skill. For centuries it followed the silk-trading routes to dazzle and scandalise in far-flung places, until British colonial rule destroyed it. It was time for me to come face-to-face with parts of my own nation's history I'd prefer to forget.

14. GREAT EXPLOITATIONS

The first time I saw a dodo, it was stuffed and in the Natural History Museum in London. And London, it turns out, is one of the best places to discover extinct fabrics as well as species. I'm hoping to track down any surviving samples of Dhaka muslin, so special that it was sold for sixteen times more than the price of silk. The 15th-century Persian poet Amir Khusrau described how a hundred yards could pass through the eye of a needle. Edward Baines, a 19th-century cotton expert, described it as 'webs of woven wind' with a weave so fine, 'it might be thought the work of fairies or of insects, rather than men'.[*]

A limited budget and a global pandemic mean that I won't be heading to present-day Bangladesh, where it originated. Even if I did, the only places I'd find this muslin are in museums, and some of the best samples – as is so often the way when it comes to British colonisation – are in London. I start at the Victoria and Albert Museum. I've visited their South Asian exhibits before, marvelling at the Moghul miniatures, named not for their size or detail, but for the predominance of a bright orange pigment, called *miniat*. Moghul princes wear tight-fitting kurtas of muslin which are virtually transparent, their brightly patterned baggy trousers clearly visible beneath. Dancing girls may be technically clothed in muslin but

---

[*] Beckert, S., *Empire of Cotton* (2014), p. 9

appear essentially topless. Poets described them as wearing 'nothing but the sheen of water'. All part of Dhaka muslin's appeal. One Moghul princess was admonished by her father for her immodesty, clothed in a mere seven layers of this gossamer fabric.

Muslin was first woven in Mosul, which, along with Baghdad and Basra, was a major cotton textile producer. It refers to cotton threads spun fine enough to create a gauzy, transparent cloth. These days it more often denotes a loose weave that also creates a gauzy effect, but not due to the thread size. Petronius Arbiter, a Roman author in the 1st century, wrote of its use in weddings, where 'the bride might as well clothe herself with a garment of the wind as stand forth publicly naked under her clouds of muslin'.* Although ordinary muslin was spun from common strains of cotton, there was only one cotton plant that could create a thread fine enough to make Dhaka muslin, and yet still retain its tensile strength. *Gossypium arboretum* was a species of tree cotton that thrived in the hot, humid conditions along the banks of the regularly flooding Brahmaputra and Meghna Rivers. Attempts to grow this tree cotton elsewhere in Bengal failed, so there were limited quantities which were cropped twice a year, in spring and autumn, with the spring crop being of better quality.

Once the cotton had been harvested, the monsoons were the best time to hand-spin, either in the early morning or late afternoon when the air was damp, which helped the fibres stretch. Before spinning, the cotton fibres were combed through the tiny teeth of a local boalia fish jaw. The cotton was then spun on a drop spindle called a *takwa,* which was much lighter than traditional spindles, weighted with only a tiny ball of clay the size of a pea. Despite their incredible tensile strength, the almost invisible cotton threads could withstand no greater weight. So fine was the thread, it was rumoured that spinners would go blind within a few years, and that a mere pound of raw cotton could be spun into a thread two hundred miles long. All spinners were women, and the natural

---

* Petronius, tr. Michael Heseltine (1925)

oils from their hands, or from combing their fingers through their hair, aided the spinning process, as did the addition of shell lime or rice starch.

Weaving was done by men. The results were astounding, with thread counts far higher than anything woven today. Even the finest muslins now woven in Bangladesh are four or five times heavier and denser than Dhaka muslin. This whole process was so laborious that production of just one bolt of muslin could take up to five months. If further decoration was needed, then additional weft threads could be gently worked into the weave using tiny bamboo needles. Strips of unadorned muslin up to ten times the length of a man were ideal for turbans; neither heavy nor cumbersome. As for muslin clothing of just one layer, varying styles were given names such as 'woven air', 'expanded smoke', or 'vapour of milk'.

Moghul dynasties, determined to ensure a royal monopoly on the finest of muslins, kept the best weavers essentially captive, often in primitive conditions, punishing them if they attempted escape or wove for anyone else.

Lower-grade muslins were more widely sold and came to the attention of the Portuguese merchant seamen, who soon learnt that Indian cotton was prized far more by inhabitants of the spice islands of present-day Indonesia than anything Europe had to offer. Soon Indian muslins, along with chintzes and calicoes, were being traded for spices. Some of this cloth became cargo on the long return journey around the tip of Africa back to Europe. Dutch and English merchants joined and then usurped this trade and, not far from Dhaka, in what is now Kolkata, a collection of British merchants founded the East India Trading Company, sowing the seeds for the destruction of India's rich cotton industry.

As I enter the Victoria and Albert Museum, dutifully donning my Covid mask, I make a beeline for the South Asia collection. It's closed for minor refurbishments. Frustrated, I try two different museum attendants, pleading to be allowed in just for five minutes to view their muslin. Exchanges on walkie-talkies take place as I peer longingly past the cordon at stunning examples of Indian chintz, still as vibrantly coloured as when they were woven two centuries ago.

In both cases the result is an apologetic shrug and I leave defeated. However, I'm not done with London just yet. It's a sunny day so I decide to walk to Joss Graham's shop, near Victoria station. He's an eccentric and particular collector of Asian antiquities, specialising in textiles, and has told me some great stories involving Turkestani robes, thievery and Laura Ashley. I wonder what he knows about Dhaka muslin. Entering his shop is always a painful exercise in covetousness. I want everything, except for the eye-watering price-tags. His assistant informs me that Joss is away in India for several weeks. 'We do have some Dhaka muslin downstairs, though, if you'd like to see it?'

I would.

Joss has acquired two bolts of antique Dhaka muslin, and the assistant carefully opens the lid of a box she's laid down on the carpet. It looks incredibly dense, which it is, in terms of thread count, but when she slides her hand beneath the topmost layer of fabric, the hand is clearly visible, her wedding ring glinting in the light. It's almost like an optical illusion how dense and yet transparent this fabric is, with up to 1,200 threads in one square inch.

'How much is this worth?' I ask.

The assistant shrugs. 'We're not really sure. I mean, there are so few pieces left. How do you put a value on something like this? Joss is in discussion with a museum for these pieces.'

We talk more, although I keep getting distracted by the gorgeous *suzanis*, robes, velvet and other desirable textiles around us. 'If there was a fire in the shop and you could only rescue one item, what would you take?' I ask.

A voice from their restorer, who is working and eavesdropping in the adjacent room pipes up, 'I'd dither and burn.'

'No, I know what I'd take,' says the assistant with quiet conviction, drawing the box of Dhaka muslin closer to her. 'It would have to be this.'

Perhaps one of the reasons I find Dhaka cotton so surprising is because usually I think of cotton as cheap. After all, it makes up the majority of my wardrobe and is so ubiquitous that it's estimated that every single person on the planet wears it. Of course, it depends how you define cheap; it's already cost Central Asia the Aral Sea.

It is everywhere, though, with cotton lint or oil popping up in cosmetics, ice-cream, cookies, explosives, soap, TV screens and money. In fact, until recently with the new plastic notes, US dollar bills were made from around 75 per cent recycled denim. Cotton even features in male contraceptives, as the toxic gossypol contained within the cotton seed can be taken in low doses to destroy the tubule linings in testicles.

In the 17th century, cotton became the first truly global consumer commodity, and by the 19th century it was the most important manufacturing industry in the world. If cotton came from sheep, we would need 7 billion of them to produce the amount of cotton we currently use, grazing on 700 million hectares of pasture. Cotton production has clearly got out of hand. How did all this begin? Where does the Cotton Road start?

Cotton is a species of mallow, and only a few varieties produce the cotton fluff that can be spun into fibre. These floated on ocean currents many millennia ago and took root in tropical regions of India, Africa and South America. Humans on these different continents – entirely independent of each other – began to clean, spin and weave this fibre, each inventing bows for cleaning and spindles and looms for transforming cotton wisps into fabric. This one plant could also illuminate the darkness, with cotton wicks dipped into lamps of cotton oil.

The main centre of cotton textile production, and the starting point of the Cotton Road, was the Indian subcontinent. In Hindu mythology, Vishnu weaves rays of the sun into a cotton garment. The Greek historian Herodotus described wild trees bearing fleeces that were even softer than that of a fine sheep. Cotton was still confined to the tropics, although the tree cotton of Dhaka fame was introduced to Persia in the 6th century BC, but failed to thrive in the drier continental climate. Eventually, imported seeds of *Gossypium herbaceum* took root in Persia and thrived. Soon it was also grown in Central Asia.

When Alexander the Great travelled through Transoxiana – the land beyond the Oxus River – he founded his easternmost Alexandria in the Fergana Valley. Here, and in the Indus Valley, his army encountered cotton, which they referred to as vegetable wool, worn by locals. They used raw cotton to pad their saddles on the long and uncomfortable journey home. Cotton was also traded along the Silk Road, and Dhaka muslin soon became popular in Rome for its sheerness, scandalising society just as silk had done earlier. Pliny the Elder complained about the hundred million sesterces that drained from the Roman coffers annually as gold was exchanged for Indian cotton as well as for silk. Cotton did not travel eastwards, though – in China, nervous silk manufacturers promptly called for it to be banned. Cotton was permitted only as an ornamental shrub. The most common route for Indian cotton to make its way westwards was by dhow along the Arabian coast and up to Egypt, passing through the Mameluke Sultanate and then changing hands in the city states of Genoa and Venice.

Cotton continued to be referred to as tree or vegetable wool; this appellation was reinforced by John Mandeville, a medieval knight who travelled eastwards in the 14th century and wrote up a fanciful account in which he reported the fusion of animal and plant in the Vegetable Lamb of Tartary. The lamb tree – Mandeville explained authoritatively – had branches tipped with ripening lambkins. As these grew larger and heavier, the boughs would bend, allowing the budding lambs to graze on the grass around them. Once their forage was exhausted, the lambs would expire and drop to the ground where they could be collected and eaten – their flesh tasting as sweet as honey. Most of their downy fleece was left behind on the tree and could then be harvested and spun. For the unconvinced, he even provided an illustration. As late as 1887, Victorian biologist Henry Lee was still writing about this Lamb of Tartary, as the trees supposedly flourished near Samarkand.

These cotton origin stories might help explain why cotton is still called 'tree-wool' in German and Czech. Speakers of other European languages adopted the Arabic word *qutun,* since they had learned about the fibre from the Arabs who were great proponents of cotton trade and esteemed cotton all the more because, unlike silk, it wasn't prohibited by the Prophet.

Just as China had spent centuries perfecting varied techniques for weaving silk, Indian artisans had developed gossamer-light muslins at one end of the spectrum, and heavy, durable calicos at the other. Then there were chintzes which were made from fine cotton that was then either block-printed or hand-painted, and often glazed by coating in starch and then polishing to make it shimmer.

Perhaps most impressive were the vibrant colours and intricate designs employed, which remained vivid even after much wearing or washing. This was thanks to centuries of perfecting mordanting and dyeing techniques. These mordants – from the French word 'to bite' – enabled the dyes to fix and to shine. First, cloth was steeped in stale urine or sour milk, which broke down any natural waxiness, allowing dyes to penetrate deeply. Then cloth was either soaked in mordants or had mordants applied to certain parts. The most commonly used mordants were metal oxides such as alum, although pistachio gall was also a favourite, as were other galls, given they are natural sources of concentrated tannin which enhances colour.

As India's cotton textiles arrived in Europe in greater quantities during the seventeenth century, their impact was huge. Europeans were wowed by the bold colours and the lightness and softness of chintzes and predictably scandalised at the transparency of muslin. There was something available for every pocket, from small handkerchiefs to entire stately rooms draped in cotton soft furnishings. Cotton clothing only came into fashion a little later, as chintz bedspreads or curtains that were no longer in the latest style were passed on to maidservants who would covet them as undergarments, being softer than linen, and retaining their colour after washing. Gradually, they were refashioned as actual dresses.

We still see the legacy of cotton through the Indian words for which we had no equivalent, and which continue in English usage today. These include: gingham, sash, pyjamas, chintz, calico, muslin, cummerbund, dungarees, mufti and khaki. As a fashion for muslin developed, risqué cartoons in the French press parodied Parisian women parading virtually naked in their new Dhaka muslin dresses, and soon the East India Company was providing Britain and its colonies with a million pieces of calico a year, which was around two-thirds of its entire export.

Everyone seemed to fall for these exotic new fabrics and their rich colours and designs. Everyone, that is, except the wool and flax weavers, retters, spinners and merchants. They were a powerful lobby and took action to protect their interests in the form of sumptuary laws. The European war on cotton had begun.

Sumptuary laws determine which type of people may be permitted the luxury of wearing certain kinds of material, as we saw earlier. They have existed for centuries, as clothing has always been one of the main ways to signify and stratify social hierarchies. In China, only certain classes within the imperial court were permitted to wear certain colours. The Ancient Greeks and Romans allowed only royalty to wear Tyrian purple. In Britain after the Black Death, the population was so reduced that labour shortages left some peasants getting ideas above their station. Sumptuary laws helped put them back in their place. Only knights and lords could wear ermine, sable, cloth-of-gold and silk velvet or brocade.

The poorer you were, the dowdier you were supposed to dress, with those at the bottom of the pile doomed to wear cheap, coarse woollens dyed a murky greige, if coloured at all.

Textile protectionism also extended to exports. Britain considered its North American colony a handy new export market for British wool. They were furious when some of the colonists managed to smuggle out sheep, rather than remain dependent on British wool. Those caught exporting sheep or lambs to the colony had their left hand chopped off and publicly displayed, with similar punishments for any illegal smuggling of wool. Colonists were defiant, though, and began hand-spinning wool from their growing flocks, wearing homespun as a symbol of resistance. Unfair laws that sought to keep the new colony from developing would eventually lead to the American War of Independence.

Soon after Indian cotton became fashionable in Europe, protectionist laws, pushed by the wool and linen lobbies, started to kick in. In Britain from 1685, hefty import duties were imposed on cotton. A year later, France completely banned all Indian cotton textiles, imposing fines on women caught parading in cotton chintz dresses or using cotton in home furnishings. By 1700 Venice had banned cotton completely, with the moral argument that cotton corrupted character. The first Calico Act in Britain banned all Indian chintz, but not muslin – favoured by the upper classes – which now included a 15 per cent import duty.

In France by 1726, not only were women caught wearing cotton fined exorbitant amounts, but men trading cotton were threatened with execution or sent to work on the galleys, a fate often considered worse than death. Yet even these draconian punishments did not deter smugglers, and around 50,000 ended up in the galleys – and those were just the ones who got caught.

Britain developed a more pragmatic approach. Rather than a total ban on cotton, they allowed for the import of raw cotton, recognising the boost this would give to the manufacturing sector. Although British-made cloth was inferior to anything coming from India, British manufacturers could respond more quickly to changing tastes in fashions, and Britain – despite being entirely unsuitable for cotton-growing – began to see how cotton spinning and weaving was an industry that could complement the wool-mills that already existed.

The rewards for factories manufacturing cotton or wool were so great that a search for speed and efficiency in both spinning and weaving led to inventions and innovations that kickstarted the Industrial Revolution. As the profitability of cotton manufacture grew, with its own lobbyists in parliament, sumptuary laws were challenged, and once the water frame had been invented by Richard Arkwright in 1769 (which used water power to spin numerous cotton threads simultaneously), all sumptuary laws were repealed. At that point, imported Indian chintz had no chance against the cheaper mass-produced cotton of Britain, which was now the manufacturing hub of the world.

While some raw cotton was still imported from India, Britain increasingly imported from the New World. The European discovery of the New World in the first place had happened partly as a result of cotton. Back in the 15th century, the Portuguese dominated maritime trade in the Indian Ocean, and their desire to find a quicker alternative route for cotton trading led Christopher Columbus on his mission across the Atlantic. He thought he had been successful when his ship arrived at a Caribbean island, and he dubbed the atoll the 'West Indies'.

Colonisation of the New World was initially buoyed by wild rumours of lost cities of gold. Eventually, the colonisers settled for growing tropical cash crops, such as indigo, sugar and tobacco. A ready source of free labour was needed to grow these crops, and cotton provided the answer.

Sea merchants returning via West Africa with cargoes full of cotton and spices had long been aware of the West African love for Indian cotton. The coastal western tribes favoured bright geometrical designs rather than floral chintz and were willing to trade for bolts of this fabric. What they traded with were the lives of other tribespeople, and these enslaved West Africans were then shipped to the Caribbean and Brazil, which had tropical climates perfect for growing cotton. Soon slave plantations grew cotton that could undercut Indian cotton in price, as there were no wages to be paid.

A quarter of Britain's cotton imports came from Saint-Domingue, one of the largest Caribbean islands. Then, in 1791, African slaves succeeded in overthrowing their French masters and establishing a free state in half the island, renaming it Haiti. It was a cautionary tale and resulted in other plantations imposing greater cruelty and subjugation on their slaves. By now there were also slave colonies in the southern states of America, but they only grew a species of sea cotton along the coastline, as it was otherwise too cold for this crop.

Then, in the early 19th century, an American, Walter Burling, discovered a cotton strain in Mexico with bolls that ripened and opened early, with a high fibre-to-seed ratio. The bolls also all ripened at the same time, making them easier to harvest. He cross-bred this strain with sea cotton and planted an experimental field in his back garden. The plants still died with the first frosts, but by then the bolls had opened and the cotton had been collected. Now, instead of growing cotton as a tree, it became an annual shrub. This was what we refer to as American Upland cotton, and today over 90 per cent of the world's cotton comes from this strain.

Now cotton could be grown in colder climes, and soon vast swathes of land in the southern US were devoted to it. The cumbersome process of separating the cotton seed from its surrounding lint was revolutionised when Eli Whitney invented the 'cotton engine', or gin for short. It sped up the ginning process to such an extent that land prices in the southern states trebled. In 1793, cotton had accounted for just 4 per cent of clothing worn in Europe and North America, but within a century that would rise dramatically to 73 per cent.

Summers in the Deep South, where cotton thrived, were long, hot and humid. Disease was rife and few could be induced to spend their days toiling in the cotton fields. Instead, enslaved West Africans were used for free labour. So, land belonging to Native American tribes was stolen by European colonists and then toiled over by West Africans, whose forbears had originally been stolen to pay for cotton cloth, which was produced in India but under the tight grip of the East India Company trade monopoly. Exploitation seemed woven into its very fabric.

Descendants of 8 million West Africans, dispersed throughout the Caribbean, Latin America and the southern states of America, were treated in abhorrent ways, picking cotton under the lash of the overseer, as families were separated, rape was commonplace and infractions were dealt with violently and publicly.

This cotton was then shipped to Britain, where children were exploited in appalling conditions in the northern mills that manufactured the cotton into cloth. The mills of Manchester and Bradford became places of such pollution, with such inhumane working conditions, that at the beginning of the 19th century the average life expectancy of a Bradford mill worker was just eighteen – 27 years below the national average. Most factory workers were profoundly deaf by middle age – if they lived that long – and many suffered from respiratory ailments such as brown lung disease, due to the cotton lint that constantly hung in the air.

This airborne lint was also a fire hazard, regularly combusting, at which point factory workers would fling themselves to the floor to avoid burns. Orphans and children from workhouses were targeted for indenture, as they could be worked for long hours and had nimble fingers and small enough frames to squeeze inside the machinery when something had snagged. The spinning jenny, water frame, flying shuttle and other industrial innovations led to widespread pollution, urbanisation and industrialisation, so that by 1830 cotton manufacture accounted for half of all British exports and yet, for the recently urbanised factory workers, their standards of living actually decreased.

Picked with free labour (although the pickers were far from free) and manufactured industrially, British cotton soon undercut its rivals, including India. Although Britain's muslin was inferior, it was half the price of Dhaka muslin and became far more popular. India, once the global centre of cotton manufacture, experienced such a systematic assault on its manufacturing capabilities by the British that it led to a new phenomenon: deindustrialisation.

At first, the East India Company had purchased Dhaka muslins from the Bengali urban trading centres. This had created a huge increase in demand that benefited the spinners and weavers. Then the Company gradually sidelined the merchants and middlemen and dealt directly with hand-spinners and weavers. Muslin took months to weave, so weavers were offered credit, which most gratefully took, not realising how high the interest rates would be. Most ended up in crippling amounts of debt and were forced to bond themselves to their British debtors. Exploitative new laws were introduced forbidding weavers to sell to anyone but the East India Company, and anyone who dared to disobey was punished, as in the case of one unfortunate weaver. 'The Company's Gamushta seized him and his son, flogged him severely, painted his face black and white, tied his hands behind his back and marched him through the town escorted by sepoys.' They announced that a similar fate would befall any other weaver attempting to break the British monopoly.[*]

The assault on Indian cotton manufacture was just getting going. Master dyers were forced to spill the secrets of their mordants and dye techniques and Indian designs were shamelessly copied by manufacturers in Britain. Cheap British chintz was then exported to India, where it flooded the market and undercut local production. If that wasn't enough, the British also imposed a crippling tax on Indian chintz exports and gave British chintz special tax privileges. Local industry simply couldn't compete, and soon, weavers and spinners who had perfected their art over generations were forced into the fields to grow food crops. It was a truly Machiavellian approach.

The financial benefits were huge when it came to buying raw cotton from India and then selling it back manufactured as cloth. Demand for more raw cotton grew, and soon new taxes were levied forcing farmers to grow cotton as a cash crop on their land as well as food crops. Bengal, with its frequent floods, was already vulnerable to crop failure, but this was now exacerbated as land was diverted for cotton. In the 1870s, when the resulting famines came,

----

[*] Thanhauser, S., *Worn* (2022), p. 61

they were devastating, killing between 6 and 10 million Bengalis, with the highest mortality rates in the regions growing the most cotton.

Now that Britain was manufacturing India's cotton, they found that the cotton tree, *Gossypium arboreum var. neglecta*, used to spin and weave Dhaka muslin, didn't work well in their machines. So, they imported American Upland seed which they crossbred with the original *neglecta* variety. This meant that *Baft hawa,* or woven wind, would never be woven so finely again. The last Dhaka muslin was woven in the late 1860s, but as American Upland cotton cross-pollinated with local varieties, including Bengal tree cotton, it had become effectively extinct.

Or had it?

Bengal Muslin is a project attempting to resurrect this fabric. They have scoured the riverbanks where *Gossypium arboreum var. neglecta* once thrived, seeking out plants that resemble the maple-like leaves illustrated in 18th- and 19th-century books on botany. They've also sequenced the DNA of dried specimens taken from Kew Gardens in London to make comparisons and have found a 70 per cent match. 'Wanted' posters of this elusive plant have been distributed in the hope that there may be undiscovered specimens still out there that are even purer.

Plantations of this resurrected tree cotton have helped revive an industry where fine threads are once more being woven into muslin. The thread count is still well below that of its forbears, but as spinners and weavers research forgotten methods and relearn this intricate art, *jamdani* saris are the dazzling result, selling for thousands of dollars. Their skill has been recognised by UNESCO as intangible world heritage.

Cotton was key to ongoing British rule in India and by the early 20th century, 60 per cent of the cotton textiles manufactured in

Lancashire were exported to the subcontinent. This fact was not lost on a young Indian lawyer, who had been working in South Africa and now returned to his homeland to campaign for its independence. His name was Mohandas Gandhi. In 1905 the first Indian Industrial Conference had already noted the unfair protectionist methods used by the British to ensure that local cotton manufacture was disadvantaged in order to keep the mills of Lancashire running. Then in 1909, Gandhi wrote *Hind Swaraj*, which was a call for independence using non-violent protest. Gandhi called on Indians of all classes to boycott British-manufactured cotton. However, they would still need something to wear, so Gandhi launched the *khadi* movement that sought to make Indian cotton self-sufficient once again.

Deindustrialisation had been so effective in many parts of the country that the only spinning wheels left were in museums or buried under storeroom clutter. The idea was a simple one: persuade Indians of all walks of life to take up spinning and weaving, and to wear homespun with pride. This would both break the economic power of the British and create employment and wealth for ordinary people who could sell their homespun. Gandhi, once a dandy dressed in tailored suits, now began to spin every day for several hours, finding the process meditative. He wore only homespun, insisting that all other members of the National Congress do the same.

Initially many of the women complained at wearing undyed, white homespun because this was the colour of mourning and people would think them widows. However, as lost traditions of dyeing were re-introduced, they were soon wearing colour. British-made suits were burnt publicly at roughly the same time as public burnings of *paranjas* were taking place in Soviet Uzbekistan.

Gandhi visited England – where he had studied as a young man – and was taken to the cotton mills of Lancashire to meet mill workers whose livelihoods were threatened by the boycott. When challenged about the resulting poverty the boycott was causing, he assured them that they had no idea what true poverty was but should come to India and he would show them. Winston

Churchill hated Gandhi and said, 'It is alarming and also nauseous to see Mr. Gandhi, a seditious Middle Temple lawyer ... striding half-naked up the steps of the viceregal palace.'

When Gandhi was invited to the palace to meet the king, journalists speculated that he would surely dress more appropriately than a mere loin cloth and homespun cotton shawl. Gandhi replied that to wear anything else while meeting the monarch would simply be disrespectful to himself, and after his visit assured the journalists with a twinkle in his eye that the king was wearing more than enough clothes for the both of them.

By the time India won independence in 1947, there were around 3 million spinning wheels at work, and today handmade textiles continue to be a huge export for the countries that made up pre-Partition India. So significant was the *khadi* movement that in the centre of the Indian flag is a cotton wheel, a reminder of the power of small things to effect big change.

The Cotton Road leading from India through Central Asia had continued to trade. Indian textile experts were brought to Samarkand to teach weaving and dyeing methods, particularly block-printing, so that Turkestan could create its own chintzes. However, Turkestani cotton lacked the tensile strength of tree cotton from Dhaka and was of a lower quality than American Upland. Yellower in colour, the bolls often didn't open before the first frosts killed the plants, so women would spend their winters at home, cracking open the bolls and trying to clean the cotton. Some was sent to Russia, which imported less than a tenth of its cotton from Turkestan, but this overland journey by camel took around six months, and by the time the cotton bales arrived, the outer layers were often too dirty to use. American cotton was far more preferable and readily available.

Until it wasn't.

The plight of cotton-picking slaves had divided American society between abolitionists, largely in the Northern states, and slave owners in the South. In 1861, the two sides went to war, and the repercussions were felt all over the world as the largest source of cotton suddenly stopped producing, precipitating a global cotton famine. Britain had favoured American cotton for its quality but also for its ease of transport across the Atlantic. Now India suddenly became more important, and cotton production was ramped up.

Imperial Russia, however, had no cotton-growing colonies it could depend on, and was far closer to India than the small island of Britain. Catherine the Great had once toyed with the idea of invading India, but now Russia began to set its sights more seriously on conquering the cotton-growing subcontinent. Britain, with its network of spies, was well aware of this, and began to make plans of its own to defend this jewel of the British imperial crown. Turkestan was about to find itself caught up in a tournament of shadows between the world's two largest empires, with cotton as the main prize.

15. FROM MOHAMMED TO MARX

When I first travelled along the Tajikistan border with Afghanistan's Wakhan Corridor on my return from the high-altitude wilds of the High Pamirs, I might have thought it remote and wild if I hadn't just come from somewhere far higher and more remote. Instead, the valley boasted actual trees, rather than the stunted willow bushes that grew higher up. Apricots were in season, the air felt thicker and warmer, and houses were surrounded by beds of flowers and carefully tended vegetable plots. We drove up to the Bibi Fatima hot springs, luxuriating in hot and fizzy water that gushed from a cleft in the rock face, happy to finally wash in warm water and chat with Pamiris who had come for a day trip spa.

Beside the springs are the ruins of a castle clearly chosen for its sweeping vistas up and down the valley. On our side were villages nestled mainly around the main road, where it was slightly flatter, and some irrigated terraces covered in apple trees. On the other side of the river was Afghanistan. Trains of camels, heavily laden, picked their way along small pathways that criss-crossed the mountainside. There was nothing particularly special about seeing Afghanistan so close. After all, the view from my bedroom window in Khorog looked out at the terraced hills of an Afghan village on the other side of the river. What was unique here was that the Afghan side of the Wakhan Valley was part of the Wakhan Corridor, a long panhandle of land that juts unexpectedly out of the north-east of Afghanistan, and which is as narrow as fifteen kilometres in some places. On the other side is Pakistan.

Why did this one narrow mountainous corridor stretch all the way to the border with China? It is a legacy of the Great Game, a 19th-century precursor to the Cold War, which was to radically change the lives and destinies of all Turkestanis. The establishment of this sliver of neutral land between the north-west frontier of India (present-day Pakistan) and Imperial Russia (present-day Tajikistan) in 1893 was vital in preventing a war and finally ending the Great Game. For both sides had agreed that if their empires ever met, then war would be the outcome.

The term 'Great Game' was first used in 1840 by Arthur Conolly, a British army captain who would eventually languish in a torture pit in Bukhara before his public execution. He had written to Henry Rawlinson, who had recently moved to Kandahar, stating, 'You've got a great game, a noble game before you.' The phrase was then used by Rudyard Kipling in his novel *Kim,* which is about Russian spies up to no good on British India's North-West Frontier.

Russia had long held expansionist aspirations. Some of its territories were won in war, such as Crimea, which was wrested from Ottoman control, while other territory was almost effortless to claim. There was a time when Russia expanded its frontier eastwards through Siberia at around a hundred miles a year. The region was sparsely populated and the indigenous and largely nomadic tribes living there offered little resistance and could be easily subjugated. Even the Pacific Ocean was no barrier to colonial expansion, and soon Russia had crossed the Bering Sea and laid claim to a large chunk of the North American continent, only later selling this territory to the United States. It is now called Alaska.

Catherine the Great was responsible for much of this expansion and toyed with the idea of extending her empire southwards as well, in order to wrest India from the British. A joint Franco-Russian invasion of India was also proposed by Napoleon. The British navy were too powerful for an ocean-based attack and most successful invasions of India had occurred from the north. So, Central Asia – that bit in between Russia and India – became of increasing Russian interest.

For the British, Russian eastward expansionism was of no concern, but they were increasingly aware of new export markets for British-made goods to Turkestan and of Russia's growing influence in this region. In the 1830s, British officer and spy Alexander Burnes travelled up from India and through Afghanistan to Bukhara. He noted the cotton chintzes sold in great quantities in the bazaar. There were no local chintz factories and these cotton prints were either of British or Russian manufacture. If better trade routes could be opened through Afghanistan, Indian chintz would soon out-class the inferior Russian-made cloth, and transport would be much cheaper than the long road by camel from the cotton factories of Nizhny Novgorod near Moscow.

'The Uzbeks are simple people,' Burnes declared blithely, having only been in Bukhara for a few days, and failing to recognise that its citizens were Tajik. Forbidden from using pen or ink within Bukhara, he later wrote, 'They believe a spy must measure their forts and walls, they have no idea of the value of conversation.'*

Burnes also spent time in Kabul and saw it as territory ripe for the colonial picking. If Afghanistan could be colonised, it would create the perfect buffer between British India and an increasingly Russian-influenced Turkestan. So, the British invaded Afghanistan and installed a puppet Emir with Burnes pulling the strings. However, his usual confidence of being one step ahead of the simple native was to prove his undoing. The new Emir was unpopular and provoked an Afghan revolt. Burnes was killed, and as the British colonists fled with their children, wives and nannies in tow, they were set upon by over 30,000 Afghans. Of the thousands of Brits who had fled newly colonised Kabul, the only man to escape alive was Doctor William Brydon, who limped into Jalalabad on a wounded horse. The rest were killed, executed or imprisoned.

Nor were Russia's colonial exploits entirely successful. At the beginning of the 19th century, Khiva was the slave-trading capital of Turkestan. Turkmen raiding parties would attack villages

----

* Burnes, A., *Travels into Bokhara* (1835), p. 187

at night and the unfortunate captives who survived the journey across the desert were then sold in Khiva. Most of the slaves were Shia Persians, and as heretics were considered fair game. Persian women commanded a particularly high price and were popular additions to harems. Russian sailors, soldiers and outliers were also captured and sold in Khiva. When Nikolai Muraviev travelled through in 1820, he sent his pistol for repairs and discovered on its return a roll of paper hidden inside the barrel beseeching him on behalf of over 300 Russian slaves to petition the Tsar to save them from their wretched and tormented state.

Liberating the slaves provided the perfect pretext for a Russian invasion. However, the British spy network learnt of this and beat the Russians to it. Captain Abbot was dispatched to persuade the Khan of Khiva to release all Russian slaves. He was somewhat dour and, having failed to impress the Khan, was lucky to escape with his life. In his stead, a dashing young Englishman called Richmond Shakespear arrived, charming the Khan and persuading him to relinquish every bonded Russian. Shakespear led them across the desert to the Caspian port fortress of Krasnovodsk and freedom, receiving official gratitude from the Tsar who was no doubt privately seething.

Eventually, though, the American Civil War and global cotton shortage meant that cotton increased in price tenfold, and pretexts were replaced by pragmatism as Russia prepared for its invasion of Turkestan. Baron G. V. Rosen, the Russian commander-in-chief of the Caucasus, talked of the need for colonised Caucasians and Central Asians to 'be our Negroes'* when it came to cotton production, and by 1865 Russia had captured Tashkent, with the Khanate of Kokand next. The Emirate of Bukhara and the Khanate of Khiva followed, although they became vassal states and were not fully integrated into the Russian Empire. The Russians did not intend to simply administrate their new territories, but flooded them with Russians who began building Russian schools, cinemas, hospitals and tramways

* Beckert, S., *Empire of Cotton* (2014), p. 345

(with the front carriages reserved for Slavs, who paid double). New Russian cities were built alongside existing native ones.

In the countryside, there were also changes afoot. General Kauffman, who had led the Russian invasion of Turkestan and was now its first governor, ordered cotton seed from America and began experimenting with it on local soil. He was not the only early adopter. Mennonite Germans – theological cousins to the Amish – had fled to Turkestan to avoid national service as they were staunch pacifists. One Mennonite colony near Khiva began planting American cotton seed, obtained from relatives who had emigrated to the Midwest. Soon, the Khorezm Oasis was one of the major centres for cotton growth, along with the Fergana Valley. American cotton yielded four times the amount usually harvested from local varieties, and Kauffman sent bureaucrats to America to learn more about production methods and yields.

Soon huge swathes of orchards, vines, paddies and fields were destroyed and replaced with cotton. There wasn't enough arable land devoted to growing food crops, but the resulting scarcity of wheat was all part of the plan. Aleksandr Krivoshein, the first Minister of Agriculture, declared: 'Each extra pud (approximately 16.5 kg) of Turkestan wheat is competition for Russian or Siberian wheat; every extra pud of Turkestan cotton is competition for American cotton.'* Siberian wheat would be transported along new railway lines to Turkestan, returning to Russia laden with 'white gold'. From 1870 until the revolution, land devoted to cotton grew by almost 50 times, ranking the Russian Empire as the fifth-largest producer of cotton globally at that time.

Russia had wanted to create enormous plantations similar to those in the American South. However, local farmers owned their own small

---

* Sokol, E., *The Revolt of 1916 in Russian Central Asia* (1954), p. 19

plots of land and had little incentive to give these up to work for wages. So, Russians set about stealing the land, using the same methods employed by the British in India. First, they pressured farmers to use their entire land for cotton-growing, and even offered incentives. This left farmers vulnerable to fluctuating prices or a bad harvest. When that was the case, loans were swiftly offered but with crippling interest rates. As soon as a farmer fell behind on repayments, their land was seized by Russian merchants and the farmers would simply become sharecroppers on the land they had once owned. Russian and local merchants were thus able to purchase huge amounts of territory, leading to a new, extremely wealthy merchant class.

Railway tracks and cotton gins were built strategically in the places where cotton was grown most. Oil presses rendered cotton-seed oil, and pressed cakes of cotton seed were moulded into jugs into which cotton oil was then poured and stored. However, most of the top jobs that all this progress brought went to the steady influx of Russian immigrants who kept arriving via the new rail networks. Those Central Asians who did get employed were paid less than their Slavic counterparts.

By the 1890s Russia was the largest global producer of cotton in the world after America and cotton-fever had gripped Turkestan to the extent that it was difficult to find or afford horse fodder, such was the demand for all land to grow cotton. Even then, the damaging effects of cotton on soil productivity had been noted, and experts suggested alternating between cotton and lucerne each year, so that the latter could help replenish the soil. They were ignored.

Annette Meakin noted the ubiquity of urban cotton gins and how most towns were strewn with cotton fluff. She visited a gin where the compressors were from Halifax. There were often no local words to describe new industrial processes and Meakin noted, 'It was amusing to have a heap of cotton pointed out to me as "good middling" by a Russian who knew no English,'[*] and who also used the English term 'cotton gin'.

....

[*] Meakin, A., *In Russian Turkestan* (1903), p. 34

However, industrial processing extended only as far as ginning the cotton. Once the cotton and the seeds had been separated, the bales of raw cotton were then sent to Ivanovo near Moscow which, thanks to its cotton mills, became known as Russia's Manchester. Here the raw cotton was manufactured into cloth, much of which was then exported back to Turkestan. By keeping Turkestan deliberately undeveloped industrially, it remained a captive market for Russian manufactured goods, with new tariffs and restrictions placed on British- or Indian-manufactured cloth. Many local workshops producing hand-spun cotton and handwoven cloth were unable to compete with Russian factories and went out of business. So, Central Asians grew used to buying back their own cotton in woven and printed form.

Just as the British had learnt to adapt their cotton designs and colour schemes for different global markets, so did Russian cotton manufacture. Russian merchants returning from Turkestan brought examples of popular local block-printed cotton and superior imported Indian chintz. Russian designers set about creating designs which they hoped might appeal to this new Turkestani market. They were able to achieve stunning results by roller printing over the same design several times with different dyes.

As well as the classic floral designs and palettes found in Indian chintz, Russian designers were influenced by William Morris and Art Nouveau, but ditched the muted colour palettes for bright florals they were sure would appeal to Central Asian tastes.

Given the Prophet's injunction against men wearing silk, men's silk robes in Turkestan were always lined with cotton, and the new Russian chintz designs proved an irresistible hit, soon accounting for half of all Russian exports to Turkestan. Before long, fabric was no longer relegated to inner linings, and whole robes were worn in these cheap but colourful designs. Uzbek and Tajik men loved nothing more than to strut around in new robes in the latest season's patterns, emblazoned with large pink roses. Ella Christie, visiting in the 1920s from Scotland, where Indian chintz was appropriated and marketed as Paisley, was not convinced by men in florals, referring to them as 'perambulating furniture'.

In the early 20th century, as modernism and Bauhaus influenced Russian design, chintz was briefly emblazoned with industrial elements such as tractors and factories, or sheaves of wheat. However, these designs proved so unpopular that designers soon reverted to colourful florals.

If there are striking similarities between pre-Revolutionary Russian chintz and English middle-class curtains from the 1980s, there is in fact a clear connection; it's that thieving Laura Ashley. As hippies travelled through Afghanistan en route to India, they often purchased beautiful Turkestani robes sold cheaply in Kabul or Kandahar. Joss Graham in London started buying up these robes and had a good stock of them in his shop. British designer Laura Ashley was fascinated by the robes, not for their outer silks but for their Russian chintz inner linings. She borrowed several robe selections and copied their designs. So, Indian chintz motifs were copied by the British, then copied again and brightened by Russians for sale in Turkestan. Then, almost a century later, they were copied and adapted once more, and made into summer dresses, sofa coverings and curtains for middle-class English women.

Not all Central Asian cotton ended up in Russia. Some was hand-spun locally and then woven into *alacha,* a robust stripey material used for cheaper robes. Khiva was one of the main production centres of this cloth, and the weavers there perfected a technique to make *alacha* shimmer and rustle like the finest Bukharan silks. Bolts of cloth were soaked in baths of foamed eggwhites and then beaten with wooden hammers. The beating would open the fibres and cause the egg-white to penetrate deep. Once dry, the cloth would then be polished with a heavy wooden beam hung vertically from a workshop ceiling and tipped with a dome of solid glass. The weight, friction and resulting heat of the polishing process would result in such a glossy finish that *alacha* was even water-resistant when new. I have an early 20th-century polished *alacha* robe from Khiva in beautiful narrow stripes of dark navy, green and purple, with an inner lining of bright turquoise roses and buddleia blossom on a red background, representing both locally sourced and Russian-imported cotton. It cost me $30 and although

I only wear it to showcase Khiva's past fashions, it's one of the most comfortable items in my wardrobe.

The Russian cotton mills were awful places to work, mirroring the misery of cotton mills in the north of England, with unregulated hours, poor wages and dangerous working conditions. One witness to the mistreatment of the working poor in England was Friedrich Engels, a wealthy German whose father owned cotton mills around Europe, including in the north of England. Engels was appalled when his father sent him to work in these mills, and in 1845 he wrote *Conditions of the Working Classes in England,* in which he highlighted the systemic injustices of the class system. Three years later another work of his was published, co-authored with someone who was to become far better known in history: Karl Marx. The book: *The Communist Manifesto.*

Marxism, as it became known, left Engels somewhat unacknowledged, and became a growing opposition ideology to the rigid class hierarchies and privilege of Imperial Russia. By 1917, the working classes tired of a war between greedy colonial powers which they were expected to fight and die for, on top of the usual economic inequalities and challenges of poverty. Some of the first workers to strike were the female cotton-millworkers in Petrograd. They were joined by thousands of others, and then riots broke out and the police fired on the crowds. Eventually there was a mutiny in the army as soldiers refused to fight their fellow workers. Just a few months later, the Tsar resigned and the Bolsheviks seized power.

The ensuing civil war was disastrous for Turkestan. It no longer produced enough grain to feed itself, as cotton had taken over, and now the trains laden with grain from Siberia stopped coming and famine broke out. 'You can't eat cotton!' was the slogan shouted by hungry protestors. This hunger and dependence on other parts of the Soviet Union became a weapon of Moscow, and up until the collapse of the Soviet Union, there was always the threat that if certain regions didn't meet their cotton quotas, they wouldn't get their share of imported grain.

Joshua Kunitz, visiting the newly created nation of Tajikistan in the early 1930s, described the thinking behind the system. 'When the peasant, together with his patch of cotton, raises enough grain and vegetables to supply his personal needs, he is more or less immune to proletarian influence. He is, relatively speaking, lord in his own domain. Specialisation entails dependence on the market, and since in the Soviet Union the market is completely controlled by the worker's government, crop specialisation means greater dependence of the peasant on the proletariat and vice versa.'[*] When the first prime minister of Uzbekistan, Faizullah Khodjaev, challenged Stalin's commitment to a cotton monoculture, and worked together with the first party secretary, Akmal Ikramov, to create less cotton-dependency and more manufacturing and economic diversity within Uzbekistan, they were both arrested, accused of bourgeois nationalism, taken to Moscow as part of the 1938 show trial, and then shot.

The Communist Party also found few allies among the peoples of Tajikistan. While some resigned themselves to whatever fate their new Soviet masters had in store for them, many joined the resistance movements, or gathered their belongings and crossed over the Amu River, to begin a new life free from Slavs in Afghanistan. At least a quarter of the population chose to move, leaving ghost villages and empty towns. After all, apart from some dialectical differences, the language, culture and, most importantly, religion were all the same.

Aware of their unpopularity, Soviet authorities prioritised Tajikistan and other Central Asian countries with tractors, as we saw earlier, albeit without the necessary fuel. Dazzling rural workers with modernity would hopefully win over hearts and minds. Once working tractors finally became part of the rural landscape, mullahs railed against these satanic machines which were – they assured the faithful – greased with pork fat, and therefore it was a sin to use them.

Central Asians weren't the only ones Moscow set out to impress. Left-leaning intellectuals and communists from Western countries were invited for heavily curated visits, carefully sidestepping the

....

[*] Kunitz, J., *Dawn over Samarkand* (1935), p. 177

devastating famines of Kazakhstan and Ukraine, to show the progress of socialism throughout the Soviet Union. This was just part of a strategy to convert the whole capitalist world to the better path of socialism, and Moscow was strategic in who to try and convince. In capitalist America, for example, it was clear that the most downtrodden and oppressed people, and therefore most likely to foment a revolution, were African Americans.

The cumbersomely named Soviet film board, Meshrabpom, decided to produce a film depicting a history of black exploitation in America. They commissioned Langston Hughes, a left-leaning African American writer and intellectual, to produce the script and he, along with fifty African American actors, travelled to Moscow in 1932 for filming. When news of this reached Washington, it alarmed the government so much that they agreed to officially recognise the Soviet Union, as long as the film project and further attempts at African American agitation were called off. For the actors it was a wasted trip, although they were given a free package holiday to Crimea in compensation. Hughes decided to stay on, and was invited to visit the cotton-growing regions of the Union in order to write about them.

He travelled to Turkestan by train, acknowledging that while the train might not have been as comfortable as ones back home, at least here, he had the same rights as anyone else to sit in the dining car or use the toilets. He met dark-skinned Tajiks who were of his hue and yet could marry Russians, hold professional positions and work in government. The egalitarianism and lack of racism was a far cry from the Jim Crow laws that still segregated most of the southern states of America.

A number of African Americans had been recruited to help improve collective farming in Soviet Turkestan. Hughes was able to celebrate Christmas with a group of twelve cotton specialists and their wives at a collective farm around 60 kilometres from Tashkent. Some were educated agricultural chemists and college graduates, while others were cotton-hands, who simply knew cotton intimately. All of them were paid well and invited to teach American methods of cotton-growing, whether in the lab or in the field. Despite the famine raging in neighbouring Kazakhstan, the Americans could procure all they needed to bake pumpkin pie, rabbit stew, mash and gravy. Under their lab work, a new strain of cotton was introduced that matured in 25 per cent less time than traditional seeds, allowing more time for harvesting before the first frosts of winter. If they had been living in the South of the States at that time, most would have been sharecroppers, 'For cotton is a crop that the Negro never shares.'*

'In the autumn, if you step off the train almost anywhere in the fertile part of Central Asia, you step into a cotton field, or into a city or town whose trees are filled with evidence of cotton nearby,' wrote Hughes in 1934. 'On all the dusty roads, camels, carts and trucks loaded with the white fibre go towards the gins and warehouses. Outside the towns, oft-times as far as the eye can see, the white balls lift their precious heads.'†

That same year, the J. V. Stalin Textile Factory opened in Tashkent, as Central Asia was finally allowed to manufacture some of the cotton it produced. Milestones such as this were widely touted and celebrated throughout Uzbekistan and the wider Soviet Union. Photographers such as Max Penner captured these great Soviet achievements. There are epic moments such as the laying of tram-tracks in Tashkent's old quarter, or the digging of the Fergana Canal, as well as ordinary elements of life, with manual labourers standing proud and noble, heads to the sunrise of a new glorious dawn. Bicycles, tractors, buses, telegraph poles and radios all speak of the modernity ushered in by socialism. A girl in an embroidered skullcap braids her hair in the mirror in which we see a portrait of Stalin hung in reverence. Russified local Communist Party members sit on chairs in suits, surrounded by kneeling village folk in their tatty floral robes, looking up, subservient and attentive. My favourite is of a happy Soviet farmer driving his tractor through a muddy field, his vision largely obstructed by a large portrait of Stalin attached to the tractor front.

---

* Hughes, Langston, *A Negro Looks at Soviet Central Asia* (1934), p. 14
† Ibid.

The photographs are clearly staged, but helped reinforce themes of progress, inter-racial harmony, modernity and prosperity. They also reinforce the Soviet racial hierarchy, with Slavs and Germans at the top and Central Asians at the bottom. Everyone should know their place, and for Central Asians, this place – as constantly reinforced through propaganda – was picking cotton. Propaganda posters regularly featured cotton-pickers, and well-known artists, such as Aleksandr Nikolaev, were expected to do their bit for socialism and create posters. Nikolaev, also known as *Usta Mumin*, produced a wonderfully man-shaming poster in which an Uzbek woman's face is shown in close-up calling out for all men to come and pick cotton. To one side of her, in darkness, surrounded by cobwebs and a malnourished donkey, are feckless farmers sitting around drinking tea and smoking their waterpipes. On the other side, in colour, hardworking women and a few enlightened men toil in the cotton fields.

Another of Nikolaev's posters shows two Uzbek men heaving bales of newly picked cotton onto a large wooden cart. A woman bends down to pick up a stray tuft of cotton and a banner above them reads in Uzbek: 'Not one gram of cotton must go to waste, not one minute of harvest must go to waste. All the cotton must be collected!'

Posters depicting the cotton harvest were quasi-religious in tone, meshing together Soviet and traditional images with local wagons processing in convoy, piled high with bales of cotton, red flags fluttering from each and with musicians at the front playing local instruments under a banner that reads: 'If the cotton is ready for harvest, then so are we!' For all the promise of education and bright futures, Central Asians were most needed out in the fields. Each September, entire urban communities would be mobilised and sent out to the countryside for two months of cotton-picking. Those working in state jobs were often mobilised, but perhaps the easiest group of people who could be co-opted for this task were those in full-time education.

For all the Soviet promises of education and betterment, Uzbeks and Tajiks knew what was truly expected of them. The September cotton-picking mobilisation included many adults working in hospitals or local government, but also consisted of a huge number of schoolchildren and students.

I talked to my friend Galya, a Tartar English teacher who lives in Bukhara, wanting to hear about her experiences of picking cotton as a student in the late 1970s. She was a star picker, managing up to 100 kilos a day. 'The boys were lazy or too busy flirting,' she told me, 'But I knew what I was doing. I'd include dirt and unopened cotton bolls in my sacks ready for the weigh-ins each sundown. There were often planes overhead spraying us with DDT, but it didn't occur to us that this was a bad thing. Anyway, we had to bathe and drink from the canals, which were laced with it, so what did a bit extra matter? In the evenings someone would play the guitar or a local instrument, and we'd all join in. We were a real Soviet family with students from all different ethnicities working together. Being away from the watchful eye of our parents meant that romances blossomed and there was something about all working together that bonded us closely. Most of the students were billeted in a barn, but I got permission to stay at home as my mother was a single parent, so I would cycle to and from the fields each day.

'Back then, we got paid 3 kopeks a kilo, and I worked hard enough to pay for student-discounted plane tickets to visit places like Kyiv and Moscow, which I would never have been able to see otherwise. I'd queue up for hours and managed to buy decent boots and a winter coat and the quality was much better than anything you could get in Bukhara. The main downside was that we spent half the academic year picking cotton. I used to bring books of English grammar into the fields with me and attempt some self-study, but in general, most students weren't as motivated and my classmates graduated without knowing much English.'

While students could benefit from extra income with only a few months' disruption from studies each year, for some Central Asians, cotton was to spell the end of life as they knew it. The days of cotton exploitation were far from over.

16. THE INTERNATIONAL
COTTON BOYCOTT

While there was a ready supply of labour in Soviet Uzbekistan, Tajikistan was largely mountainous and the arid plains, now planned for reclamation as cotton fields, were sparsely populated. Five-year plans needed fulfilling and communities living in the remoter mountain areas were doing little to further Soviet aims. So, some were given financial incentives to leave their ancestral homes and travel down to the plains with carts and livestock. They were often promised that their new lands would be 'Gulestan' – a place of flowers – which couldn't have been further from the truth. Those first arriving in a new area often had no accommodation and had to build homes themselves, along with canals, schools and other infrastructure. It was a hard life, and during flyblown, sweltering summers, many longed for the clean mountain air and icy cold streams of pure water that they'd known before. Understandably, many who stayed in the mountains, having heard about the real conditions of these cotton-pickers, were quite happy to remain where they were.

So, between the 1950s and 1970s there were regular forced relocations of mountain peoples, particularly the Yaghnobi, those linguistic heirs of Silk Road Sogdian. Helicopters would show up unexpectedly, and soldiers would round up entire villages, giving them just enough time to grab a few possessions, before flying them down to the plains. Inspired by my truncated call with Jeff in Tajikistan, I decided to combine a visit to Uzbekistan in the spring of 2022 with a side-trip to Tajikistan. I'd meet up with my American friend, Zack, who runs a fruit juice business, and we'd hike for a few days in the mountains before heading to Zafarabad to see Jeff.

'And the great thing is that now you don't need a visa; you can just rock up at the border and get a stamp in your passport,' Zack had explained on a call before I left the UK. The border was only half an hour from Samarkand and I arrived ready to dredge up my hazily remembered Tajik. There were no problems on the Uzbekistan side, but the Tajik border guard – who also spoke Uzbek – frowned as he searched my passport for a visa.

'I don't need a visa,' I explained breezily. 'I'm from Angliya.'

'Angliya,' he mouthed, brow furrowing as he ran his finger down a list.

'Or it might be Buyuk Britaniya,' I added, and then suggested, 'Can I come round and look at the list with you?' He grudgingly agreed and we both scanned the type-written Cyrillic list of 52 countries. I passed Jamaica, Vatican City and Lichtenstein, but there was no England, Great Britain or United Kingdom.

'Back,' said the guard, pointing in the direction of Uzbekistan. 'If you don't have a visa, you have to go back.'

I managed to borrow a phone on the Tajikistan side and call Zack, who was still driving from Dushanbe.

'I'm so sorry,' he said. 'I know Americans can come through. I thought Brits could, too. I should have checked.'

'We both should have checked,' I replied, annoyed with myself.

My dreams of interviewing Yaghnobis began to fade. All was not lost, though. Zack still visited Zafarobod and, armed with a list of questions, was able to interview two Yaghnobi elders who had both been forcibly relocated from the mountains. Seated on wooden platforms under a vine, and plied with bowls of fresh yogurt, Zack settled down to record their stories.

The white-bearded Kholov Sayeed had nothing positive to say about the forced relocation. He was three when the helicopters came and had spent over 50 years living in what had been desert but was now irrigated cotton fields. They had to leave almost all their possessions behind.

'Back home, the air was clean, the water fresh and the mountainsides were covered in grass during the summer. We'd send a boy with the goats to camp at higher ground and we would harvest the meadow grass around us ready for winter. Here, our water is brown, the air is thick and dusty and we have to pay for hay to feed our livestock. The worst thing for us is that we've lost our language and our community. If I can't speak Yaghnobi then what am I? You're nothing without your language. We still speak it at home, but our children are losing it and learn Tajik in school. Before, we were all in one place, but now we're dispersed. If you scatter burning sticks from a fire, they soon become just smoking embers. There are still a few families who returned to our mountains even though it was forbidden. They speak Yaghnobi properly, not like us where we mix it with Russian and Tajik.'

Many of the older people and children died during their first summer on the plains, unused to the intense heat and inadequate shelter.

Juraboy is now 60 and was only seven when the helicopter came and took his family. His memories of life in the mountains are less rosy, recognising the tough, long winters, the lack of fruit trees as it was too cold for them at 2,400 metres altitude, and the lack of arable land up in the mountains. 'The authorities told us that the mountains were unstable and would fall on us and destroy our villages,' he explained. 'What did we villagers know? We believed them and thought that the move was for our own good.'

When Juraboy arrived on the plains, he didn't speak any Tajik or Russian and had never seen cotton growing before. There was no water except what was brought in on trucks, and they had to build a canal themselves before the land could be irrigated. Despite these hardships, he thinks that life in Zafarabod is probably better because now they have schools and more land and better farming technology. Still, he laments the loss of his language and a community where no one asked what was theirs or a neighbour's, as everyone shared everything. I wonder at the irony of such naturally socialist communities being destroyed in the name of socialism.

By the Brezhnev years of the 1970s, Uzbekistan was under increasing pressure from Moscow to increase its cotton yields and to overfulfil already unrealistic cotton quotas. Sharaf Rashidov was chairman of the Uzbekistan Communist Party at the time and wanted to keep his job. So, he gave Moscow what they wanted – in word, at least. In 1975, the tenth five-year plan was announced, stating that cotton production would rise from 4 million tonnes annually to 6 million tonnes. Rashidov assured Moscow that this was doable but had a plan of his own which he put into action.

Trains that supposedly groaned under mountains of cotton departed from Tashkent to Moscow but were actually empty. Officials were bribed to report them as full, and fictitious reports of overfulfilled quotas arrived regularly to Moscow along with the usual photographs of joyous Uzbeks in the fields busy cotton-picking. To maintain this fiction, more and more officials at high levels had to be bribed. Even Brezhnev's own son-in-law was implicated when the reality of what became known as 'the cotton affair' came to light. It was actually Soviet satellites that gave the game away. When trained on their own lands, it soon became clear that empty fields stood where cotton was supposedly overflowing. As Moscow realised it had been duped, the investigation began, with over 2,600 arrests and over 50,000 people fired. Some higher-up officials committed suicide, and some speculate that Rashidov himself, who died in 1983 just as the rumours of a cotton cover-up began to circulate, may have done so at his own hand.

It was out of the ashes of this scandal that a young man called Islom Karimov, raised by the state in an orphanage – a usual requirement for Central Asian Soviet leaders – came to power as chairman of the Uzbekistan Communist Party. After the collapse of the Soviet

Union, he swiftly reinvented himself as Uzbekistan's first president. Karimov's economic policies changed very little from the Soviet model. The state still owned all the land and set cotton-growing quotas for each region, while the farmers were essentially sharecroppers. The decision of where to plant cotton and how much to plant was made by local mayors and collective farm bosses, who were also responsible for ensuring quotas were met. This meant that they often resorted to intimidation and even violence when needed, remunerating themselves generously from the cotton pot, and leaving the dregs for the actual farmers and harvesters.

The state was also the only legitimate customer for the cotton produced, purchasing it for around a third of its true global market rate – if they paid up at all. Empty promises of payment were common, as was paying in kind with whatever happened to be surfeit, leaving it to the farmers to try to resell and recoup some of their losses. Often cotton was graded as being of poor quality, which meant farmers were paid less, but was sold as high quality. An impoverished rural class barely managed to eke out a living, relying on vegetable plots and remittances from sons in Russia to make ends meet. During the late Soviet era, there had been a drive to mechanise the cotton harvest and around half of the fields were harvested mechanically, but in post-Soviet Uzbekistan, with high unemployment and a surfeit of cheap labour, the cotton would all be picked by hand.

Unlike China, America, India and Pakistan, who all manufacture the bulk of the cotton they grow, over 70 per cent of post-Soviet Uzbek cotton was exported raw. This made it easy for gate-keeping individuals within government to reap huge rewards, creating cotton barons among the ruling oligarchs, such as the infamous Rustam Inoyatov who was also head of the secret police and oversaw a systematic policy of torturing pious Muslims and anyone who dared speak out against the Karimov regime. At this point, Uzbekistan was the second-largest cotton exporter in the world, bringing in a billion dollars a year.

By 2005, when the Environmental Justice Foundation released a report that highlighted the chronic exploitation taking place within the cotton sector, farmers were earning as little as $7 a month in wages and many simply crossed the border to Kazakhstan during harvest time as cotton-pickers were paid a little better there. The labour shortfall was made up by schoolchildren.

By 2007, the state exploitation of ordinary Uzbeks was not dissimilar to their plight 100 years earlier under Tsarist rule. It was as if the Soviet rise of the proletariat had never happened. A million students, children, state medical workers and public sector employees, as well as farmers, were sent to the fields each autumn to harvest cotton. There were growing calls for change from advocates such as the former British Ambassador to Uzbekistan, Craig Murray, and increasing numbers of anti-slavery and child-labour charities. A coalition of NGOs, independent trade unions, retail associations, academics and ethical consumer groups, calling itself the Cotton Campaign, banded together to push for a worldwide ban on the import of Uzbek and Turkmen cotton.

Over 300 international brands and retailers signed the cotton pledge, refusing to sell garments made with Uzbek cotton until significant changes were made. Any large clothing retailer that didn't sign up risked ethical shaming and damage to their brand.

In 2014, the Karimov regime began to yield to international pressure, and no longer press-ganged schoolchildren into harvesting cotton. However, college students, including those aged sixteen to eighteen, as well as university students, were still sent to the field, along with doctors, nurses, teachers and other state workers. The government also denied that there was an issue with forced labour, despite an increase in rural coercion to make up for the new shortfall in pickers.

Around this time, I led my first tour group to Uzbekistan. It was September and the fields were white. Our bus passed a field of cotton-pickers and I asked the driver to stop so that we could take photos, and also for the group to pick a little cotton themselves, just to see what it was like. Our local guide's eyes widened and he told the bus driver to keep driving.

'Are you crazy?' he hissed. 'Don't you know what happened two years ago? A tour group stopped at a cotton field to help the students. Some were studying English and told the tourists how much they hated and resented being forced to the fields to pick 80 kilos a day, or paying for the shortfall out of their own pockets. One of the tourists wrote a newspaper article about it and even used his own name. Of course, the secret police traced back which tour group he'd been on, and who'd been the driver and the local guide. They both lost their jobs.'

He pointed out as we passed further fields that there was always a car parked beside them with someone from the secret police sitting inside, monitoring and ensuring that there were no attempts at resistance.

In March 2022, the Cotton Campaign finally agreed to halt its boycott of Uzbek cotton because of the significant changes brought about under President Mirziyoyev. New measures offer a sliding pay scale that starts lower at the beginning of the harvest, when the picking is easy, and gets higher by November, when the cotton is scarcer and the picking gets harder. Wages have increased, and harvesters can earn around $150 a month if they work hard. Wages are more often paid in full and on time, making voluntary cotton-picking a more attractive proposition. There's also been a significant reduction in the number of medical and educational workers forced to the fields. There's also a growth in the use of mechanised cotton-harvesters.

The Cotton Campaign acknowledged that there are still numerous cases of coercion from collective farm bosses or regional mayors, but that this is no longer systemic. The campaign thanked the courage of civil rights campaigners within Uzbekistan who continue to face government opposition to their activities, but who nevertheless bring new cases of abuse to light. The Covid pandemic created higher levels of unemployment for Uzbeks who normally went to Russia for work, which contributed to a willing labour market in 2020 and 2021, meaning coercion simply wasn't needed.

What will happen now that the spotlight is no longer on Uzbekistan, and with no trade unions or systems to protect farmers, remains to be seen. While farmers are no longer forced to sell cotton only to the state, the private firms are largely owned by people in government. The only hotline for complaints demands that all callers give their full name, address and passport number, making whistle-blowing difficult. It seems virtually impossible to separate cotton-growing and exploitation.

After fifteen years of boycotting Uzbek cotton, the Cotton Campaign has turned its sights on Turkmenistan, where forced labour continues, and on Xinjiang province in China, where the Xi Jinping regime has enslaved Uighurs and other Turkic people to pick and manufacture cotton as well as other goods. The United States has taken a stand against Uighur slavery, putting the onus on any manufacturers of cotton goods sold in America to prove that slavery was not part of their production process.

Cotton exploitation in Xinjiang has gone hand in hand with the destruction of Uighur culture, language, reproductive rights, religious observance and community. Communist Party Secretary Chen Quanguo, fresh from his impressive track record of terrorising and subjugating the people of Tibet, was brought into Xinjiang in 2016 to continue his work. He turned Urumchi, the regional capital, into a surveillance state and incarcerated over a million Uighurs and other Turkic minorities in what are referred to euphemistically as 're-education camps'.

Eighty per cent of China's cotton is grown in Xinjiang Province, causing irreparable ecological harm in this water-scarce region. History is repeating itself as a communist colonial power destroys the environment and forces the colonised to grow and harvest cotton, no matter what. The Taklamakan desert, which dominates the middle of Xinjiang, has recently grown by up to a third, and providing water for thirsty cotton is putting additional strain on the retreating glaciers within the region and raising already worrying levels of water scarcity to new heights.

I asked my Uzbek family in Khiva about their own memories of cotton-picking and was surprised at how nostalgic they were.

'We had a great time,' said my host mum, Zulhamar, who'd picked during the Soviet times. 'I lost my father young and I was the oldest child, so my mother got permission for me to still stay at home. I just cycled out to the fields each day. I was one of the star pupils, picking like a machine! One time I managed to pick 200 kilos in a day, and won a prize and gave most of my earnings to my mum. They used to bring us things to buy with our cotton-money that you couldn't get in the bazaar, like this beautiful material that I had made up into dresses. The cotton was much taller back then and you could be in the middle of a field and no one could see you. Now it's all short and you have to stoop down to pick it.

'I started aged thirteen and picked until I left school. They brought us cotton-seed oil and meat and this Russian bread that we didn't like, so then they brought us flour and one of the older girls made proper Uzbek bread that we could eat. The worst bit was in November when there was hardly any cotton left, but we still had to go out into the fields and make sure that none got wasted. By then, the food had mainly run out and I remember one time, we were hosted by a villager and all we had left was Russian bread that no one wanted. The villager had dried chillies hanging up outside his house to keep away the evil eye, and we tried rubbing some of these on the bread to give it flavour, but it just burnt our mouths. Still, we had a great time and they'd bring out musicians to play for us in the evenings.'

Her children, Malika and Zealaddin, both went-cotton picking under the Karimov regime. They were slow pickers, managing less than 30 kilos a day, and their dad ended up owing the school money because they hadn't picked enough to cover their food costs. 'Back then, we went as a family to visit Malika in the fields, bringing lots of home-cooked food with us. She was billeted in a village classroom, cleared of desks and covered in cotton-stuffed mattresses. A large cauldron of greasy macaroni bubbled outside, and the school toilets are best left undescribed. There were no showers.'

Out in the fields, I helped Malika with some cotton-picking of my own. For about fifteen minutes I was a foreign novelty among her classmates. Once the boys discovered I was from England, they wanted to know if I lived in Chelsea, Manchester or Liverpool and were disappointed by my lack of football knowledge. As we picked and chatted, they taught me some of their tricks. They would try to start picking at five in the morning while the cotton was still damp with dew, and then covering the pile over so that it wouldn't have dried out by weigh-in. Peeing on it also helped. Of course, the cotton couldn't be too wet or you'd get downgraded. Stones were another option, but you'd have to position them right in the middle of your bundle to avoid discovery.

At first, there was something quite satisfying about tugging out the cotton boll, making sure that the whole thing came out in one piece. It reminded me of picking my nose or removing the entire peel of a satsuma in one piece. In fact, I'd say that cotton-picking is quite an enjoyable pastime – for around five minutes. After that, I could imagine the tedium and repetition of it, and yet the need to work fast, zeroing in on a boll, tugging it in a series of rapid jerks and then dropping it into the increasingly heavy satchel before repeating and repeating and repeating. After half an hour of picking I was happy to be called to the car by Koranbeg, my Uzbek dad, and said goodbye to Malika and her classmates. Later, when I washed my hands, they stung, and I realised that the tiny guard-hairs around each boll had been scratching me each time.

Zealaddin was aged sixteen, having already spent three autumns in the cotton fields, when the government capitulated and stopped taking schoolchildren to the fields. 'We were the last class of my age to pick cotton. I think that's significant,' he told me, now a young man and a father.

Surprisingly, the biggest defender I know of Uzbekistan's policies to send children to the cotton fields is my old friend Jane, a tough-as-nails English teacher from Guildford who accompanied her pupils to the fields every September for six years during the 1990s. We first met at her incredible home in the old Jewish quarter of Bukhara. She and her partner had purchased the house for just a thousand dollars or so, from an emigrating Jewish family in the early 1990s who had taken little other than the mezuzahs that had been attached in each doorway.

A vine snaked up one corner of the courtyard, shading a traditional seating platform with sun-bleached bolsters and mattresses around a food-cloth. To the right was the main guest room with beautiful carved wooden doors, a high ceiling of carved beams, and walls of intricate plasterwork covered in verses from the Hebrew scriptures, with plaster niches for teapots and bowls.

The rest of the courtyard consisted of a doorway into a cramped kitchen, a cosy winter living room with thick walls, and a small, windowless bedroom that led off it. Outside was a rickety staircase that led to a flat roof and a small bedroom where Jane and Andrew slept. A semi-owned cat prowled. Their one concession to modernity was the addition of a sit-down flushable toilet under the outside staircase, and a shower.

Jane greeted me with a wild nimbus of curly hennaed hair, wearing a dress and baggy pants of Soviet atlas silk in a riot of colour. Andrew, brown as a nut, shaved his head and wore a traditional skullcap entirely embroidered with silk cross-stitch in the Shakhrisabz style. Later, when he took me for my first visit to the 15th-century hammam, I noticed that he had the same stark skullcap tan-line as all the other older men.

'Oh, don't tell me you think we've gone native, too,' said Jane witheringly, as she invited me in and busied herself laying out rounds of fresh bread, bowls of homemade jam, fresh cream and the ubiquitous cotton-flower teapots and tea bowls. Jane, I discovered, did withering particularly well, especially when talking about foreign volunteers and their expectations of luxury. 'Why should the community respect you if you come here, spend the first six months just renovating your house into a palace and then start telling them how they should live?'

The fact that I lived with a local family met with her approval, and she was even willing to overlook my vegetarianism. I asked them more about their life in Bukhara and sat, jaw sagging open as Jane breezily recounted her experience with some of the local water-borne organisms. I already knew about the famous *risht,* a type of guinea-worm that was endemic to the region until the Soviets introduced a sanitation system. The male was relatively harmless, but the female could grow inside you up to a metre in length.

'With me, something happened to my major organs ... starting with kidneys and then moving to the lungs and heart. I started swelling up like a Michelin man, my heart failed and I developed a clot on my lungs. My body turned against itself and started to close down,' Jane explained. 'I was connected to all these tubes and breathing apparatus and they called Andrew in a couple of times to say goodbye to me. That's when I went insane.'

'What?' I asked, setting my drinking bowl aside.

'I don't know if it was the medication, but I lost my mind. I'd tell Andrew that everyone in the hospital was trying to kill me and he had to send my uncle in a helicopter to rescue me.'

'Or she thought the hospital was bugged, so she kept writing notes to me,' Andrew added, 'but she'd write on the same line over and over again and it was impossible to read. Oh, and she wanted to know why everyone in the ward had been given free Uzbek-air videos, and where were hers?'

'Eventually, they found a doctor who knew tropical medicine and he recognised that I had a rheumatic fever and got me on the right treatment and I recovered.'

'And you still came back here?' I asked, incredulous.

Jane shrugged. 'We all have to die at some point and I'd rather die out here doing something useful than getting run over by a bus in Guildford.'

I share this story because it helps give background to the conversation I had with Jane about this book and her own experiences cotton-picking. We've stayed in touch all these years and we're both passionate and obstinate, so our definition of an animated discussion is what Andrew refers to as a row.

'Of course I went with my students to the cotton fields. Why should I have had special treatment for being a foreigner?' she demanded. 'And now there's all this handwringing and international boycotts of Central Asian cotton. It's such a typically Western mentality.'

'What, so you think it was okay for the state to bus children off to some flyblown village, have them all sleep in a barn or a classroom and then toil the fields from dawn to dusk, with no washing facilities, and nothing to eat but stale bread and greasy macaroni three times a day? How is that not exploitation? My host sister didn't make her quota, so not only was she paid nothing, but her dad had to pay the school for the privilege of her spending two months toiling in the fields.'

'Yes, but it was only the soft city kids who complained. Most of my class were from the villages anyway and they were used to sleeping in one room with all their family. At least with the cotton drive they got a camp bed and didn't just sleep on the floor. And as for washing facilities, most of them didn't wash for months at a time. They put me up with a woman who lived next to the barn where my students were sleeping, and I was desperate for a shower after my first day in the fields. There was nowhere, so I tried a makeshift bucket bath in her pit-latrine. My hostess complained because I'd splashed water onto their bucket of mudbricks which they used for wiping. She told me to go to the village hammam which was open on certain days of the week.'

'How is that not exploitation, to expect kids to work in those conditions and with no choice in the matter?'

Jane gave a loud, exasperated sigh. 'Because they knew it wasn't all about them. Listen, the Soviet Union had collapsed and the whole command economy with it. Uzbekistan was struggling not to become a failed state before it had barely begun. Their one export crop was cotton, and everyone was expected to pitch in to pick it. How's that exploitation? It's just the responsibility of being a citizen.'

'Yeah, but it wasn't the country that benefitted from this free labour, it was corrupt politicians who were making their fortunes.'

'So, you deal with government corruption. You don't have to boycott cotton.'

'But that's how you deal with corruption. Who else will those politicians listen to?'

Jane was not to be persuaded. 'There was such a sense of camaraderie. The parents dropped their kids off with big bundles of fruit and nuts, so they weren't just eating greasy macaroni. And anyway, that's what most of them would have had at home. It was a chance to make new friends and some of the village kids actually made a little pocket-money.'

'By picking how much?'

'The really fast ones could harvest 100 kilos or more a day. My record was 50 kilos in one day, which was considered very good for a teacher. Students would hide stones in their bags, but they always got found during the weigh in. Then in the evenings someone would play a dutar or beat a tambour, and everyone would join in and sing or dance. They were wonderful times.'

'Are you sure you're not just remembering the best bits? What about the actual back-breaking labour?'

'My hands would crack and bleed, and all the outer skin would peel off,' Jane stated matter-of-factly. 'You have to sort of zero in on the cotton boll with your fingers,' she made a five-fingers pincer movement. 'But that means brushing against the guard bristles, and when you do this thousands of times a day, it really starts to affect your skin.'

'Sounds utopian! And that's just your skin. My friends Joel and Claire were working at Kokand University and were sent to the fields with their students. Joel got into a row with their overseer because they were made to work in the heat of the day, with no drinking water. The overseer just pointed at the ditch and told him to drink from there.'

'What's wrong with that?' Jane demanded. 'These soft little foreigners coming out wanting bottled mineral water! I drank from the ditch, just like everyone else, and I'm still alive.'

'Yeah, but you almost weren't,' I pointed out.

'Yes, but the locals are hardy. They're used to drinking ditch water and living in those conditions. It was only the city kids who bribed doctors to write health-exemption notes.'

There was clearly no changing Jane's mind, nor matching her gruelling six harvests, but for this book, I thought I should spend more than half an hour cotton-picking. I'd loosely arranged to join cotton pickers in one of the Uzbek-speaking villages near Osh, but then found myself planning sunscreen, sunglasses and a cap, making sure I had a really large water bottle and podcasts to listen to on my phone. It was beginning to look distastefully like poverty tourism, as I'd never have a truly authentic experience of what it's like to pick cotton unless I had no choice in the matter, whether through local government coercion or simple poverty and a need to put food on the table.

You don't choose to be out in the fields stooped over cotton bushes, a cloth satchel dragging from one shoulder, the glare of the sun in your eyes, the pressure not to slow down, and the damage being done to your fingers – you do it because you have to. Because no one gets rich from picking cotton. Wages are low for the workers who pick and who manufacture cotton because T-shirts need to remain cheap and virtually disposable. As a result, most Westerners now own far more clothes than they need or use, and the textile industry accounts for a tenth of global carbon emissions and a fifth of global wastewater. This pressure to keep textiles cheap means that their true cost is often hidden. And this same pressure to cut corners even affects beautiful, handmade textiles, as I was to discover …

17. EMBROIDERING THE TRUTH

It's May 2022, and white mulberry trees are in fruit in Uzbekistan. Where the soft fruits have fallen onto hard pavements they leave sticky blackened patches, thick with flies. The air is filled with the intoxicating scent of *jigar* blossom. The flowers are tiny and yellow, contrasting with the pale green leaves, and locals claim that if you sit underneath a *jigar* tree in bloom, it'll make you horny, and if you fall asleep under one, you'll turn crazy.

I'm in the front seat of a shared taxi with a family of four crammed in the back. We leave the industrial city of Navoi behind us and head towards scrub-covered hills, passing a shepherd boy with his flock of fat-bottomed Karakul sheep that wobble along. It's been an unusually wet spring and the steppes are studded with wild irises and poppies. In the hills, we pass a flock of goats wagging their small tails like puppies, and local families picnicking among a detritus of plastic waste left by previous visitors. We pass a life-size cardboard cut-out of a camel. I assume this is an attempt at decoration similar to the statues of camel caravans that have proliferated in Uzbekistan's tourist cities, but when we pass a carboard cow, a cardboard sheep and then six or seven actual camels ambling across the road, I realise that these are animal-crossing road signs.

The jagged peaks of the Nuratau mountain range are ahead of us, but before that lies our destination, the oasis town of Nurata. The family in the back have come to visit on pilgrimage and want to be dropped off at the holy spring.

I ask the father what benefits he hopes this pilgrimage will bring.

He shrugs. 'It's a day out and a chance to visit somewhere different,' he replies, unspiritually.

We're dropped off at the spring complex, which has been deemed worthy of Uzbek municipal treatment and now features a shadeless park full of browning conifers that seem an unwise planting decision for a desert oasis. Through an archway is a mosque, and beside it is the holy spring that provides Nurata with most of its water. Spring water bubbles up into a large pool which is a deep shade of turquoise. Scaleless fish – often quite large – dart beneath it, considered holy and never fished or eaten.

A large channel from the main spring passes an old hammam where pilgrims and locals can bathe in the water. Visitors fill ten-litre bottles of spring water to take home with them, along with some locals, who depend on the spring as their main water source. Most houses are rationed to two hours of water a day. After all, the browning conifers needs to be irrigated.

Behind the complex is a hill topped with the impressive ruins of a fortress built by Alexander the Great. The bricks can still clearly be seen, and there are a few mouldering towers and outcrops. This has long been a place of local pilgrimage. However, as Uzbeks and Tajiks learn more about Sunni Islam, this shrine-visiting and the veneration of Muslim saints is questioned as suspiciously Shia-like. And as for the tradition of tying votive rags on the shrubs and bushes around the fortress ruin, this is a Buddhist practice that is now forbidden in most urban pilgrimage sites according to lists of prohibitions displayed in Uzbek and English. Praying to saints at their tombs or leaving money on the tombs has also been outlawed, although both still occur regularly.

For the pilgrim unsure if a spring and fortress count as properly Muslim sites of pilgrimage, you can always salve your conscience with Islamic tat, available from the numerous stalls along the way. Plastic prayer-beads are popular, particularly the green glow-in-the-dark ones. There are Mecca compasses, brass plates with Islamic suras written on them, shiny plastic gold rear-view mirror decorations, usually with 'Bismillah' written in Arabic. There are bracelets of small black-and-white evil-eye beads, as well as the imported blue Turkish ones, and amuletic chillies to keep the evil eye at bay. Black leather triangles with talismans in them hang beside gimmicky plastic keychains. There's a brisk trade in pious perfume that is oil-based rather than alcohol-based. I've found similar stalls before with Mecca snow globes. For kids, there are scrunchies, Rubik's Cubes, novelty magnets, hair bands, Barbie dolls, pens, handbags and disposable plastic toys.

None of this surprises me. What does is that not one single stall is selling *suzanis*. After all, Nurata, along with the village of Shofirkhon – an hour from Bukhara – are the main source of all *suzanis* currently embroidered in Bukhara, Samarkand and Tashkent today. And *suzanis* are the reason that I've come here.

The word *suzani* comes from the Persian for needle and refers to dowry embroideries produced among the patchwork of Uzbeks and Tajiks living in the Fergana Valley, Western Tajikistan and Southern Uzbekistan. The oldest-preserved *suzanis* date from the mid-19th century, and they steeply declined in quality under Soviet rule. *Suzanis* produced during this relatively short period before the Soviets have become highly collectible, and well-preserved examples from the 19th century sell for four-figure sums at auction.

They were originally produced by families with enough means to keep the female members in seclusion. When a girl was born, her mother would begin work on her dowry embroideries, eventually joined by her daughter, and usually employing the help of other female relatives. The dowry would include larger *suzanis* for wall-hangings – considered indispensable decorations. Wedding sheets were another essential, embroidered around the sides with the central part left white and unadorned to be hung up publicly after the wedding night to display the virginal blood spilt. *Namaz* prayer *suzanis* were sometimes included, with an arch to point towards Mecca. Then there were smaller *suzanis* for wrapping around fresh bread, or holding a mirror, or covering cradles.

Why lavish such incredible embroidery on these largely utilitarian items? There were three main reasons. First, particularly in older surviving pieces, there is an incredible amount of talismanic embroidery and these were produced to offer magical protection. The second reason was to impress – *suzanis* certainly managed that. They were supposed to demonstrate the beauty and skill of a bride who would not be seen by her future husband until the wedding night. Given that they were a communal effort and that wealthy families often purchased particularly beautiful *suzanis*, this wasn't very accurate. The third was that *suzanis* had a high resale value as there were always families who hadn't prepared long enough in advance for a wedding and would happily pay for a completed *suzani*. There was also growing demand for *suzanis* from abroad, making them investments that could be sold if times were tough.

The embroidery was done with silk threads – sometimes produced from silkworms tended by the embroiderers themselves. The background was usually plain white cotton, white symbolising happiness and purity. As for the silks, initially they were dyed exclusively with natural dyes, including imported cochineal and indigo. However, by the 1880s, chemical dyes had made an appearance. There was plenty of colour clashing but somehow it worked.

A larger *suzani* was so intricately embroidered that it would take two to three years of full-time embroidering to complete. As a result, the work was usually parcelled out. Firstly, several strips of white cotton or linen would be roughly sewn together, and then either the maternal grandmother or a professional artist would draw out the design on the cloth. Once completed, the individual cotton strips were separated again and then distributed to various aunts and cousins. Occasionally relatives would be paid, but more often, everyone remembered who owed whom and could then call in to help when their own daughters needed additional embroiderers.

Different women embroidered with different tensions, which meant that when the strips were re-sewn, there was often a mismatch in the join. Nor did every woman remember the agreed-upon colour scheme, which led to further disparities between strips, and no one would complete their strip in its entirety, as completion meant that the embroiderer was finished and could now die.

The result was a curious blend of exquisite skill and slapdashery. Three or four main stitches were used. These was a couching stitch, now referred to in English as Bukharan couching, which created blankets of colour. An alternative to filling in large spaces was a very fine chain-stitch, achieved using the tambor method of a stretched frame and a tiny handheld hook. Then there were border-stitches which often surrounded vegetal motifs.

Because the *suzani* designs were hand-drawn, freestyle, no two were ever the same. Typically, a design consisted of a frame and then a central field, a little like a carpet. The primary motifs were floral, but not all was as it appeared.

The 1930s saw a rapid decline in the quality of *suzanis*, as working from home was outlawed in a Soviet drive to emancipate women and collectivise and industrialise Central Asia. Olga Sukhareva, a textile historian in the 1930s, was able to interview this last generation of great master embroiderers and *suzani* designers, gaining unique insights into their work. She discovered that, while most women were illiterate, designers rarely forgot a pattern they'd drawn, even if it had been for a client many years previously. These women taught Olga how to read a *suzani*.

To the uninitiated, the designs looked largely floral. But that was often just camouflage. Olga learnt that what she had thought were long, narrow leaves with an upwards curl at the end were symbolic knives to pierce the evil eye, and was even told by her host, as she stepped out into the night, to whisper the words 'kitchen knife' under her breath while walking home in the dark, to keep her protected. Other kitchen items to receive floral treatment included the pad used for slapping flat rounds of dough into a tandoor oven, and the perforated metal skimmers used for stirring cauldrons.

Chili motifs proliferated, as did almond leaves, as mountain almonds were considered bitter enough to keep the evil eye at bay. Pomegranates symbolised fertility; willows, known for their medicinal properties, were symbolised by their leaves which promoted healing. Those considered afflicted by the evil eye were often beaten with willow boughs in leaf, as they were thought to be powerful enough to drive out the malignant spirit. Lamps represented fire, which was still considered holy – a legacy of Zoroastrianism. Sometimes camouflaged amid embroidered foliage were animals. What at first glance might appear to be a leaf was in fact a bird or a fish, or even a tortoise or scorpion.

By the early 20th century, samovars, trains and teapots featured in abstract floral ways. Nurata was known for beautiful framed *suzanis* with open space in the central field where four or five bundles of different flowers were embroidered. Unique to Nurata were large lozenge medallion *suzanis*, consisting of solid embroidery radiating out from the centre and containing repeated motifs of teapots and ewers, perhaps because water was so highly valued in this desert oasis with its sacred spring.

Due to the spiritual nature of *suzani* creation, only the chosen few were permitted to become professional designers. Designers passed their skills down the female line, but if a daughter showed little interest or skill, then another female relative or neighbour might be apprenticed instead. Either way, to graduate from being an apprentice required a ritual meal which could only be prepared when the master felt her apprentice was ready. She would cook the food herself, and during the meal she would pray blessing over her apprentice, in a graduation ceremony of sorts.

Occasionally, if a master embroiderer died unexpectedly, the ritual feast would be cooked by the apprentice, and she would invite other designers who would posthumously invoke the master's blessing. Deceased masters were said to appear in their apprentice's dreams, instructing them and suggesting new patterns. Impatient apprentices who refused to wait for their master's eventual blessing would usually meet untimely ends, and such tales were often repeated to keep young women in their place. After a master had died, her successors were expected to use their profits to prepare feasts held in her honour, and receive blessing from beyond the grave.

I never thought much about embroidery before moving to Central Asia, finding it fussy and part of a stuffy aesthetic that felt dated. So, I was as surprised as anyone at how enamoured I was by pre-Revolutionary *suzanis*, not just because of their skill, but because they had a tribal kind of energy and dynamism that I'd never seen in embroidery before. Should I confess that I blew the advance I got on this book on an early 20th-century *suzani*, which I think is either from Nurata or Shakhrisabz? It was a bargain, and I keep telling myself that I can always sell it on for a profit. It's large and would make a spectacular bedspread, but I don't want the cat shedding on it. I still don't know it well, but keep discovering new elements about it. Two tiny evil-eye beads have been sewn on to it in different places, and parts have been left incomplete. A whole panel has been done in the 'wrong' colours, with the large rosettes in brown rather than plum and crimson. It's unmistakeably unique.

Given the almost exclusive use of silk for embroidering *suzanis* up until the Soviet times, I'd initially planned for this chapter to appear under the silk section. However, as I discovered in Nurata, cotton is the only consistent material in a world where pressurised embroiderers try to cut corners.

I climb Alexander's fort and admire the view from the top. Having found no *suzani* at this place of pilgrimage, I then leave the spring behind me and go wandering into the neighbourhoods, asking passers-by where I can find embroiderers. It's a small town and every-one knows everyone else. Soon enough, I'm knocking on the gate of a compound, answered by a young woman who leads me into a spacious courtyard of fruit trees and chickens to her mother-in-law, who sits in a simple room with an earth-packed floor covered by a grubby *kilim*, embroidering.

Her name is Shodmongol and she's 63 years old. She's Tajik, as are most people in Nurata, but speaks Uzbek fluently. Once she's got over her initial disappointment that I'm not a potential client, she hears that I'm researching *suzanis* and starts to warm to me, telling me her story. It's one I hear variations of from other older women in Nurata. During Soviet times she worked in a state shop. By then women were allowed to embroider *suzanis*, but as hobbyists and not for commercial gain. Shodmongol was able to procure dyed silk threads and cotton and would embroider *suzanis* in the evenings. Then one day, she visited the Registan in Samarkand and saw *suzanis* for sale and watched as the few groups of heavily shepherded foreign tourists who had come with the Soviet Intourist company paid for *suzanis* in hard currency. After they had left, she spoke to one of the sellers and returned a few weeks later with several com-pleted *suzanis*. Such trade was considered black market profiteering, but in the twilight years of the Soviet Union with the advent of perestroika, most officials turned a blind eye to such petty trading.

This illegal sideline enabled Shodmongol to afford the occa-sional luxury. Then, when the Soviet Union collapsed and the state shop closed, she panicked, wondering how she would feed her chil-dren. Then she remembered her *suzanis*. As more tourists visited independent Uzbekistan, demand for them grew and she took on apprentices and now employs 40 or so village girls to help her. A freelance designer in her neighbourhood draws up the designs for her, and she receives orders with photos of the required designs via messaging apps such as Telegram or WhatsApp, from sellers in Samarkand or Bukhara.

'What materials do you use?' I ask, prepared for the swift glance of a seller sizing up what she thinks you want to hear. Instead, she gives me the truth.

'Viscose,' she states. 'Occasionally silk, but it's so much more expensive, so we only use silk if there's a specific order willing to pay more. It's the same with all the other *suzani* businesses. We all use viscose.'

'Even on these nicer *suzanis* with *adras* as a backing cloth?'

She shrugs and nods. 'We barely make any profit as it is, with the sellers constantly squeezing us. They don't care what material we use, as tourists will believe anything.'

'Now there's a problem with viscose,' her daughter-in-law adds, carrying in a stack of dirty cups and plates. 'Something about the war.'

I frown. 'Does your viscose come from Ukraine?' I ask. 'I would have thought it was produced in China.'

'It is,' Shodmongol explains. 'But Ukraine buys it and does something to it, maybe they spin it into the right sized thread? I don't know. I just know that since the war in Ukraine, they can't get shipments of it and that's made it harder to find.'

Her daughter-in-law also embroiders, but favours the tambor and hook over a needle. She shows me her tambor, a metal frame on legs, which keeps the fabric taut. The tiny hook then goes up and down through the fabric, creating exquisitely fine chain-stitch. 'I like it because it's easier to work with a hook when you're watching TV in the evenings,' she explains with a tired smile.

'Why don't you sell any *suzanis* here in Nurata?' I ask. 'I just came from the spring and they had stalls selling everything else but not the one thing Nurata should be most proud of.'

Shodmongol shakes her head in dismay. 'Don't,' she says with a wave of her hand. 'Didn't you see the row of empty shops with carved wooden pillars fronting them? Whenever there's an important delegation, we're all rounded up and forced to set up stalls there. The delegates never buy anything, though. It's a complete waste of our time, and local people aren't interested in *suzanis*. It's just the tourists.'

I knew that some of the cheaper *suzanis* were made with viscose. It has a different sheen to it, and a slightly plastic look, but

I hadn't realised that even the higher-end *suzanis* with silk/cotton backing were viscose as well.

In the next workshop I visited, Shahodat, also in her sixties, gives me a skein of silk threads and another of viscose to feel. There's a difference, although I have to concede that the finished viscose embroideries still look great. Shahodat employs a hundred women who all work from home in the evenings in the more remote desert villages. Her export business is thriving. My eye wanders to stacks of square cloth, each embroidered with a grid of twelve symbols and underneath, in English, the embroidered names of the tribes of Israel.

'We had an order for 5,000 pieces, all the same, from Israel. Something religious, I don't know more than that.' I tell her that each of the emblems represents one of the tribes of Israel and she shows mild interest. Next to them are racks of long flowing cotton gowns with *suzani* embroidery down the sides. 'They're for Arabistan,' she explains.

'Which part?' I ask.

'Qatar?' she says, uncertain that it's a real place, but I nod. She also has orders from Turkey, Romania and New Zealand. Her daughter sells their *suzanis* online through Etsy. As well as wall-hanging *suzanis*, they make handbags, cushion covers and gowns. 'The gowns are really popular now and I get lots of orders from Bukharan souvenir stalls for them, but the problem with Bukharans is that they're always trying to pay less for our products, so I make more money with export orders. Do you have any clients for me?' She's not one to miss an opportunity.

'Who does all your designs?' I ask.

'My son,' she replies.

I raise an eyebrow. 'I thought the designers were always women.'

'Who says they have to be?' she asks testily, as if she's answered this question a few too many times before. She then offers to take me to his house to meet him.

Shirali is in his thirties, sporting a religious beard, and his wife wears hijab rather than the traditional gypsy-style scarf. He's been working on designs since he was a child, and doesn't care if people think it's women's work.

'The designs come to me in dreams. I'll dream them and then wake up and grab a pencil and immediately sketch them out on paper so I don't forget.' He likes working on black backgrounds of cotton or polyester, using a pen full of white correction fluid to draw the designs with.

I remember watching a *suzani* designer at work in Shofirkhon, who drew directly onto sheets of silk/cotton *adras* with a ballpoint pen.

'But what happens if you make a mistake?' I'd asked.

With an eyebrow arched in scorn she replied slowly, 'I don't make mistakes,' and I was silenced. Typically, designers use rulers for drawing out the thick outer frames that give *suzanis* their carpet-like look, and then tea bowls or soup bowls for drawing circles of varying sizes which then become petalled and variegated. Shirali favours a CD for his circles. He has a steady hand and within minutes he conjures floral wonders where before there had been just a dark void of cloth.

'And what about you?' he asks. 'You speak Uzbek. Are you Muslim?'

I tell him I'm not, and he then asks if I've watched Dr Zakir on YouTube, as he speaks English and will soon convert me to the true path of Islam. I smile politely.

By the time I leave Nurata, I'm not as heavily laden as I thought I'd be. Now that I know that these beautiful *suzanis* are nearly all made with viscose, I think about all those tourists happily handing over large amounts of money for something they've been sold as silk but is actually not. If sellers were honest about the viscose, maybe I'd feel differently, but actually what is being sold is a fake.

It also means that those who are genuinely selling silk *suzanis* will lose out, unable to compete with their cheaper rivals. I experience something similar a few months later while trekking in Nepal.

Leech-bitten and sunburnt, I spend my last day in Pokhara shopping for souvenirs. Many of the shops are run by Kashmiris, but most supposed cashmere is blended with viscose or acrylic. Having watched a YouTube video on the different residues left by burning wool, silk, viscose or acrylic, I flourish a cigarette lighter and the chastened seller then shows me his selection of actual cashmere, which is always four or five times more expensive.

In Uzbekistan, the old quarter of Bukhara is now one enormous boutique shopping centre. However, other than the Islamic miniatures – which are arguably the best in the world – most products are not made locally or even in Uzbekistan. There are still two smithies where you used to be able to buy beautiful hand-worked knives and stork-shaped scissors, but now most of the scissors come straight from a factory in China. Some enterprising Bukharan has visited Kashmir with Central Asian *suzani* designs and commissioned embroideries from there which are now passed off as locally made, although they look quite different, employing a totally different style of stitching. You can buy Aladdin-style lamps that have come from either China or India, and a profusion of cheap Indian scarves that sell for the same price you'd pay from a British market stall. Of course, ask the sellers and everything is made locally, probably by their grandmother. It's always antique, naturally dyed and pure silk or baby camel wool.

The most successful scammer is Sabina, who started selling ceramics on the street beside the Friday Mosque and from a young age learnt to haggle and flirt in several languages. Now she runs a huge emporium full of carpets from India, Afghanistan, Pakistan and China. She offers a generous cut to local guides from each sale, as their clients are plied with green tea, raisins and bullshit. 'All of the carpets you see here are made in our workshop,' she explains with wide-eyed innocence, 'which is just one hour outside of Bukhara.'

Conveniently inconvenient to visit. There's a loom in a corner with a girl working at it. One glance will show you that her carpet looks nothing like the others for sale, which also look nothing like each other. Still, most tourists are trusting and those who do buy carpets usually end up paying far more than they would for the same carpet in their own country. Apparently, Sabina recently got done for selling a huge $30,000 carpet which she told her clients was pure silk. They had it examined by a specialist back home and it turned out to be viscose, so they made an official complaint and opened a legal case against her. I confess that this news pleased me.

Tourist demand for beautiful textiles is both a blessing and a curse. In Bukhara during the early 1990s, souvenir sellers realised that their finite stock of older *suzanis* was rapidly dwindling. Tourists preferred the natural colours of older pieces, so they went back to villages such as Shofirkhon and asked around for the old women who could still remember how to use a hook or needle. International organisations such as UNESCO as well as smaller-scale NGOs began reviving felt-making, carpet-weaving, atlas silk produced with 19th-century designs, and so on. It was UNESCO who funded the silk carpet workshop I started. I sit there with Madrim, who runs it now, and tell him about my experiences in Nurata. He listens with growing frustration.

'Tourists are always complaining that our *suzani* cushion covers are too expensive, and that they found cheaper silk ones in Bukhara. But if they're all just viscose, how are we meant to compete?'

'We need to get hold of some viscose and let people feel the difference between a skein of that and a skein of silk. We can also teach them how to burn a few strands and smell the difference.'

Fakes are not the only issue tourism is creating for the workshop.

Madrim asks: 'Aslan, do you remember those big old women who would stride into the workshop and demand that you employ their granddaughters?' We both chuckle. 'Well now, we have no waiting lists and we're struggling to recruit new embroiderers and weavers. It's the women in Khiva. They've become spoilt. No one wants to work hard anymore. Why sit at a loom for eight hours when you can run a souvenir stall or scroll on your phone at a hotel reception desk?'

Madrim is interested to hear how most of Nurata's *suzanis* are embroidered by women out in villages. His wife, Mehribon, has done the same and is now training village women far from the prosperity that tourism has brought Khiva. Those women who show talent are given cotton squares, and silk threads are weighed out for them to transform into embroidered cushion covers.

'Village women work harder. Everyone knows it,' Madrim declares. 'The wives of my friends who have sons of marriageable age are all looking for village girls as prospective wives because they'll work hard and don't have the cheek and the airs of girls from Khiva.'

While tourism has arguably revived much of the handicraft heritage lost during the Soviet era, there is also a growing distance and disconnect between where a product is made and where it is sold. Even in the 1890s, Annette Meakin observed that the quality of *suzanis* made commercially rather than for dowries was much lower, and the same thing happened with Turkmen woollen carpets. I wonder if Khiva or Bukhara will become like the Grand Bazaar in Istanbul, or the Souks of Cairo, or even the streets of London, where most of what is sold comes from elsewhere. Tat in a London souvenir shop will usually be made in China.

Have we irreparably entered the age of viscose?

As we near the end of the Cotton Road, there are signs of hope. Bangladesh is trying to revive Dhaka muslin, and India is largely manufacturing its own cotton cloth now, exporting beautiful handwoven cotton textiles globally. The end of colonialism spelt the end of Britain's cotton manufacturing industry, and now the brick mills of Northern England which once housed so much misery are smart offices or spacious flats. International pressure and boycotts on cotton products from China and Turkmenistan remain in force. Even Uzbekistan, once the heart of Soviet cotton-production, is slowly weaning itself off such heavy cotton-dependency. Cotton fields are being ploughed up and orchards replanted. Maybe one day the famed golden peaches of Samarkand will once more be available for export.

However, cotton clothing continues to be far cheaper for consumers than is fair for either the pickers or the environment.

LOOSE ENDS

Writing my first book, *A Carpet Ride to Khiva*, was a kind of therapy. Having lived there for years and made it my home, I'd left Khiva for three weeks and then wasn't allowed back in. I was devastated and heartbroken and unable to simply pick up the threads of my life. I felt guilty for having abandoned Madrim to run the two workshops, and I didn't know if I'd see him again, or my wonderful Uzbek family. There'd been no proper goodbyes; no time to savour my last few days in Khiva, or the breath-taking dawn view from the flat roof of my house, where I slept in summer, minarets and madrassahs gleaming gold in the rising sun. So, I relished these moments on paper instead, and found somewhere to put all the love and grief that I felt towards Khiva and the people who'd been a community for me.

It was in the wake of the Andijan massacre of 2005 that all Westerners working for international development organisations were gradually expelled and blacklisted. I thought this was a permanent state of affairs, but six years later we started hearing rumours that our blacklisting was just for five years, and some previously expelled people got back in on tourist visas. By then I had moved to Kyrgyzstan and was preparing to start a woodcarving workshop in Arslanbob. My partner in the project was Andreas, one of the best violin-makers in Germany – if not the world – who had taken early retirement to come and share his knowledge and skill. I wanted him to see examples of woodcarving workshops using traditional designs, but all the ones I knew of were in Uzbekistan. We decided to apply for tourist visas and to attempt a land border crossing near Osh. Usually I'm willing to give things a go, but I still felt scarred by my expulsion from Uzbekistan and didn't want to experience that again.

So, I cocooned myself in scepticism, not packing properly or bringing enough money, and planning to go hiking with some Swiss friends after a short trip to the border and then back to Osh again. I could hardly believe it when – after just a one-hour interrogation – I emerged on the other side of the border, back in Uzbekistan again.

Returning to Khiva after seven years was surprisingly cathartic. There were joyous reunions and exclamations of how beautifully fat I'd become – a traditional compliment that I was hoping was inaccurate – and I revisited the silk carpet and *suzani* workshops and saw how they were faring. In my seven-year absence not only had I changed, but so had Khiva. Girls now wore smart knee-length skirts that would have been unthinkable before. Everyone had smart phones. I found myself regularly thinking, 'In my day ...', realising that it wasn't my day anymore, and that the place I'd selectively remembered wasn't all sunshine and roses either.

I kept quiet about any room I saw for improvement in the workshops. Madrim, who knew me too well, finished our tour with a furrowed brow. 'Why aren't you telling me what needs to change? I need your help.'

'Because you've kept the workshops going all these years. Who am I to turn up and start criticising?'

Madrim rolled his eyes in frustration, and I realised that I had made a mental list which I then shared.

I next visited my Uzbek family in Khiva on a farewell tour of Central Asia, as I prepared to move back to the UK. I told them that, while I could now return on tourist visas, I had no idea when that might be, as I didn't know what I was going to do in terms of work, and although my CV was very colourful, I wasn't sure how employable I'd be.

'But Aslan, why don't you just become a tour leader?' said Zulhamar. 'You speak English and Uzbek, you know the history better than we do, and you've written a book.'

It was a good idea, and soon I led my first tour back to the region. I then returned every year, at least once, until the Covid pandemic, which meant I didn't visit for almost three years, the longest I'd been away from Central Asia since I first visited in 1996. So, in May of 2022, I was excited to connect with my Uzbek family, close friends and the workshop again, not least because my visit coincided with a very special occasion.

I wake up in Meros B&B, my host family's house beside the harem in the walled inner city of Khiva. I'm not in my old bedroom, though. Other tourists are staying there and I've been put in the downstairs room which isn't as popular. I hear the sounds of tourists eating breakfast in the cavernous dining room outside my bedroom door and smile as I remember the frustration I felt, trying to persuade my Uzbek family to turn their two spare rooms into a small bed & breakfast. Eventually they started to realise how lucrative this could be, and now they've extended the house and have seven guestrooms. I pass through the dining room, glancing up at the beautiful painted wooden ceiling that Koranbeg was working on when I first moved in over two decades ago. There are echoes of him everywhere and I still miss him. It feels fresh every time I return, even though it's been four years since I got the phone call from Jaloladdin, his eldest son, telling me that his father had died of a heart attack that morning while in the shower.

Now there's a new Koranbeg in the family living room. He toddles over to me when I seat myself cross-legged on a cotton-stuffed seating mattress beside the low dining table. His mother, wife of Zealaddin, Koranbeg's youngest son, gets up as I enter, returning shortly with a plate of fried eggs and potatoes. The TV is always on, but now there are around twenty channels to choose from, and most of them are commercial. Heavy-handed nationalism, which made up the bulk of TV viewing when I lived here, has been replaced by more entertaining programmes and an endless stream of adverts, largely for natural remedies of dubious efficacy. My favourite is Venofish, a strangely named cream for varicose veins.

Zulhamar walks in holding the hand of her latest granddaughter who everyone agrees is a complete nightmare.

'Bayramingiz bilan,' she says, congratulating me on the special occasion we'll be celebrating at lunchtime. Before that, I need to visit the factory for the blind in Urgench with Madrim.

This has been a mission of mine for several years. After Farkhad, our weaving master, got offered a job as vice-director of the Khiva blind school, there's been no one to weave the cotton backing for the *suzanis* and Madrim has resorted to buying factory-woven cloth from the bazaar. It's horrible and too thin, and I've complained about this situation for ages, as naturally dyed silk embroidered onto factory cotton cloth seems just as bad as chemically dyed viscose embroidered onto good-quality *adras*.

It's easy for me to nag, but Madrim has his hands full overseeing all the natural dyeing, as well as running the workshop, which is a more than full-time job. There's just one workshop now, as the rental price on the second madrassah we converted as our *suzani* workshop was too expensive to keep. There's also a lot more space in the carpet workshop as so many weavers now want to work from home.

We head together to Urgench, the regional capital, to visit the factory and see if they're still hand-weaving cotton or whether we can buy one of their metal looms so we can make our own. We barely recognise the factory, which has sold a lot of its land but is thriving under a new director. She welcomes us into her office and we soon sense that this is someone we can work with. She's quite emphatic about not selling any looms, but she'd be willing to set one up in the carpet workshop and have one of the faster blind weavers from Khiva work there.

'We'll pay their wages, though,' she says. 'Then you buy the cloth they weave from us. If you need more than one person who can weave, that's no problem. We have plenty of weavers right now.'

She takes us downstairs and we see the looms in action. Madrim runs his fingers over the warp and weft produced by one woman and shoots me an impressed look. When we visited years before, the quality had been shoddy, and we'd refused to purchase anything. Now, we agree to experiment with a few metres of cloth, and if it works well for the embroiderers, we'll hopefully start weaving cotton in the workshop again.

Flushed from our success, we arrive back at the north gates of Khiva's walled city in good spirits. We just have time to drop by my house to collect two tins of assorted chocolates that I brought from the UK, and then head to the workshop.

We're about to celebrate the workshop's twenty-year anniversary.

Madrim's daughter-in-law has been overseeing the cooking of *plov*, a greasy rice, carrot and mutton dish, which is a must for any celebration. She mouths silently to Madrim and uses her hands to indicate that we'll need another fifteen minutes.

'Why don't you just let her speak?' I ask him, wondering how they've managed for almost a decade now, living in the same house but with her not allowed to speak to her father-in-law.

'Don't,' says Madrim, rolling his eyes. 'She's very traditional. I gave her permission to speak to me after she had her first child, but she still won't. At least she talks to my wife.'

Moments like these remind me that, however much I still feel at home in Khiva, I'm different and struggle particularly with the gender disparities. We're distracted by a cackle from the doorway as Nazoqat and several other weavers make an entrance. Nazoqat is the exception to local women 'knowing their place', and always has been. Once rake-thin, she's now gained weight and heft and is on her third or fourth marriage. She remains indomitable as ever, and her latest husband seems to have meekly succumbed to the fact that she has no intention of changing. She's one of the weavers who now works from home.

The weavers and embroiderers greet each other with kisses, happy to be all together again. They lay a food-cloth in one of the madrassah cells and cover it with salads, cakes and bottles of fizzy drinks. I scan the faces and am happy to recognise some of them. Sharofat, who worked with us from the start, has now moved from weaving to embroidering, which she prefers. She even achieved brief stardom in a YouTube parkour video based on Aladdin that was filmed in Khiva and Bukhara. She had to look shocked as Aladdin tumbled out of our storage room and somersaulted over the embroiderers, chased by baddies.* Safargul, Feruza and Bakhtigul are also part of the old guard, along with a few others who joined us in the first three years under my tenure.

'Aslan, more tea?' Bakhtigul has taken on the role of hostess and hovers around everyone, adding more plates to the food-cloth. I spend most of the lunch asking after former weavers and how they're doing.

When the meal is drawing to an end, I ask if I can make a speech. I congratulate everyone, and then I point out that over the twenty years since I started the carpet workshop, most of that time, Madrim has been the one keeping everything going. I note how the new carpets being woven have a much finer knot count and that the quality remains exceptional. I finish with a plea for more women to come back and work here in the workshop itself as, although many prefer the flexible hours of domestic work, it's beginning to look almost deserted when I show my tour groups around.

Madrim then makes a speech, which isn't really his forte and is mainly about reminding the weavers not to waste so much silk

---

* https://www.youtube.com/watch?v=JPQNm2d3QIQ

when they make their knots. Still, there's polite applause as we raise our tea bowls to another twenty years.

When I got kicked out, there were over 80 people – mostly women – in the workshops. We had a waiting list of about the same number of women, as word had got out that it was a good place to work (no one had to bribe me, sleep with me or be related to me to get a job) and wages were actually paid and on time. Among the weavers there was a spike in divorce rates, as those who suffered from domestic abuse – which was commonplace – realised that they didn't have to put up with bullying mothers-in-law or black eyes from their husbands. A steady income had given them financial autonomy, power and the option to get out.

Fewer women are working at the workshop today simply because they have more employment options and can afford to be picky. Tourism has taken a massive hit over the past two years of a global pandemic, and I've discussed with Madrim the need for an online presence rather than simply selling to tourists directly. But the carpet workshop has weathered this storm, which is more than can be said for the sister project started in Bukhara by UNESCO. I'm well aware that the UNESCO name has contributed hugely to the workshop's continued existence, as it has offered serious protection from greedy mayors or others who might seek to appropriate the workshop for themselves, or milk it dry with extortion.

I look around the madrassah courtyard, which feels so familiar, and my heart swells with pride. These women and many others who have worked with us have, I hope, seen their lives improve from being here. I've seen the way new apprentices watch in mild surprise as tourist groups from all over the world gasp and gush over the carpets they're weaving and *suzanis* they're embroidering, recognising the skill and artistry that apprentices have just taken for granted. Each woman usually ends up walking with her head held a little higher after that, for they are weaving and embroidering treasures and future family heirlooms.

As I sit cross-legged at the food-cloth with a bowl of green tea in my hand, I think about all the ways in which textiles have been synonymous with exploitation in this part of the world, if not in every part. There's growing pollution as well as the ecological devastation in this water-scarce region, yet we still see the rise of fast fashion in Western countries, with more and more clothing being treated as virtually disposable. Just over a century ago, in those same Western countries, most people simply had one set of work clothes and then their Sunday best. I think about my own wardrobe, full of far more than I need. What happened to 'You who have two robes give one to those who have none'? I wonder if I wear anything that was made by a Uighur slave in China, or what the life-stories and working conditions might be for those who picked the cotton for the T-shirt, underwear and shorts that I'm wearing.

I'm glad that in our workshop we're making things that are beautiful and costly, and created to outlast the person who buys them and to be passed on to the next generation. And I'm reminded that textiles can also empower and create income and dignity and beauty, and I find myself hoping that the same fierce intelligence we've applied to the survival of our race of naked apes, who are naturally deficient in fur or fat to protect ourselves from the cold, might be used to help us improve; to clean up the messes we've made, to change our spending habits, to mend things and not simply dispose of them, and to truly value the artistry of beautiful textiles and not create a world where corners must always be cut and truth is always embroidered.

'Aslan?' Madrim asks, putting a hand on my arm.

'I'm fine. I've just got something in my eye,' I lie, and smile. Then we take a selfie together and then more photos with all the weavers and the dyers and the embroiderers. For we have been stitched together into a community, and we share the warp and weft of each other's lives.

EPILOGUE
A New Road

This was where I planned to finish the book, in the carpet workshop, celebrating our twentieth anniversary. But then a new road begins construction right under my feet, connecting my two worlds. It starts just after our workshop celebration in Khiva as people pester me about six-month visas to Britain. Everyone wants to know how to get a fruit-picking visa without paying the $3,000 bribe. They're inevitably disappointed that I know nothing about this visa scheme, so I do some research online and discover that Brexit has left British farms with no one to pick their fruit or vegetables. Farmers were banking on a large portion of labourers coming from Ukraine, but the Russian invasion has put a stop to that. So the net has hastily been cast wider and now the UK government is granting six-month seasonal visas to labourers as far afield as Indonesia and Nepal, as well as many Central Asian countries. I smile bitterly to myself at the irony of xenophobic farmers voting for Brexit and ending up with people far less like themselves than they had before.

'The best thing you can do is to talk to someone from Khiva who's already been to Angliya and find out what their experience was like before you jump into anything,' I caution anyone who asks me.

I take my own advice and track down Dilmurad, who runs a souvenir shop near the workshop and who went to the UK the previous year.

'It was awful,' he tells me. 'Like being in a gulag during the Stalin years. I paid the $3,000 bribe to this woman in Tashkent who used to work for the British Embassy. She prepared all my documents and then I bought the plane ticket. It was really expensive but worth borrowing the money as we've had so few tourists during the pandemic … I ended up going to a farm in Boston, Lincolnshire.'

'We had to pay for everything; the caravan, which was £70 a week each, and then the gas and electricity, the blankets, and as for food, they were meant to drive us once a week to a supermarket but told us to just buy from the farm shop where the prices were jacked up. But the worst thing was the Romanian, Bulgarian and Ukrainian supervisors. Most of them didn't speak much English and they certainly didn't speak Uzbek. We had to pick broccoli and spent most of the time bent double in the mud. You needed to be able to stand up and stretch your back every now and then, but if you did, then the supervisors would come over and start yelling. Seriously, it was like a prison camp. One Romanian picker got in a fight with the supervisor and they chucked him in the freezer unit to "cool off". He was sick in bed the next day. I only lasted a month and then I took my wages and fled.'

'What's your English like?' I ask, as we're speaking in Uzbek. 'Could you speak to someone and tell them what was happening?'

'There were a few English girls in the office but they didn't care and they had the same look you get from people in Moscow who just think you're a dirty immigrant and must be stupid.'

'But what about all the money you spent on the bribe and the airfare? Did you even get to see London?'

He laughs hollowly. 'I saw Heathrow airport and the farm. That's it. I lost so much money but it was better than being a slave.'

Before I leave Uzbekistan, I email the British Embassy asking if they are aware of the bribery around visas and they tell me that they are. I write back to ask what they're doing about it but get no response. The plane home has just one tour group on it and the usual smattering of wealthy Uzbeks. Every other seat is taken by village men from Uzbekistan and Tajikistan, all heading to farms around the UK. I speak to a few in the Tashkent transit lounge and am shocked at how unprepared they seem. Most have no idea how they'll get to their farm from the airport, and some haven't even checked a map to see what part of the UK they're going to.

So, at our baggage collection carousel in Heathrow, I call out loudly in Uzbek, 'Who needs help to find their farm? Who needs to change money or buy SIM cards?'

I'm soon surrounded. No one seems to know more than one or two words of English. Virtually no one has a credit or debit card. Some are in groups going to the same farm, while others are on their own, including a poor Tajik who has to get himself to a farm near Edinburgh.

'Do you realise that's in Scotland?' I ask.

He smiles and says, 'Viliam Vallace.' Most Central Asians have seen the film *Braveheart*.

'It's a long way away but I don't think we can get you a flight there as you don't have a debit card.'

I help him book an overnight bus ticket. Others plan to take a taxi for the two hours to their farm. 'This isn't Central Asia. Do you realise how much that will cost you? Over two hundred dollars.' Their eyes widen in alarm and I direct them to the bus or train stations and help them change enough money for their tickets.

An English tourist from the plane sidles up to me.

'Excuse me, are you helping the migrant workers?' she asks. I nod. 'Well, we're driving back to Devon and we've got room for three in the back seat if anyone needs a lift.'

In Arrivals, there's a representative with a clipboard from one of the four sponsoring bodies who liaise between farms in the UK and Central Asia. He's there in person because the first plane-load of Mongolians is about to arrive.

'Why is there bribery involved in Tashkent for getting these visas?' I ask him.

He shakes his head. 'We're going to stop working with Uzbekistan because of the corruption. It says clearly on all our websites that no one should pay any money to anyone else local, and if they're asked then they should report them.'

'What about the money your farmers charge for accommodation? With six workers crammed into a caravan out in the sticks, the farmer is getting more than they'd pay living together in a nice three- or four-bedroom house with an indoor bathroom.'

'No,' he assures me. 'They're not paying seventy quid a week, it's seventy quid a month.'

'That's not what my Uzbek friend told me he paid.'

'Your Uzbek friend?' he asks, as if I'd be stupid to believe anyone from Uzbekistan.

The man dismisses me and goes to help another group of arrivals. I find out later that everyone is paying between £60 and £70 a week in rent, usually sharing with five others and usually living in caravans. I hand out my phone number to anyone who might need it, telling them to call me if they get into trouble. There are two Uzbeks who are heading for farms near Cambridge and I invite them to travel with me by train, but I explain that the bus is cheaper even if it takes longer. They opt for the bus.

Over the next few days I don't hear from anyone, and feel relieved. Then Shirali, who is now on a farm in a village near Cambridge, contacts me and asks if I can help him find a different farm as this one isn't giving him enough work. I tell him that I don't think it will be easy to change farms but offer to come and visit. It's just twenty minutes by bike from my flat. I arrive to drizzle on a Sunday afternoon – their one day off each week. Shirali is chubby and smiley and leads me back to a caravan he shares with other Uzbek men and a Kyrgyz couple.

It's the first time I've seen Kyrgyz and Uzbeks living together and I wonder if there's any of the racial tension I'm used to from Southern Kyrgyzstan. Not at all. In the land of the Brits, even a Russian is a brother, as the old cultural and linguistic Soviet ties are stronger than any other alliances. We sit in the cramped living room and I'm plied with raisins and nuts – parting gifts from their relatives and neighbours back home. Shirali explains that the strawberries still haven't ripened so they're not getting the hours they were expecting, plus they have to pay for food and accommodation, and they're meant to be sending money back home.

I've managed to contact one farmer and he says that it would be difficult for a labourer to transfer farms. I pass this on and Shirali shrugs stoically. I also let him know that from what I've heard, once the strawberries ripen they'll be working really long hours, and he brightens. I tell them about charity shops and the joys of picking up a second-hand bargain, and then we go online so they can order discount cards for the big supermarket near them.

A few weeks later, I take some of them punting, which I think is what all visitors to Cambridge should experience. They sit and take pictures of the beautiful college buildings as I stand at the end of the flat-bottomed boat with a pole to push us along. I'm with a bunch of Uzbeks, but now I'm the host and they're the guests.

Almaz, a friend of mine from Arslanbob who works in tourism, emails me out of the blue, sounding desperate. He's stuck on a farm near Colchester and he's desperate to get out. He was expecting to improve his English but the only people he's met on the farm are Romanian or Bulgarian, and they have a quota system where everyone has to pick a certain amount of fruit a day. Failure to comply results in a letter of warning. After a third warning, you get the boot and have a week to vacate your caravan.

He's already seen several Kyrgyz and a Kazakh get expelled. They've disappeared into the black economy in London where they're even more likely to be exploited as they're now working illegally. I try to persuade Almaz to contact the GLAA, the Gangmaster and Labour Abuse Authority. I send him the number and email address and tell him that if he doesn't speak out then the situation will never improve and others will also continue to suffer. He maintains that if they come to inspect the farm, the supervisors will lie and make everything look nice, and the workers will all be too afraid to say anything.

I contact RFERL, a news outlet that specialises in researching stories from the former Soviet Union, with a whole news desk
devoted to Central Asia. I hear back from Farangis, a Tajik journalist, and we correspond. She wants to visit the UK to cover this
new wave of Central Asian migration and I arrange for her to visit
Shirali and the others at the farm.

We arrive to a rickety wooden picnic table and benches covered
in an assortment of items that I know well. There's a steaming plate
of *peroshki*, a popular Russian fried dumpling, in this case filled
with a nicely spiced potato filling. Soon, several dishes of *plov* will
emerge, although there's no cotton-seed oil to give it its signature
flavour and they've used a different kind of rice that isn't as good
as the Uzbek variety. Then there are some spinach pastries that I
made, and instead of the beautiful rounds of fresh Uzbek bread,
stamped with pin-hole designs, there's an uninviting stack of pla-
sticky cheap white sliced bread – an English staple. I'm given a
chipped mug of Lucozade, as they don't have glasses. On it I read,
'I'm a WAG'. My worlds collide on one table.

Farangis hears from various Central Asians how they're faring.
It's been hard working in greenhouses, particularly as Britain is
experiencing record summer temperatures, and it's usually at least
10 degrees warmer inside the greenhouses.

'I hope that whoever buys my strawberries washes them properly first,' Shirali jokes. 'It gets so hot in there that we're all dripping with sweat and the strawberries probably taste salty!'

Farangis asks if they're given work clothes, but they aren't. 'All
I can say is that it's a lot better than Russia,' says one older man
from Andijon. 'Here, the police don't go after us just because we're
brown and have beards. Yes, we have to pay for national insur-
ance, and gas, and accommodation, and all our food, but it's still
more than I was earning in Russia and at least they don't cheat us
out of our wages, which used to happen to me.'

Shirali takes a plastic tube from his pocket and shakes some of
its contents onto the palm of his hand.

'Where did you get *nuss* here?' I ask him, as he tips a palm's-
worth of a dark green tobacco-like powder into the space

between his bottom lip and lower gums, which makes his speech slurred.

'I got it from one of the more recent arrivals. We're setting up chatgroups and we can order what we need for the new people to bring out with them. Next week we'll have some proper Uzbek bread,' he sighs, and his round face crinkles in a satisfied smile.

He also knows people who've ditched their farms and are now working illegally in London. I warn him against this as he'll be even more vulnerable to exploitation. 'When my visa runs out and I go home, I'm going to spend the winter learning English. That's the hardest thing for us. We can't communicate with anyone. Then, when I come back next year it'll be easier for me, and now I know the system I know I don't have to bribe anyone to get my visa.'

A young guy from Margilan speaks some English. 'Have you thought about requesting to be made a supervisor?' I ask him. 'They need people who can speak Russian and a Central Asian language. The salary is probably better, too, although make sure you're a nice supervisor and not like some of the ones I've heard about.'

Bit by bit, brick by brick I'm watching this new road, or perhaps bridge, take shape. For the first time in such significant numbers, ordinary Central Asians are stepping outside the orbit of the former Russian Empire and forging this new path for themselves. It isn't easy, but they're resilient.

'Next time I'll bring my wife, too. She'll work even harder than me. My mother can look after the kids. Who knows how long we'll have this opportunity for?' says another.

This new road is just a small branch of the Migrant Road, a web that criss-crosses the globe, spanning all continents. Like the other branches, this road between Britain and Central Asia is ever-changing, offering the same dreams and dangers, opportunities and obstacles, as the textile roads that have preceded it.

I wonder how it will develop, but the future is unknown.

GLOSSARY

Appliqué In textiles this is the stitching of fabric onto more fabric to create a pattern or design.

Aul A settlement of nomadic felt houses.

'Bayramingiz bilan' The equivalent to 'Happy Holidays'.

Beshik A Central Asian cradle into which swaddled babies are strapped.

Borsok deep-friend diamond-shaped pieces of dough popular amongst both sedentary and nomadic people throughout Central Asia.

Caravanserai A courtyard large enough to accommodate a caravan of camels surrounded by a ground floor of shops or storage facilities and an upper floor for hospitality.

Chuval A type of large Turkmen storage bag hung on the lattice walls of a yurt and typically containing clothing.

Field and frame Both carpet terms, the field refers to the main design within the central rectangle of a carpet, and the frame is the border of the design that frames it.

Flatweave A term used for heavier textiles that do not include knotted pile.

Flywheel A mechanism to increase movement momentum while providing stability in machinery.

Gul Flower, both literally and as an abstract floral motif in textiles.

Hammam A steam bath-house, usually communal and gender seg-regated.

Hank A coiled unit of yarn, like a skein.

Haram Something that is against Islamic practice.

Hujum An Uzbek term meaning 'attack' or 'assault' and commonly used to describe the Soviet campaign against Islamic practices regard-ing women of the 1920s onwards focussed on female unveiling.

Ikat A style of dyeing in which warp threads carry the pattern, having been resist-dyed.

Isfan A dried herb which gives off a pungent smoke when burnt and is reputed to drive away evil spirits or microbes, depending on your worldview.

Jinn A devil or demon.

Kalpak A hat, usually referring to felt hats worn by traditionally nomadic Central Asians.

Kilim A flat-woven floor covering which, unlike a carpet, has no knotted pile.

Kino The Russian term for a film or movie, sometimes also applied to soap operas.

Kumiz The national drink of Kyrgyz and Kazakhs made from fer-mented mare's milk.

Kurta A long shirt or tunic that covers the lower thigh and some-times the knee as well.

Laghman Thick, hand-stretched noodles, usually served in a meat and vegetable broth.

Madder root Madder is a straggling weed, known as *royan* in Uzbek and *Rubia tinctorum* in Latin; the roots, once matured, give a pinkish/brick-red colour that can be enhanced by the use of mordants and tannins, such as oak gall.

Madrassah An Islamic school of learning, usually based on a courtyard layout with residential cells for studying and living in.

Medallion Used in carpet terminology to describe a large central pendant design surrounded by smaller, floral designs.

Mihrab An archway at the front of a mosque, pointing the faithful in the direction of Mecca.

Mullah An Islamic cleric or leader of a mosque.

Namaz A Muslim prayer, recited five times a day facing Mecca.

NGO Stands for 'non-governmental organisation' – usually doing development work of some kind.

Oak gall Nut-sized round nodules formed by certain types of oak in reaction to wasp eggs laid in their trunks. High in tannin, they work with madder root to create vivid reds.

Organza A fine, gauzy weave, usually of silk.

Overspun threads A technique which creates threads too tightly wound to lie flat, with a natural tendency to coil up.

Paranja An all-enveloping cape worn by urban women in Central Asia along with a horsehair veil, and campaigned against by the Soviets in the 1920s and 30s.

Pattu A handwoven blanket worn as a shawl and popular amongst Afghan men.

Perestroika 'Restructuring' in Russian, referring to a reduction in the power of the Soviet State both economically and politically under the leadership of Mikhail Gorbachev in the 1980s.

Pile The effect created by the ends of thousands of knots in pile carpets as opposed to flatweaves which have warp and weft but no pile.

Plov The national dish of Uzbekistan, consisting of rice, carrots and mutton, with regional variations.

Ply Threads that have been spun individually in one direction which are then spun together in the opposite direction to create a stronger thread that is typically two or three ply.

Puttees These are feet wrappings that provide warmth and are an alternative to and predecessor of socks.

Ramazan The Uzbek name for Ramadan – the Muslim month of fasting.

Resist-dyeing A form of tie-dyeing in which parts of a fabric or warp threads are bound to prevent dyeing and other parts are left open to receive the colour.

Sericulture The rearing of silkworms for silk.

Shalwar kameez A thigh or knee-length tunic over baggy trousers.

Shashlik Skewers of meat cooked over charcoal.

Shyrdak A Kyrgyz and Kazakh decorative felt made with stitched appliqué.

Suzani Literally means 'needlework' in Tajik and describes the embroidered tapestries of Southern Uzbekistan and Tajikistan.

Tumar A triangular amulet usually with tassels hanging from its bottom side, stuffed with cotton, wool and talismanic writing.

Tunduk The wooden wheel which forms the aperture of a yurt from which spokes of the dome radiate.

Turkestan A historic term used to describe the area of Middle Asia now occupied by the former Soviet Central Asian states, Northern Afghanistan and Western China.

Usta Someone skilled in a craft as opposed to an apprentice.

Vellum Skin from the stomach of a sheep or goat and superior to paper in book-making.

Wahabi The term used to describe Islamist fundamentalists, referring to the strict Saudi Wahabite sect which advocates jihad.

Warp A weaving term describing the vertical threads that make up the backbone of a carpet.

Weft A weaving term describing the horizontal threads that weave between the warp threads.

BIBLIOGRAPHY

Titles I have drawn on heavily are in bold type and suggested for further reading.

Allworth, Edward, *The Modern Uzbeks – from the fourteenth century to the present* (Hoover Institution Press, 1990)

Babur, Zahiru'd-din Muhamad, *The Babur Nama* (Everyman Library, 2020)

Bailey, Lieutenant-Colonel F. M., *Mission to Tashkent* (Jonathan Cape, 1946)

Barber, Elizabeth Wayland, *The Mummies of Urumchi* (Macmillan, 1999)

Barber, Elizabeth Wayland, *Women's Work – the first 20,000 years* (Norton and Company, 1995)

Bates, E. S., *Soviet Asia – progress and problems* (Jonathan Cape, 1942)

Beckert, Sven, *Empire of Cotton – a global history* (Knopf, 2014)

Blunt, Wilfrid, *The Golden Road to Samarkand* (Hamish Hamilton, 1973)

Boulnois, Luce, *Silk Road – Monks, warriors and merchants* (Odyssey, 2004)

Burnes, Alexander, *Travels into Bokhara* (John Murray, 1835)

Butler, Alan, *Sheep – The remarkable story of the humble animal that built the modern world* (O Books, 2006)

Cameron, Sarah, *The Hungry Steppe – famine, violence and the making of Soviet Kazakhstan* (Cornell University Press, 2018)

Chochunbaeva, Dinara, *Kyrgyz Felt of the 20th and 21st centuries* (Textile Society of America, 2010)

Christie, Ella, *Khiva to Golden Samarkand* (J. B. Lippincott, 1925)

de Clavijo, Gonzalez, *Narrative of the Embassy of Ruy Gonzalez de Clavijo to the Court of Timur at Samarkand* (1403–6)

Conquest, Robert, *The Harvest of Sorrow – Soviet collectivization and the terror famine* (OUP, 1986)

Coulthard, Sally, *A Short History of the World According to Sheep* (Anima, 2020)

Edwards, Anne, *Throne of Gold – The Lives of the Aga Khans* (William Morrow, 1996)

Fee, Sarah (ed.), *Cloth that changed the world – the art and fashion of Indian Chintz* (YUP, 2020)

Feltwell, Dr John, *The Story of Silk* (Alan Sutton, 1990)

Finlay, Victoria, *Fabric – the hidden history of the material world* (Profile, 2021)

Forsyth, Mark, *The Etymologicon – A circular stroll through the hidden connections of the English language* (Icon Books, 2011)

Galeyev, Ildar & Penson, Miron, *Max Penson – Photographer of the Uzbek Avant-Garde 1920s to 1940s* (Arnoldsche, 2011)

Gillow, John, *Textiles of the Islamic World* (Thames and Hudson, 2013)

Graham, Stephen, *Through Russian Central Asia* (Cassell & Co, 1916)

Hansen, Valerie, *The Silk Road – a new history* (OUP, 2012)

Harvey, Janet, *Traditional Textiles of Central Asia* (Thames and Hudson, 1996)

Hopkirk, Kathleen, *A Traveller's Companion to Central Asia* (John Murray, 1993)

Hopkirk, Peter, *The Great Game – on secret service in High Asia* (John Murray, 1990)

Hosking, Geoffrey, *A History of the Soviet Union* (Fontana Press, 1990)

Hughes, Langston, *A Negro looks at Soviet Central Asia* (Co-operative Publishing Society of Foreign Workers in the USSR, 1934)

Hughes, Langston, *I wonder as I wander* (Hill and Wang, 1956)

Iaroslavtsev, Nicholas, *Langston Hughes' visit to the Soviet Union (1932–3)* (www.blackpast.org, accessed 8 March 2018)

Kalter, Johannes, *The Arts and Crafts of Turkestan* (Thames and Hudson, 1984)

Kalter, Johannes & Pavaloi, Margareta (eds), *Uzbekistan – heirs to the Silk Road* (Thames & Hudson, 1997)

Kamp, Marianne , *The New Woman in Uzbekistan – Islam, modernity, and unveiling under communism* (UWP, 2016)

Kerven, Carol (ed.), *Prospects for Pastoralism in Kazakstan and Turkmenistan* (Routledge, 2003)

King, David (des.), *Ikats – woven silks from Central Asia – The Rau Collection* (Basil Blackwell, 1988)

Koestler, Arthur, *The Invisible Writing* (Collins, 1954)

Krist, Gustav, *Alone through a forbidden land* (Faber and Faber, 1939)

Kunitz, Joshua, *Dawn over Samarkand* (Van Rees Press, 1935)

Lentz, Thomas W. & Lowry, Glenn D., *Timur and the Princely Vision – Persian Art and Culture in the Fifteenth Century* (Los Angeles County Museum of Art, 1989)

Leoni, Francesca (ed.), *Power and Protection – Islamic Art and the supernatural* (Ashmolean Museum, 2016)

Macartney, Lady, *An English lady in Chinese Turkestan* (Ernest Benn,1931)

Maclean, Fitzroy, *Back to Bokhara* (Jonathan Cape,1959)

Maillart, Ella, *Turkestan Solo* (Putnam, 1934)

Mair, Victor, *The Mummies of East Central Asia* (Penn Museum Expedition Magazine, 2010)

Mannin, Ethel, *South to Samarkand* (Jarrolds, 1936)

Meakin, Annette M. B., *In Russian Turkestan – a garden of Asia and its people* (George Allen, 1903)

Meller, Susan, *Russian Textiles – printed cloth for the bazaars of Central Asia* (Abrams, 2007)

Meller, Susan, *Silk and Cotton Textiles from the Central Asia that was* (Abrams, 2013)

Middleton, Nick, *Extremes along the Silk Road – adventures off the world's oldest superhighway* (John Murray, 2005)

Muravev, Nikolai, *Journey to Khiva through the Turkoman Country* (Avgust Semyon, 1822)

Navalkin, Vladimir and Navalkina, Maria, *Muslim Women of the Fergana Valley* (Indiana University Press, 2016)

Nazaroff, Paul, *Hunted through Central Asia* (OUP, 1932)

Northrop, Douglas, *Veiled Empire – Gender and Power in Stalinist Central Asia* (Cornell University Press, 2003)

Olufsen, Ole, *The Emir of Bokhara and his country* (William Heinemann, 1911)

Pahlen, Count K. K., Mission to Turkestan 1908–9 (OUP, 1964)

Paine, Sheila, *Amulets – a world of secret powers, charms and magic* (Thames and Hudson, 2004)

Paine, Sheila, *Embroidered Textiles – traditional patterns from five continents* (Thames and Hudson, 1990)

Petronius, tr. Michael Heseltine (William Heinemann Ltd, 1925)

Pinner, R. & Eiland, M. L., *Between the Black Desert and the Red* (Fine arts museums of San Francisco, 1999)

Postrel, Virginia, *The Fabric of Civilization – How textiles changed the world* (Basic Books, 2020)

Richardson, David and Sue, *Qaraqalpaqs of the Aral Delta* (Prestel, 2012)

Riello, Giorgio, *Cotton – the fabric that made the modern world* (CUP, 2013)

Robbins, Christopher, *In Search of Kazakhstan – the land that disappeared* (Profile, 2007)

Roxburgh, David J (ed), *Turks – a journey of a thousand years 600–1600* (Royal Academy of Arts, 2005)

Shakespear, Captain Sir Richard, *A Personal Narrative of a Journey from Herat to Ourenbourg, on the Caspian, in 1840* (Blackwood's Edinburgh Magazine Vol. LI, June 1842)

Shishkin, Philip, *Restless Valley – revolution, murder, and intrigue in the heart of Central Asia* (YUP, 2013)

Sokol, Edward D., *The Revolt of 1916 in Russian Central Asia* (John Hopkins University Press, 1954)

St Clair, Kassia, *The Golden Thread – How fashion changed history* (John Murray, 2018)

Stockley, Beth (ed.), *Woven Air – The Muslin and Kantha tradition of Bangladesh*, (Whitechapel, 1988)

Sukhareva, O. A., *Suzani – Central Asian decorative embroidery* (IICAS, 2013)*

Suleman, Fahmida, *Textiles of the Middle East and Central Asia* (Thames and Hudson, 2017)

Thanhauser, Sofi, *Worn – a people's history of clothing* (Allen Lane, 2022)

Thomas, Alun, *Nomads and Soviet Rule – Central Asia under Lenin and Stalin* (I. B. Tauris, 2019)

Thompson, Jon, *Carpets – from the tents, cottages and workshops of Asia* (Barrie & Jenkins, 1983)

Thompson, Jon, *Silk, carpets, and the Silk Road* (NHK Cultural Centre, 1988)

Tyler, Christian, *Wild West China – The untold story of a frontier land* (John Murray, 2003)

Vambery, Arminius, *Travels in Central Asia* (John Murray, 1864)

Vambery, Arminius, *Arminius Vambery – his life and adventures* (T. Fisher Unwin, 1884)

Whitfield, Susan (ed.), *Silk Roads – people, cultures, landscapes* (Thames and Hudson, 2019)

Whitlock, Monica, *Beyond the Oxus – the Central Asians* (John Murray, 2002)

Wiener, G., Jianlin, H. and Ruijun, L., *The Yak*, 2nd edition (UN FAO, 2006)

Wood, Frances, *The Silk Road – two thousand years in the heart of Asia* (UCP, 2003)

Yafa, Stephen, *Cotton – the biography of a revolutionary fiber* (Penguin, 2005)

Kyrgyzstan Enquiry Commission: https://reliefweb.int/sites/relief-web.int/files/resources/Full_Report_490.pdf

Report on the UN investigation into the inter-racial violence of Southern Kyrgyzstan (2010): https://reliefweb.int/sites/relief-web.int/files/resources/Full_Report_490.pdf

*Although the research is brilliant, the English translation is quite a challenge. Perhaps one for the enthusiasts only.

ACKNOWLEDGEMENTS

First of all, thank you to all the people I was able to interview or include in this book that made it so much more interesting than if it was just my own experiences.

I'd also like to thank the Society of Authors for awarding me a grant through the John Heygate Award to help published authors of travel writing. The grant really helped me with my research at a time when libraries were closed due to the Covid pandemic. I'm also very grateful for Lois and Bill who run a watermill in Posara, Tuscany, for letting me stay for a few weeks and be their writer in residence, and introducing me to the wonderful world of aperitifs, in particular a good negroni.

In general, I try to get my manuscripts read by a fairly wide range of people before handing over to my editors as that initial feedback is so helpful, particularly when I get consistent feedback from different people. So, I'm very grateful to the following for their helpful insights and feedback: Jeanette Won, Richard Gould, Eileen Griffith, Richard Norman, Rachael Warrington, Coco Mbassi, Tim Stevenson, Fiona Ryan-Watson, Ann Wakem, Margy Lewis, Jane Chard, Susan O'Brien, Carrie Baker, Sheila Stevenson, Roger Dines, Agris Krumins, Paul Wright, Erin Crider, Tim Perry, Claire Harri, Tricia Ellingham, Niel Knoblauch, Robin Waley, and David McArdle.

Thanks also for picking up at least some of the typos before I handed in the manuscript. My favourite was, '… black embroidery on shite felt', which was supposed to have been white felt.

Thanks to Anna Morrison for a stunning front cover, and to Hanna Milner, Duncan Heath and Sophie Lazar for their trimming and polishing and knowing when I've included just one 'and an interesting aside to this …' too many.

And lastly, thanks to any of you who, having read this book, decide to live a bit differently, whether it's planning a trip to the -stans yourself, or paying more attention to where your clothing is sourced from, or even just leaving a positive book review.

INDEX